'In this stimulating and provocative book, Debbie Garvey has provided inspiring and practical narratives, underpinned by neuroscientific evidence and a clear values set, which creates a reflective and action-focused agenda for all those who work with young children. I believe anyone who reads this book will be inspired and motivated to challenge and extend their thinking and professional practice, adopting the critical and nurturing stance which lies at the heart of quality services for children and families.'

– Professor Chris Pascal, Director, Centre for Research in Early Childhood

'In this remarkable book, Debbie Garvey has brilliantly analysed both the reasons and the techniques for nurturing PSED. From theory and neuroscience to lifelong practice via well-meaning, wellbeing and the importance of listening, Debbie explains it all in a thoroughly engaging, affable style. Most importantly, she inspires genuine, and sometimes challenging, self-reflection on practice, using some novel, intriguing and effective methods.'

– Kathy Brodie, early years professional and trainer

by the same author

Performance Management in Early Years Settings
A Practical Guide for Leaders and Managers
Debbie Garvey
ISBN 978 1 78592 222 0
eISBN 978 1 78450 507 3

Leadership for Quality in Early Years and Playwork
Supporting your team to achieve better outcomes for children and families
Debbie Garvey and Andrea Lancaster
ISBN 978 1 90581 850 1
eISBN 978 1 90581 883 9

of related interest

Observing and Developing Schematic Behaviour in Young Children
A Professional's Guide for Supporting Children's Learning, Play and Development
Tamsin Grimmer
ISBN 978 1 78592 179 7
eISBN 978 1 78450 450 2

Learning through Movement and Active Play in the Early Years
A Practical Resource for Professionals and Teachers
Tania Swift
ISBN 978 1 78592 085 1
eISBN 978 1 78450 346 8

Promoting Young Children's Emotional Health and Wellbeing
A Practical Guide for Professionals and Parents
Sonia Mainstone-Cotton
ISBN 978 1 78592 054 7
eISBN 978 1 78450 311 6

NURTURING PERSONAL, SOCIAL AND EMOTIONAL DEVELOPMENT IN EARLY CHILDHOOD

A Practical Guide to Understanding Brain Development and Young Children's Behaviour

Debbie Garvey

Foreword by Dr Suzanne Zeedyk

Jessica Kingsley *Publishers*
London and Philadelphia

Contains public sector information licensed under the Open Government Licence v3.0.

First published in 2018
by Jessica Kingsley Publishers
73 Collier Street
London N1 9BE, UK
and
400 Market Street, Suite 400
Philadelphia, PA 19106, USA

www.jkp.com

Library of Congress Cataloging in Publication Data
A CIP catalog record for this book is available from the Library of Congress

British Library Cataloguing in Publication Data
A CIP catalogue record for this book is available from the British Library

ISBN 978 1 78592 223 7
eISBN 978 1 78450 500 4

Printed and bound in the United States

For the wonderful Fingers, T-bone and Little Wolf,
I am always amazed and inspired by you.
Wellbeing is time spent with you guys.
Always be just who you are!

Contents

Foreword

I have come to think of this as a book of stories. Debbie Garvey has taken the findings of science and turned them into stories. In undertaking this risk, she has taught me something important: we need more such stories.

We need them because stories are transformational. That is their purpose. Stories are not simply descriptive. They do not merely report an event, real or imagined. The function of stories, throughout the arc of human history, has been to craft a pathway to deeper truths, to richer meaning. And that is what Debbie Garvey offers us. She gives us stories that illuminate the insights at the heart of contemporary neuroscience.

That's a big task for an author to set herself, given that even the word 'neuroscience' feels scary to many people. Moreover, stepping into the neuroscience arena has become controversial, as some commentators are worried our increasing knowledge of the brain generates more anxiety than benefit. So, I am grateful an early years practitioner should have taken the plunge to explore new ways of helping the field move from theory to practice, from knowledge to understanding.

This is what the many stories in this book teach us: if we approach children's behaviour, first and foremost, from a place of compassion, rather than knowledge, then we are best placed to make use of scientific discoveries. Listening to Debbie Garvey's stories takes courage, though, because they not only enable us to see children's behaviour anew, they force us to see ourselves anew. So, let me begin this foreword by celebrating not just the author's courage, but that of the readers. It's going to be a bit of a bumpy ride.

The discoveries made by neuroscientists are now regularly reported to the public, via the media and social media. Any internet search will easily yield basic developmental processes. Babies are born already able to communicate, and they engage socially with other people from the outset. Their brains are much more observant than our culture realises, and brains develop more rapidly within the first few years of life than they ever will again. The growth of synapses between neurons in the brain is driven largely by a child's experiences of their world, and the growth of those synapses happens at a rate faster than anything we can realistically imagine. The central nervous system of babies and toddlers remains immature, leaving them unable to self-regulate the physiological reactions they have to their environment. They need help and support and reassurance from others in order to cope well with daily life.

As relevant as these insights are for those who care for young children, it is striking how many obstacles remain to their being incorporated into adult behaviour. This is, in part, because not everyone has shared in this knowledge. Information on babies' brain development is not yet standardly included within ante-natal classes for parents or childcare degrees for professionals. Even when the information is made available, it is not always easy to apply when your toddler is having a tantrum in the middle of the supermarket or biting another child in his play group or when you are the nursery manager devising a staff rota that truly facilitates continuous relationships with children. That, then, is precisely what Debbie Garvey sets out to do: help readers translate the neuroscience so it becomes useful when responding to the ordinary, daily behavioural challenges presented by young children. Why *do* they bite? What *is* an emotionally healthy drop-off policy? Why *are* some children so resistant to new foods? What do you do when a child *refuses* to be put down, but you have other children to attend to?

Perhaps we would expect a book with the words 'practical guide' in the title to offer us answers to such problems. What we might not have expected is how Garvey's stories lead us to question the unconscious assumptions about behaviour with which we started. Why are we so very bothered by children's biting? What is it like for children to walk into an unfamiliar space? Where did the modern penchant for nursery graduation ceremonies come from, and does it serve children or adults? Why is our emphasis so often placed on children's behaviour, rather than their feelings, even though we don't usually treat adults in this way? Why does it seem so hard to fully embrace the idea that young children are *never* naughty? Why haven't I, as the reader, ever before asked myself some of these questions? Many seem obvious, now that they have been pointed out. Others are so surprising they feel provocative.

I have rarely seen a professional practice guide do what Debbie Garvey has done in this one. She gently but persistently turns the reader's attention back on him or herself, insisting on self-reflection. This is where her skill as a storyteller comes to its fore. By beginning with stories of her own ordinary experience – her broken foot, her emotions on entering unfamiliar buildings, her behaviour when tired and grumpy – she invites the reader's compassion for her struggles. Once she has called that forth, it feels a natural step to extend the compassion outward, to the children and parents she is describing on the page. The reader joins Garvey in wondering about children's feelings when standing on a busy street, or when they are tired and grumpy and overwhelmed, or when they are rendered dependent on a stranger and feeling vulnerable. Debbie's stories are transformational because they are based in compassion and curiosity.

In today's world, where childcare and parenting practice is increasingly informed by neuroscience, this storytelling approach becomes valuable for two key reasons. The first concerns shame and denial. Most of us feel ashamed when we realise, upon 'getting' the relationship-based message at the heart of neuroscience, we have sometimes failed to consider children's internal emotional experiences. Even more uncomfortable is the idea we might have caused children hurt or damage. Self-reflection of the type Debbie Garvey leads us to – and that I believe the neuroscience itself leads us to – inevitably causes us moments of shame. We do not usually intend to wound or undermine children, and it takes courage to face up to the realisation we have sometimes done just that. It is even harder to accept that our unintentional behaviour might have had lasting ramifications. Debbie's gentle but relentless wondering enables us to step into courage. That step is essential, because if we can't come to terms with the idea we could do damage to another person (whether a child or adult), we are left only with the option of stepping into denial. We turn to denial to protect our sense of self as a good person.

Unfortunately, it is not only individuals who turn to denial to protect their sense of self. Whole professional sectors can slip into denial, as demonstrated in 1950s hospitals, when psychologist James Robertson had difficulty getting staff to recognise that their policy of separating parents from ill children was creating long-term psychological damage (Robertson and Robertson 1989). How will we respond when the science points to hazardous areas of policy today: touch, play, transitions? Denial may be helpful to grownups, but it is never helpful to children, who are dependent upon us for care. That is why, as I said at the outset, the early years field needs more stories that facilitate curiosity. Compassion overcomes shame and denial.

The second reason we need stories like these concerns the value of neuroscientific explanations, which has become a topic of controversy. For example, critical theorists Hilary and Stephen Rose (2016) argue that too much blame and also too much hope has ensued from contemporary neuroscience. Poverty, inequality and political economies are being ignored amidst claims about enhancing a child's 'mental capital'. The Roses are particularly critical of the divisive rhetoric governments now use to serve claims about 'poor parenting'. Neuroscience has, in their view, presented a new way of wrapping up age-old judgements about deserving and undeserving citizens. Jan Macvarish (2016) and John Bruer (2002) take a similar view, arguing strongly against the contemporary penchant for 'training' children, which they see as growing out of an overzealous and misplaced emphasis on the significance of the early years. They worry parents and professionals are being misled, and that with so much pressure now attached to 'stimulating' young children's brains, family life is suffering. Developmental psychologist Alison Gopnik (2016) adds her voice to these concerns, despite her fascination with infant brain development. Her message is that parents should stop 'parenting', allowing themselves to give up anxiety and control over their children's learning and giving children more freedom to guide their own learning through play. Gopnik feels so strongly about this she challenges even the language we now all use. She contends that 'parent' is a wonderful noun, but a terrible verb. She loathes the idea that 'parenting' has come to be regarded as a kind of work, rather than a kind of relationship.

I agree with the concerns expressed by these commentators. Modern society is too easily seduced by neuroscientific explanations, with 'neuro' terminology often proving more persuasive than actual information (Weisberg et al. 2008). Political rhetoric is certainly too judgemental, with many governmental policies now as dehumanising as were Victorians' class-driven beliefs about the 'undeserving poor'. Parents have become highly anxious about getting their parenting 'right', confused by too many sources of expert advice and danger stories about how it could all 'go wrong'. However, I disagree that these outcomes are a consequence of neuroscience itself. The problem comes from the ways we make use of this information. We too easily decontextualise behaviour, failing to take account of the interaction between a person and their environment. We make harsh judgements about the value of a person on the basis of behaviour in a single moment, without knowing their personal story. I would argue that the concerns central to many critical analyses are not a consequence of the science but of our own humanness. When allied to compassion, neuroscience is helping us make deeper sense of human behaviour. Debbie Garvey's stories show us that the most important insights to have emerged have less to do with the components of the human brain than with the importance of relationships to its healthy functioning. Western society needs all the help it can get in valuing relationships. If neuroscience can help us in doing this, my view is we should welcome its contribution to policy and practice. I leave the reader to judge whether, after reading Garvey's approach to her material, they agree with me.

In short, this book is not ultimately about caring for young children. It is really about why human relationships matter throughout the lifespan. Garvey makes that link explicitly by weaving in attention to adolescence, adulthood, dementia and Parkinson's disease. Readers also find themselves looking backwards at their own infancies, as when Garvey reminds us we all experience emotions like disappointment, frustration and anger, but we often don't remember the journey by which we learnt to cope with such emotions. Nor does she ever allow us to forget that, like children, parents have personal, social and emotional development (PSED) needs and that childcare staff are as responsible for thinking about those as they are the needs of children. Essentially, Debbie Garvey is trying to show us that, when viewed through the lens of relationships, a book about children is never just about children. It is always ultimately about human beings.

This contrast between the words 'child' and 'human being' illustrates the point made repeatedly by linguist Benjamin Lee Whorf (1956). 'Language shapes the way we think and determines what we can think about.' The language choices we make have dramatic impacts on the way we conceptualise ideas. In these pages we glimpse a range of the linguistic cul-de-sacs we have unintentionally created for ourselves in the early years sector. A good example is the language of 'skills'. The education sector currently talks about PSED as an area of 'skills development' that requires to be 'taught'. However, once we understand the body's self-regulatory system, we realise how fully physiology underlies behaviour. What happens if we use the language of 'physiological capacities', rather than 'behaviour skills' – and use the terminology of 'support' rather than 'teach'? How do such linguistic shifts help us create the kind of relationship-led care Garvey is calling for? And if the word 'people', as opposed to the term 'children', appeared in our policy documents more often (even a tiny bit more often?), how might that change 'practice' in the early years sector? Might we even begin to do away with the word 'practice', replacing it with the term 'relate'? That single term is a great help to early years staff in the middle of difficult moments. Their task is not then to remember 'best practice guidelines', but simply to be aware of how they are 'relating', in the moment, to the young 'people' in their care.

The stories of laughter and anxiety and accomplishment and uncertainty that Debbie Garvey offers us throughout these pages are indeed transformational. They enable us to see the world not only through children's eyes, but through new eyes of our own.

Dr Suzanne Zeedyk

References

Bruer, J.T. (2002) *The Myth of the First Three Years.* London: Free Press.

Gopnik, A. (2016) *The Gardener and The Carpenter.* New York: Farrar, Straus, and Giroux.

Macvarish, J. (2016) *Neuroparenting: The Expert Invasion of Family Life.* London: Palgrave Macmillan.

Robertson, J. and Robertson, J. (1989) *Separation and the Very Young.* London: Free Association Books.

Rose, H. and Rose, S. (2016) *Can Neuroscience Change Our Minds?* Cambridge: Polity Press.

Weisberg, D.S., Keil, F.C., Goodstein, J., Rawson, E. and Gray, J.R. (2008) 'The seductive allure of neuroscience explanations.' *Journal of Cognitive Neuroscience 20*, 3, 470–477.

Whorf, B.L. (1956) *Language, Thought and Reality.* Cambridge, MA: MIT Press.

Acknowledgements

First of all, thank you to Marie and Andy, and Sarah and Johnathan; I feel blessed and privileged that you allow me to be such a big part of your children's lives. They bring me so much joy and I have learnt, and continue to learn, so much.

Many people have been at my side, to offer help, support, feedback, challenge and encouragement. Throughout, this has been done with sensitivity and honesty, as well as respectfully and ethically, and for that I offer my sincere thanks, appreciation and gratitude to:

Dr Suzanne Zeedyk: you have long inspired me, I am delighted and privileged that you agreed to write the foreword; it is a pleasure and an honour to know you.

Professor Francis McGlone: thank you for your help, guidance and assistance. The work you do is incredibly important to early childhood. You have been immeasurably supportive, and given readily and freely of your time, and for that I am ever grateful.

Professor Chris Pascal, Professor Tony Bertram, Professor Lynda Erskine, David Wright, Kathy Brodie and the Dads Rock team: my sincere thanks and gratitude to you. Each of you gave your time, knowledge and support, openly and willingly, and helped me to unravel my, sometimes, confused and tangled thoughts. Thank you for sharing so enthusiastically the expertise that each of you has.

Yvonne Butterfield: your thoughtful, caring and empathetic approach to early childhood, and life in general, is always a joy to be a part of. I truly value your support and expertise, and am honoured to call you my friend.

Andrew James at Jessica Kingsley Publishers: my thanks as always, you are one of the most sincere, calm and honest people I have ever worked with, and I genuinely thank you for your ongoing support. On to the next project?

My thanks also to the rest of the JKP team; your continued help, support and guidance is truly welcome.

My husband: from supporting me when my physical injury got in the way of my PSED, to helping my sometimes disorganised and chaotic emotional brain make sense of my thoughts. Your unique view of the world encourages me to explore paths I would never otherwise consider. Thank you. I couldn't do any of this without you.

Merry and Pippin: without you this book would never have been written. Time spent with the two of you is always good for my PSED.

As always, there are a whole host of other people that helped to make this happen. My thanks to everyone who assisted along the way.

Preface

A conversation with Andrew James, Senior Commissioning Editor at Jessica Kingsley Publishers, in Spring 2016 resulted in the agreement to write two books, both for the ECCE (Early Childhood, Care and Education) sector: one book on performance management and this one on personal, social and emotional development (PSED). What became clear fairly quickly was that they both had the same core messages, that relationships are fundamental; as I described it in the performance management book:

> So, if we are in the ECCE sector to make a difference, to improve children's life chances, and impact on outcomes, all the research shows that it is the staff that make the most difference. It all comes back to:
>
> - relationships, personal development, training, staff support, such as supervision, and the right environment = *quality outcomes for children and families.*
>
> Which is exactly what we have examined throughout this book:
>
> - relationships, personal development, training, staff support, such as supervision and the right environment = quality outcomes for *practitioners and staff.*
>
> And so the message is simple; *you can't have one without the other!* (Garvey 2017, p.242)

Additionally, both books had the same central belief, that knowledge and understanding of neuroscience is vital to working with humans (whether they are little ones or grownup ones). The difficulty was going to be how to extrapolate three decades of research, theory, practice, knowledge and understanding from inside my head and decide which bits needed to go in to which book. There are of course some things that are so important that they need to go in both books; however, there is a major difference. The performance management book considers the impact from an adult perspective; *this* book considers the impact on young children. However, the central messages for all my work (whether in books or on training programmes) are clear: the elements of quality early childhood experiences are all interrelated, interlinked and inextricably interwoven. Staff, children, parents/carers, PSED, neuroscience, environments, theory, research, leadership/management, performance management, etc. all add to the mix. In addition, if we experience difficulties in one area, then the chances are that other areas will be affected too.

I have tried, wherever possible, to not simply repeat areas of performance management or my previous book, *Leadership for Quality in Early Years and Playwork* (Garvey and Lancaster 2010, and affectionately referred to as L4Q), but obviously, there are times when I have added to, or used, sections from one of them to emphasise points within *this* book. If I have quoted word for word from either of them, I have, as policy dictates, referenced appropriately. Additionally, there are some areas where it just does not make sense to try to re-write an already written and useful section, so, for example, the sections below under terminology, etc. are simply lifted, either word for word, or with slight variations, from my Performance Management book.

Terminology

Just a note on terminology before we go much further. The term 'personal, social and emotional development' is explored at length elsewhere in the book, but there are also other 'phrases' or 'wording' that I just want to explore a little.

We and Us

It can be really difficult when writing a book to know which term to use when referring to the readers of the book. Therefore, when I use the term 'we', I mean 'you and I'. For example, by saying 'we have probably all had experience of…', I mean you, the readers, and I have probably had experience of… I think of this like a 'virtual' conversation. It is a two-way thing – I can share research and ideas, and together we can explore what that might mean for practice.

And If Not – Why Not?

Throughout this book, you will find this question repeated and repeated and repeated. It is meant as a supportive question – not a criticism. This is my way of trying to ensure that all the theory and research we examine constantly relates back to real practice for you, your setting and your staff team, and the children and families you work with. It is simply offered as a question, to help you pause a minute and just think…

Leadership and/or Management

There has been, and I suspect there will continue to be, much debate about the terminology and wording of leader and/or manager. In L4Q (2010), we explored this, and came to the conclusion that in all reality, maybe it does not actually matter; indeed Jonathan Wainwright in the Introduction of L4Q (p.8) stated that:

> Maybe there are some differences between leadership and management. Earlier thinking says that there are, but perhaps worrying about these differences may simply act as a distraction from our tasks.

Additionally, this view is being acknowledged elsewhere:

> Thus, we are inclined to agree with the perspective put forward by Garvey and Lancaster (2010) that seeking to separate leadership and management is another unhelpful dichotomy. (Campbell-Barr and Leeson 2016, p.79)

So, it is with the understanding that the words are interchangeable, that the terms leader/manager and leadership/management are used throughout this book.

ECCE

ECCE (Early Childhood, Care and Education), or ECEC (Early Childhood, Education and Care) or EY (Early Years) or EYFS Settings (Early Years Foundation Stage Settings) or EC (Early Childhood or perhaps Early Care?)…and so the list goes on, but which to use? Some will be more familiar than others, and some are easier to read and say, whilst some feel a tad clumsy. There does not seem to be a 'preferred' term, so my personal preference is ECCE (Early Childhood, Care and Education). This is not about whether care or education is more important, which should come first or any other 'hidden agenda'. Quite simply, of all the abbreviations I find ECCE easier to say, read and type. Throughout this book the term ECCE will be used to describe anything and everything to indicate children under five years old receiving some form of care/education from people who are professional practitioners.

In addition, you will also see the term 'Early Childhood' used, as in the title, for example. This is because sometimes the term ECCE can be seen as the professional 'arena' of working with children; however, much of what we discuss within this book is applicable to all areas of early childhood. Yes, this book is primarily aimed at practitioners working in the ECCE sector, but there are also other people interested in early childhood too. Parents/carers, etc. would not use the term ECCE, so for this book, both ECCE and early childhood are used.

Children

Very young children come in all shapes and sizes (literally), they have a range of abilities, develop at differing rates and learn different things at different times. What one child finds easy, another child may find incredibly difficult (emotionally or otherwise), just as we as adults have differing strengths. Please consider throughout this book the range of children you may be working with. I have not generally gone into lots of details in terms of 'defining' children, and tend to use the words babies, very young children, young children and children. However, there will also be children with Special Educational Needs and Disabilities (SEND), children with additional languages, children from chaotic home lives, children with medical needs, and so on, and so on. It is your role as practitioners to understand the children you are working with, or could possibly find yourself working with. Therefore if, for example, a reflective practice question asks you to consider 'how are the children feeling?' you will need to bear in mind the wide range of children you work with currently, or could work with in the future.

Practitioners

Practitioners is a term used throughout the book to describe anyone working in a paid or voluntary, but professional, capacity with young children – whether student, early years practitioner, nursery nurse, EYP/EYT, senior, room leader, teacher, leader or manager, etc.

Staff

The word 'staff' is used to cover anyone and everyone who works with children in a paid or voluntary, but professional, capacity. This includes practitioners, but also includes other staff who are sometimes forgotten. Cooks, kitchen staff, cleaners, gardeners, caretakers, administration staff, finance staff, and so on, should be included in development plans, consulted for their views and be involved in wider developments. Additionally, these staff are likely to come into contact with children, so they should be included and supported to understand the ethos, and their impact, within the setting.

Parents

There are a range of people who settings work in partnership with to support children, such as mums, dads, foster carers, adoptive parents, childminders, nannies, grandparents, aunties and uncles and adult siblings. At any point in time, any one of these 'carers' could be in the 'parental' position of, for example, picking a child up from a setting. In terms of writing, 'parents/carers' looks and feels clumsy, so I have used the term 'parent/s' with the following proviso in mind: the term 'parent/s' should also be understood to include other adult carers in a child's life.

How Can This Book Be Used?

Feedback on previous books indicates that they are practical books, that can be read from cover to cover, or dipped into for information on a particular aspect. Therefore, this book is written in the same way. The aim is to offer leaders, managers and practitioners, or anyone interested in early childhood, a range of theory and good practice, supported by case studies and reflective practice examples to support you in exploring and developing your own critical thinking when supporting young children. Additionally, it does not matter if the policies, procedures, processes, etc. you are using are developed locally by you and your team, or centrally by a head office, for example; the approaches that I am suggesting throughout this book can still be used.

This book is designed to help you reflect on your practice. This book, and indeed reflection, isn't about right or wrong. In very simple terms, reflection is about considering what you do, why you do it and what you might do next, or in the future, for example. Throughout there is acknowledgement of various debates regarding the topics covered and analogies regarding the way young children are often treated very differently to adults. This includes, for example, how there are often seemingly double-standards just because you are a little person rather than a grownup person. Therefore, this book can be used to help you consider whether the practices currently used are suitable, and if not, why not?

At the very end of the book, in the appendix, is a sample Reflective Action Plan for Practice (RAPP) for you to record your thoughts, reflections and intended actions. The RAPP is designed for you to reflect on your journey through this book. There are two examples of the RAPP. One RAPP is offered as a sample, which has suggested questions and pointers to support your reflections. The final RAPP is blank for you to record your own reflections. And, the reason for the term RAPP? Just because I like the reference to the way a director will say 'that's a wrap' at the end of shooting a movie. In other words, it signals the end. However, in the case of the action plan, it may be the end of the book but hopefully, the reflection will continue.

Who Is This Book For?

This book is for anyone working in the ECCE field, anyone interested in early childhood, such as parents/carers, and anyone else who is interested in exploring how PSED plays a pivotal role in lifelong development.

INTRODUCTION

So, let me start by explaining how my interest in personal, social and emotional development (PSED) developed. In the middle of a summer heatwave, without warning, and with little time for preparation, my husband and I found ourselves caring for a brother and sister, who were just five-and-a-half weeks old. Thankfully, it was a quiet time in the Early Childhood, Care and Education (ECCE) world, and I had the time to spend at home with them while they adjusted to us and we adjusted to them. I was supposed to be writing new training programmes, but as the days turned into weeks, I found myself simply watching them as they grew. They were such bundles of joy and energy, and they took us on a journey through a range of emotions. They made us laugh with their antics, worry if they were eating/sleeping enough, marvel at their determination and when the little girl caught a serious tummy bug and almost died, then we cried too.

As time went on, it soon became apparent that the little girl was much braver, physically, than her brother; whereas the little boy was much braver emotionally than his sister. I watched fascinated as they encountered differing physical, social and emotional obstacles; she was the first to learn to get up and down stairs, but she was not keen on cuddles and recoiled if we tried to touch her. With her brother, it was the other way around; he fell so many times trying to master the stairs, but he loved cuddles and was so affectionate. When people visited, he would be curious and interested, and eager to say hello in his own way, whereas his sister hid away until the visitors had gone.

They are much older now, and although she is still wary of strangers, she will allow some cuddles from us, but only on her terms (usually at bedtime). He did of course master the stairs, but he is still a little clumsy, and has a habit of falling off the bed occasionally. They soon became a big and important part of the family, and they still are. They taught me many lessons about PSED, and they still do.

In case you have not worked it out yet, the five-and-a-half-week-old duo we ended up caring for are now our two adult-middle-aged cats. Allow me to introduce you to Pippin (our female, black and white Tuxedo cat) and Merry (our tabby and white male cat). Yes, they are named after the hobbits in *Lord of the Rings*, yes, they have distinct characters and, yes, I could be accused of anthropomorphism (giving animals human characteristics and emotions). But bear with me...

The two tiny five-and-a-half-week-old kittens we ended up with had been brutally taken from their mother, at almost half the age that is recommended, and well before they were ready. Kittens at such a young age still need their mother's milk, their mother's protection and their mother's help to learn the skills they will need later in life. They were too little for 'cat food', did not know how to use a litter tray, and did not know how to drink from a water bowl.

They were so tiny, so helpless and had been horrendously treated by humans who should have protected them. Their eyes (like human babies) were still blue, and you could fit them into the palm of your hand. Along with their three brothers and sisters they were abandoned in a box... Thankfully, they were discovered by a very caring young man, who successfully found homes for all of them, including, of course, the two that came to live with us.

One of the first things we did was arrange a visit for Pippin and Merry to the vets: we found that Pippin was a girl and Merry was a boy, but thankfully apart from being tiny, they were perfect. The issue was going to be getting them to eat. So, we took them home, and fed them every two hours, from a tiny syringe, with soya baby milk (contrary to popular belief, cats are actually lactose intolerant, and cow's milk can make them very ill). At one point Pippin became seriously ill; the only way we could check if she was actually getting any food was to weigh her on digital kitchen scales every few hours.

Over time we had to teach them the things that cats need to know. We taught them how to lap water (and to this day they both still put their paws into a water dish first, which makes me wonder if this is due to seeing us put our fingers in the water to show them). We taught them how to eat 'grownup food' (a little bit of food on their noses encourages them to lick). We had to teach them how use the litter tray (yes, physically moving their paws so they got the idea) and clean their bottoms (think cotton wool and warm water). In other words, all the things that they would have learnt from their mother. It was hilarious, terrifying, wonderful, scary, rewarding and frustrating at any given moment.

As I watched them grow and flourish, over that first summer, I saw more and more characteristics and actions that reminded me of the young children I had known. Physically, Pippin, although much smaller, was more advanced, she took bigger risks, jumped higher and further and climbed anything and everything, whereas Merry hung back and watched. Emotionally, Merry loved people, he sat on anyone's knee, rubbed against any leg, and he would meow loudly from the top step every time either of us came into the house. Pippin, however, was, and still is, wary of most people, she hides from visitors, and meows unhappily and loudly at the vets. Merry did, and still does, purr for most people, even at the vets, where to this day they have still not heard his heartbeat. A couple of years ago, one of the vets actually commented that Merry was, emotionally, the most secure cat she had ever met... So, I guess, the veterinary world is interested in PSED too!

As Merry and Pippin approached the six-month-old age bracket, we had a conversation with the vet about neutering. The operation for a female cat takes longer and is more complex; however, the danger of having Merry neutered first could mean that Pippin could still come 'into season', and possibly escape the house, meaning the chances of pregnancy were very real. The vet felt that it was more important to have Pippin spayed first, even though, technically, she was under the recommended weight. The vet's concern was that, as such a tiny cat, pregnancy could put her in life-threatening danger. Reluctantly we agreed to have Pippin spayed first.

After the operation, we picked Pippin up, and took her home to recuperate. The vets had put one of those 'conical-lampshade cat collars' around her neck. The ones that are designed to stop cats licking any wounds or stitches. The idea behind this is a sensible one; cats' mouths are full of bacteria, and the collars are designed to help keep the wound area clean. However, Pippin was having none of it. She was traumatised. I can only describe watching her, and hearing the heart-rending cries she made, as an animal in trauma. The collar made her unbalanced, so she bumped into things, she could not reach the food in her bowl, she could not get comfortable to go to sleep, and she could not jump up to sit next to us. After what seemed like an eternity of witnessing her distress, she was obviously exhausted, and my husband had had enough. He picked Pippin up and sat her next to him, and took off the collar. Pippin made an attempt to lick the stitches, my husband gently moved her head away from the area, making soothing noises, but firmly saying 'no'. Now, I know animals cannot speak, I am not some crazy cat lady! But, I can say what I saw: Pippin curled up next to my husband, and went to sleep... Additionally, she never once tried again to lick the wound, and it healed beautifully. I am absolutely certain that Pippin was traumatised by the collar, the relief of having it taken off was instantly obvious, and I am sure, in her own way, she 'understood'.

So…how does this link to young children and PSED? Well, the more I watched the cats develop, and their 'personalities' emerge, the more interested I became in PSED. For instance, watching Pippin with the collar, and afterwards without it, reminded me of working with children who cannot yet speak. Although these very young children may not have full use of language, they often understand much, much more than they can say, and use their non-verbal skills to express themselves, and show us their needs. Similarly, watching the cats' different approaches to people was fascinating: Merry's social confidence, curiosity and obvious delight in meeting people, compared to Pippin's obvious mistrust. More and more I began to wonder if anyone had researched if there were any links between PSED in children and animals (but specifically mammals, and this will come up occasionally through the book). So, I started to read, and found a few books such as the 1872 book by Charles Darwin, *The Expression of the Emotions in Man and Animals*, which is a fascinating read. However, whilst I did not find huge amounts of information about the links between PSED in humans and mammals, I did find research, books and other information that caused me to question my professional beliefs, and sent me on a reflective journey to re-examine my approach to early childhood practice.

The more research, theory, papers, etc. I read, the more I questioned some of the well-meaning, allegedly 'caring' and unintentionally but potentially damaging practices we use as standard in early childhood. Research from across early years, early childhood, social sciences, neuroscience, cognitive psychology, development psychology, and other 'brain-related' fields were all adding to the knowledge base of understanding in regards to early brain development. I started to discuss some of the findings I had read about, with colleagues, other professionals, and with practitioners on my training programmes. I found that people were extremely interested in the messages I had picked up, and so the idea for this book was born – it has just taken a while to be in a position to do the actual writing.

There is now more emerging information on emotions in animals; researchers have identified that mammals have a similar reptilian brain to humans, and importantly, some level of an 'emotional brain' too. Hence the term 'mammalian brain' which we will explore more in Chapter 1. For example, several recent studies have shown a range of mammalian species appearing to mourn, or show grief, when a closely related animal dies. In an article in *National Geographic*, Traci Watson looked at some of the research regarding how several species of whales have been observed continuing to hold the dead bodies of a 'pod-mate' or close relatives:

The most likely explanation for the animals' refusal to let go of the corpses: grief. 'They are mourning,' says study co-author Melissa Reggente, a biologist at the University of Milano-Bicocca in Italy. 'They are in pain and stressed. They know something is wrong.' (Watson 2016)

Similarly, the article considered other species which are suspected to show emotion:

Scientists have found a growing number of species, from giraffes to chimps, that behave as if stricken with grief. Elephants, for example, return again and again to the body of a dead companion. (Watson 2016)

In the *National Geographic* article, Watson goes on to acknowledge the ongoing debate regarding brain development in animals:

Such findings add to the debate about whether animals feel emotion – and, if they do, how such emotions should influence human treatment of other creatures. (Watson 2016)

Likewise, TV programmes such as *Planet Earth* (BBC 2012), *Planet Earth II* (BBC 2016a) and *Spy in the Wild* (BBC 2016b), as well as other wildlife documentaries, are more and more showing that perhaps the way we, as humans, consider other animals needs some thought too? Whatever the reason, I can only conclude that my animals appear to show emotional responses to some situations. Both Merry and Pippin purr when they seem 'happy' and content, and cower under the bed during a thunder storm, or on Bonfire Night, for example. Merry can often be found 'playing' in water, which he seems to 'enjoy': he is fascinated by anything wet, including rain water, puddles, showers, sinks, baths and even snow. Yet, he has an inexplicable reaction to the window cleaner, and bolts out of the cat flap, his body low on the ground, ears flat against his head, and looking what I can only describe as terrified, whenever the windows are cleaned. Whatever it is, emotional reaction or otherwise, I owe my thanks to Pippin and Merry, because without them, I would not have explored PSED, and possibly would never have discovered the wealth of information about how our human brains develop.

So, due to observations on two tiny, helpless kittens, my interest in PSED developed. Yes, I had previously considered some early childhood-related PSED concepts, but not to the depth that I went on to research. I am not, nor do I claim to be, an academic; the information I have collated here is an amalgamation of an eclectic mix, collected over years of practice, and is based on values that are close to my heart. Throughout my observations, research and collections of over three decades of 'information' I discovered that PSED appears to be the basis of all other development (and we will explore this throughout this book), and I also discovered that perhaps this was about more than just young children. In my previous book with Jessica Kingsley Publishers (*Performance Management in Early Years Settings*, 2017), one of the central threads was around the concept of using sound ECCE principles and theories in our work with adults. In *this* book, I am going to turn that on its head and consider how, if, we treated adults the way we sometimes treat children, there would be uproar!

Chapter 1 on brain development, neuroscience and PSED is a reconfiguration of Chapter 1 in my previous book *Performance Management in Early Years Settings*. In *this* PSED book, however, there is a focus on young children. This leads into Chapter 2, which explores the influences on PSED, and considers some of the challenges children face as their personal, social and emotional brains, knowledge and understanding develops.

Chapter 3 considers the well-meaning ways in which adults believe they are supporting children, often with unintentional consequences. Leading on from this, Chapter 4 examines ways in which children's wellbeing can be promoted and supported in effective, encouraging and empowering ways.

Chapter 5 studies the importance of listening to children, and how children use a range of ways to 'speak' to adults. Throughout all of the chapters we will refer back to the research of neuroscience and how this can support early childhood practice.

The final chapter brings all of the previous chapters together and looks at the importance of PSED and neuroscience, not just for young children, but for everyone around us. We will consider how what we know in early childhood can have a positive influence on lifelong practice and therefore wider society as a whole.

Chapter 1

BRAIN DEVELOPMENT, NEUROSCIENCE AND PSED

This chapter is a reconfiguration of the chapter about 'brain development, neuroscience and supporting staff' in my book *Performance Management in Early Years Settings* (Garvey 2017). In essence, the two chapters are very similar; the Early Childhood, Care and Education (ECCE) sector is giving wider recognition to research, and developing understanding of the importance of brain development in our work with young children, and I wanted to explore this from two very different angles. In my previous book, I considered how early childhood practice could support leaders and managers in working with adults. For the purpose of this book, and this chapter, I am going to consider how some knowledge and understanding of brain development can support adults in understanding and supporting personal, social and emotional development (PSED) in early childhood.

There are ground-breaking discoveries being made in a range of areas, such as Biology, Neurobiology, Neuroanatomy, Neurochemistry, Neuroscience (and branches such as Cognitive Neuroscience, Behavioural Neuroscience, Social Neuroscience), Developmental Psychology (which explores changes in humans and cultures over time), as well as Cognitive Psychology (which considers areas such as learning, thinking, memory and perception). This rich diversity of research means our understanding and knowledge of human brain development is expanding rapidly. For example:

> The first few months after birth, when a child begins to interact with the environment, are critical to human brain development. The human frontal lobe is important for social behavior and executive function; it has increased in size and complexity relative to other species, but the processes that have contributed to this expansion are unknown. Our studies of postmortem infant human brains revealed a collection of neurons that migrate and integrate

widely into the frontal lobe during infancy. Chains of young neurons move tangentially [loosely] close to the walls of the lateral ventricles and along blood vessels. These cells then individually disperse long distances to reach cortical tissue, where they differentiate and contribute to inhibitory circuits. Late-arriving interneurons could contribute to developmental plasticity, and the disruption of their postnatal migration or differentiation may underlie neurodevelopmental disorders. (Paredes *et al.* 2016, p.81)

In other words, what Paredes and the team found is that during the first few months of life, babies' brains are physically still being formed as not all of the neurons are in the correct place at birth. They also suggest that some of the routes the neurons have to take are 'treacherous', and that their role within their destination of the frontal lobe (cortex) is to help support the 'balance [of] the brain's need for stability, with the ability to learn and change' (Weiler 2016). To me, this very new area of research generates a whole barrage of questions, not least as to how we best support parents and our very youngest children, but also how this research has huge implications for anyone interested in early childhood. The research also raises concerns regarding other influences on such young brains during this sensitive period, such as neurons that are 'late arrivals' and possible 'disruptions' along the journey. Again, this has huge implications for those of us interested in early childhood, which could perhaps include some of the areas we will consider in Chapter 2, as well as other issues for consideration elsewhere in this book:

> The first months of life, when an infant first begins to interact with its environment, is a crucial time for brain development, Huang said. 'The timing of this migration corresponds very well with the development of more complex cognitive functions in infants. It suggests that the arrival of these cells could play a role in setting up the basis for complex human cognition.' (Weiler 2016)

All of this new and ground-breaking research and scientific understanding adds to our growing knowledge and understanding in early childhood. Therefore, throughout this book, there will be opportunities to consider various aspects of research and how this may be beneficial to us as adults in terms of how we support personal, social and emotional development, and behaviours, in early childhood. However, it is then understandable that when faced with such huge amounts of new material coming from a variety of different angles, there can be some confusion.

Brain Development vs Neuroscience vs Psychology

It is perhaps useful, at this point, to clarify the terminology that will be used in this book. Much has been written about the use of 'neuroscience' to influence policy and practice, and whether indeed this has been correctly used and interpreted. Della Sala and Anderson (2012) talk of 'neuromyths' and cite Landau (1988), Bruer (2000), Goswami (2006), Purdy (2008) and Fischer (2009) as places to go for further reading. They offer one perspective on this ongoing debate:

> ...while the use of 'neuroscience', is attractive in education it seems to us the 'cognitive psychology' does all the useful work or 'heavy lifting'... There is indeed a gap between neuroscience and education. But that gap is not filled by the 'interaction' of neuroscientists and teachers (nearly always constituted by the former patronizing the latter). (Della Sala and Anderson 2012, p.3)

Regardless of external debates, I believe that the term 'neuroscience' is well-known in ECCE, however it is being used. Much of the knowledge I have gathered is an amalgamation from across all the disciplines discussed, and I suspect that is the case for many of the practitioners working in the ECCE sector. In my head, I see this range of theories, knowledge, understanding and even debates, under the encompassing umbrella of 'neuroscience'. If you are interested in this debate, there is a range of information on this in the bibliography, if you wanted to explore this further. I was discussing this with Professor of Neuroscience, Francis McGlone, who suggested we could use the term 'cognitive neuroscience':

> *Cognitive neuroscience* is the scientific field that is concerned with the study of the biological processes and aspects that underlie *cognition* [thought, reasoning and learning], with a specific focus on the neural connections in the brain which are involved in mental processes. (F. McGlone, personal communication, 2 March 2017)

Many people interested in early childhood are interested in the function of the brain, and how it works. We are interested in the 'changes in humans and cultures'. We are interested in 'learning, thinking and memory', and how this supports our work with children (and, perhaps, adults too). Therefore, I believe 'neuroscience' is a word that is accepted and understood in the early childhood field to mean 'the science of brain development'. I do not want to overcomplicate or confuse matters further, therefore, it is with the widest meaning and understanding, as discussed here, that I will refer to the term 'neuroscience' throughout this book:

Neuroscience has traditionally been classed as a subdivision of biology. These days, it is an *interdisciplinary* science which liaises closely with other disciplines, such as mathematics, linguistics, engineering, computer science, chemistry, philosophy, psychology, and medicine. (Nordqvist 2016, emphasis added)

The science of the function and development of the brain (neuroscience) is a developing one, and therefore only slowly revealing its secrets. This means there is much debate in and around the areas of neuroscience as to *how* important the early years are:

The best chance to turn this around is during the *1001 critical days*. At least one loving, sensitive and responsive relationship with an adult caregiver teaches the baby to believe that the world is a good place and reduces the risk of them facing disruptive issues in later life. (All-Party Parliamentary Group 2015, p.5, emphasis added)

In 2002, the Organisation for Economic Co-operation and Development (OECD) published a report and came up with the term 'neuromyths':

The genesis of a neuromyth usually starts with a misunderstanding, a misreading and in some cases a deliberate warping of the scientifically established facts to make a relevant case for education or for other purposes. (OECD 2002, p.71)

The OECD report *Understanding the Brain: Towards a New Learning Science* is worth a read, to anyone interested in neuroscience and early years. Not least because it challenges our thinking. I do not want to get into too much of an academic debate about neuroscience, and whether or not the early years are 'vital', 'windows of opportunity' or 'sensitive periods' – terms which are bandied about in any article, journal or book with any vague connection to early years and neuroscience.

Despite all this intense research, the brain is so very complex that our knowledge, despite constant new technologies, is rudimentary and highly conjectural. No one has any kind of overall theory about how the brain works. So it is hardly surprising that, as yet, neuroscience does not add up to a coherent explanation of how we think and become the way we are. (Penn 2014, p.87)

To explain this debate in simple terms, the dispute comes when some people try to use existing research to *prove* that it is *only* the first three years of life that count. This argument implies that any learning and development cannot happen after this, or indeed that any 'damage' cannot be repaired later – and this is simply not true. (Think about learning to drive, or adults overcoming a fear of, say spiders, for example, which is well after the first three years of life!) This is usually referred to as 'brain plasticity', meaning the brain's ability to change. What is acknowledged and generally agreed is that the early years are important, and as those of us interested in early childhood know only too well, we can make a difference:

> This means that the best time for shaping brains is during the early years, before the age of three. This doesn't mean that it's all over by three years. The brain continues to develop until the early twenties, and even then, it still has massive capabilities to change and adapt. But, the brain will never again adapt as quickly and robustly as it does during the early years. (Zeedyk 2014b)

I do, however, want to acknowledge that this debate is very relevant and very real, and one, that in early years, we need to be aware of. Much of the understanding of brain development comes from work undertaken on and with animals, or posthumously on human brains. Additionally, our understanding and knowledge of human brain development is still evolving. Furthermore, we need to continue to be curious, inquisitive and challenge assumptions. In other words, don't believe everything you read…check out the research, consider what you know and observe about young children and challenge when what you see and hear does not appear to make sense.

Bearing all of this in mind, and for the purpose of this book, I am going to use the term 'sensitive periods', and we know that a child's early years are a sensitive period in terms of development. I feel this recognises the debate and the neuromyths agenda, but also acknowledges the importance of the early years as a whole. In terms of nurturing PSED and understanding behaviours, I feel the following quote is helpful:

> A fundamental paradox exists and is unavoidable: development in the early years is both highly robust and highly vulnerable. Although there have been long-standing debates about how much the early years really matter in the larger scheme of lifelong development, our conclusion is unequivocal: What happens during *the first months and years of life* matters a lot, not because this period of development provides an indelible blueprint for adult well-being, but *because it sets either a sturdy or fragile stage for what follows.* (Shonkoff and Phillips 2000, p.5)

Brain Development

Scientific (and indeed medical) research tells us that the brain is a complex organ, of which only a small amount is understood, and new discoveries are continuing to be made.

> Since Paul McLean suggested in 1970 that there was a 'triune' brain, or three-brains-in-one, there has been general recognition that the brain is structured by evolution, starting with a reptilian brain, on top of which developed a mammalian emotional brain, and finally a human neocortex. (Gerhardt 2015, p.51)

There is still much debate amongst neuroscientists and neuroanatomists as well as other scientists from a range of disciplines about the exact makeup of the brain. For example, it is now widely accepted that many reptilians have some form of developed cortex, and that some cells in the limbic system react to the position of the head and not just emotions. For example, Najafi *et al.* (2017) are offering 'a large scale network' rather than one area or the 'emotional brain'. They go on to say:

> Although research on the brain basis of emotion has often focused on particular brain regions, the investigation of associated larger-scale circuits is growing at a considerable pace. This is not only the case in human research with fMRI but also with genetic and molecular techniques that afford increasing control and enhanced monitoring of neuronal populations in non-human animals.

Furthermore, we need to be careful that we do not always say 'oh, that's the mammalian brain' or use the example of 'gut reactions' of the reptilian brain purely as an excuse for certain behaviours.

> One final problem with the triune-brain model is that it treats the brain as if it were organized along strict hierarchical lines. Just because the cerebral cortex is where conscious thought takes place does not mean that it sits at the top of a pyramid and controls all the lower levels of the brain. On the contrary, some deeper structures in the brain (the brainstem in particular) exercise significant, continuous control over activity in the cortex – for example, by modifying the synchronization of its neurons according to whether the individual is asleep or awake. (The Brain from Top to Bottom 2012)

I am also conscious that many of us interested in early childhood are not scientists (me included), but we have to have some language we can use, without overcomplicating the subject. Therefore, it is with this understanding in mind, that I will use the terms:

- the brainstem (sometimes referred to as the reptilian brain)
- the limbic brain (sometimes referred to as the mammalian brain)
- the neocortex.

It is of course always useful to keep up to date with current thinking and new discoveries, and acknowledge that what means something to one person (or discipline) may mean something completely different to someone else – or indeed may even be considered outdated. Therefore, for the purpose of this book, I think this language is something we in early childhood can feel comfortable with, can work with, and have some level of understanding of, at this moment in time. I acknowledge that this is a very simplified version of neuroscience, but this is only intended to be an introduction and an overview to brain development and exploration of how this knowledge can support practice in the early childhood field. In addition to this I will explore the theory, evidence and research regarding the function and role of the Reticular Activating System (RAS) Filter, sometimes called the Reticular Formation.

I recognise that these areas of the brain do not operate in isolation, and have a complex network of connections, synapses and neurons that influence and support each other. Many medical and academic descriptions, as well as a range of terminology, are available to consider the various parts, areas and functions of the human brain. If you are looking for further information on this, the websites 'The Brain from Top to Bottom' or the 'DANA Foundation' are perhaps useful places to start. Additionally, I was delighted when Dr Suzanne Zeedyk agreed to write the foreword for this book. Suzanne's work of bringing science to the public is hugely accessible and understandable, and further details of where to look can be found in the bibliography.

Furthermore, the help, support and guidance I have received from Professor Francis McGlone has been exceptionally valuable. His help, support and vast knowledge of the neurosciences and associated fields has been incredibly useful. I would urge anyone interested in this area to look at research by Professor McGlone and continue to keep a watchful eye on the media for his name.

Additionally, anything written by Sue Gerhardt is very readable, interesting and easily relatable to ECCE practice (with adults, as well as with children). The hugely influential, often quoted as a 'leadership' book, *Emotional Intelligence* by Daniel Goleman, also has a whole section dedicated to the emotional development of the human brain, and is equally helpful. Interestingly, although Daniel Goleman is often quoted in terms of leadership, much of his work is actually about understanding PSED, and Emotional Intelligence in children:

> Perhaps the most disturbing single piece of data in this book comes from a massive survey of parents and teachers and shows a worldwide trend

for the present generation of children to be more troubled emotionally than the last: more lonely and depressed, more angry and unruly, more nervous and prone to worry, more impulsive and aggressive. (Goleman 1996, p.xiii)

Alternatively, if you prefer watching to reading, Allan Schore is a researcher in the field of neuropsychology. Often described as the 'American Bowlby', Schore has numerous publications as well as some easily understandable videos on YouTube. There are, of course, numerous other writers and researchers (see the bibliography section) and as you look into this subject more, you will find favourites that you find helpful (or not) as the case may be.

There is also new research appearing almost daily, which just goes to prove how much there is still to discover about the workings of the brain. What is known, and is fairly easy to understand, is that it is the nervous system that carries the messages around our brains and bodies, and that the nervous system transmits information gathered from the five senses.

The Importance of the Five Senses

Let us consider how information is received by the brain; this can only happen by use of one of the five senses:

- sight
- hearing
- smell
- touch
- taste.

One, or more, of the five senses has an 'experience' and this information is channelled through the nervous system into the spinal column and up into the brain. This is why the ECCE sector acknowledges, champions and demonstrates the importance of children learning through experience. ECCE practitioners provide a range of experiences that enables, empowers and encourages young children to explore their world by what they see, hear, smell, taste and touch. For example, very young babies begin to learn, almost from birth, by putting things into their mouths; interested adults provide safe ways for babies to develop this. Hand-held toys, sensory baskets and heuristic play are all examples of open-ended resources that allow babies to explore. As babies grow, adults respond to the growing senses, for example, by offering foods that allow exploration of new tastes, smells, textures, etc. and, similarly, understand that not everything will be liked on first offering.

However, in terms of PSED, how often are lunchtimes rushed and stressful (for adults as well as the children), and simply a part of the day to be completed as quickly as possible in order to clear away and tidy up and move on to the next thing? Imagine though if this happened to you as an adult. How would you feel if you had to rush your evening meal because someone was determined to clear up as quickly as possible? How would you feel if your meal time consisted of someone constantly telling you to sit still, sit up, behave, stop talking, etc.? Sadly, this is the reality for many children, and we will explore this further in Chapter 3.

In terms of PSED, it is vital for adults to consider how we are supporting children to engage with all of their senses. If we know that it is the senses that carry messages to the brain, then how do we support children to use those senses in order to learn, develop, flourish and thrive? Some children will respond more strongly if their sense of smell is engaged, while for others it may be their hearing. Therefore, practitioners are finding innovative ways of introducing lavender or music into settings, for example, in order to facilitate a calming atmosphere for the children. As we know, children learn by doing, exploring, copying, taking risks, making mistakes, repetition and so on, and the messages children's brains are receiving, via their five senses, are full of interesting and exciting things to explore, learn about, be intrigued by, be inspired by and feel valued by. In other words, we offer a range of ways for supporting the Characteristics of Effective Learning (Early Education 2012, p.5). In this way, children are supported to learn and develop, they are encouraged to explore their world through their senses and messages can then travel further into their brains.

Reptilian Brain (Brainstem)

The reptilian brain, is as its name suggests, largely equated with the functions of the brains found in early primitive reptiles. It sits close to the top of the spinal column, at the base of the brain. In simplistic terms, the reptilian brain controls our bodily functions and our responses to what is happening around us (especially danger). The reptilian brain needs food, warmth, sleep, routine and people who help it to feel safe, and once all these things are in place the reptilian section of the brain feels secure. We know the importance of this for children, but do we always consider how the reptilian brain may well be causing the reactions/behaviours we see in children? How often are children 'accused' of being 'naughty', when actually they are tired, hungry, cold or even afraid? Imagine the scenario if an adult was treated in this way.

REFLECTIVE PRACTICE: CASE STUDY

Reptilian Brain Behaviours

You are running late for work. You have slept badly due to a head cold. The boiler was not working, and therefore you did not have any hot water. You accidently dropped the last of the milk and so have not had breakfast. The roadworks on the High Street caused the bus to be late and now you have run the five minutes from the bus stop and have arrived at work, out of breath, hot and sticky, slightly apprehensive and a little grumpy.

As you arrive at the building, there are lots of parents and children and other staff around. You run down the corridor to get to the lockers as quickly as possible, in order to get into your area as soon as you can.

Suddenly your manager comes out of the office and shouts: 'We do not run inside. Please walk nicely.'

Consider the above scenario:

- How would you feel?

- How do you think your reptilian brain would be feeling?

- How often do we do/say similar things to children?

- Considering this now – how does that make you feel?

It seems ridiculous when put into this context, and we will explore this more elsewhere in this book, but this (and similar examples) happen to children all the time, and it happens a lot. It is acknowledged that this and similar situations are not intended to cause stress, fear, hurt and anger and so on – but that does not help the poor reptilian brain...

In early childhood, it is well recognised that the needs of the reptilian brain are vital for children's wellbeing, learning and development. Children who are cold, hungry, unsure what will happen next, or untrusting of the adults or the environment, for example, are *unable* to learn, develop, flourish and thrive. Therefore, ECCE practitioners, by having regard to each 'unique child' and developing 'enabling environments' and 'positive relationships', are supporting the young reptilian brains in their care to feel safe, and ensuring that 'Development Matters' (Early Education 2012) for each child.

However, do we *actively* and *consciously* consider the needs of the young reptilian brain? Do we stop to think 'is this child cold/hungry/frightened/ hot/tired', etc.? Or do we move straight into almost 'blame' mode – and react to stop the child behaving/acting in a particular way? Imagine the scenario of being late for work; how different would that feel if your manager turned and said 'hey, you look a little frazzled, go sit down for a few minutes and give yourself time to breathe'? I am sure that the majority of us do give children 'time to breathe', but I am also sure that unintentionally we also shout 'we do not run inside' (or similar well-intended phrases) without thinking about what the reptilian brain might be experiencing, or without considering other factors that may be involved.

For example, are we aware of the potentially stressful encounters the small reptilian brains may have already experienced before they even enter, or arrive at, our settings? The reptilian brain needs to feel safe and secure in order for it, and the rest of the brain, to function correctly, yet, sadly, we will have all supported children who, for a variety of reasons, are struggling to feel safe and secure. Sadly, many children face issues or 'other factors' that influence their brains. Therefore, we offer protection, warmth, love and affection, and do our utmost to ensure, that with us at least, children have the safety and security they so desperately need. In other words, we build strong, respectful and trusting, as well as positive, relationships. We build caring and supportive environments where each child can be unique. However, we do not always know which children need additional support in order to feel safe and secure. We do not always know which children are frightened by our environments, for example. Are we aware of the children experiencing difficulties at home? Or, consider the children you know, the ones who perhaps cannot talk yet, or the ones who are quieter, or the children perhaps with Special Educational Needs or Disabilities (SEND); how do we support the PSED of these children? How do we ensure the reptilian brains of these children feel safe and secure?

You have probably noticed the obvious and intentional references here to *Development Matters* (Early Education 2012), and the highly effective triumvirate of:

- Unique Child

- Enabling Environments

- Positive Relationships.

These well-regarded, familiar and highly effective areas of early childhood practice are the bedrock of our beliefs in how children learn, develop, flourish and thrive. We quote them and refer to them constantly, but do we consider them in relation to brain development? Do we consider how each unique child, the environments we provide and the relationships we form have a direct impact on how children's brains develop and, indeed, react?

The Fight, Flight or Freeze Response

One of the main roles of the reptilian brain is to decipher the many millions of pieces of information received constantly, and highlight any that may be about to cause a threat. The reptilian brain's response to a threat is to help our brain decide on the most appropriate course of action to keep it safe: whether it is a case of fight, flight or freeze. Consider how animals behave when they are scared, perhaps when sensing, or coming across, another animal who may see them as food. They have three basic options:

- Fight: is there any possibility of being bigger or stronger than the perceived threat?

- Flight: is there any possibility of out-running the perceived threat?

- Freeze: is there any possibility of standing completely still and not being noticed?

So, for example, a deer, meeting a lion, would very quickly decide that winning a fight is probably out of the question, flight could be a possible option, if there is enough open space to out-run the lion, or maybe standing still against the trees and hoping not to be noticed is the best choice. The analogy of a 'rabbit caught in the headlights' is useful here. Rabbits often freeze in terror and seem unable to run away to safety when suddenly finding themselves on a road at dusk, and facing an oncoming car.

In terms of humans, the response is similar. With young children, when they meet a real or perceived threat, they work out the best response: fight, flight or freeze. Consider toddlers finding their way in an ECCE setting and trying to understand group dynamics, for example; some will fight, some will choose flight and some, just like the rabbit in the headlights, will freeze in terror. Additionally, at different times, the same toddler may try any or all of the responses to see which is the best option. The question to ask ourselves here is – do we as adults recognise these reactions as the reptilian brain response?

Now let us consider adult responses to threats, which also can be real or perceived. The key here is to understand, that as mammals (human or otherwise), there is rarely a considered, thoughtful or measured response in these situations. It is usually a primal instinct, driven by the reptilian brain to ensure safety. Dr Suzanne Zeedyk (2013) talks of the metaphorical fear of 'sabre-toothed tigers' and the primal instinct to stay alive and not be eaten.

As already discussed, the brain's response to threats is unconscious, but there is also a physical (or physiological) response to fear, which is also beyond our control. Imagine walking alone down a dark street late at night, you hear footsteps behind you. Your heart starts to beat faster, your mouth goes dry, your pulse quickens, your muscles start to tense, you start to sweat and your breathing becomes faster and shallower, and so on. Within a split second your brain has perceived the threat, moved your body into a state of high alert and considered whether to fight, flight or freeze, all without you making any conscious effort... And this response is the same in children who are afraid, worried or anxious, whether or not that fear is real or perceived.

In today's modern world, as Zeedyk (2013) rightly points out, although there are no 'sabre-toothed tigers', there are however other threats, both real and perceived, that cause the brain to react in much the same way as it would have done in primeval days. Parents, practitioners and leaders and managers in the early childhood world spend a huge amount of time trying to ensure threats (both real and perceived) are minimised for children, wherever possible.

One way in which we consciously do this is through Observation, Assessment and Planning (OAP). Practitioners continuously observe children, and consider why they are responding (or should we say – behaving?) in the way they are to a given situation or experience, then plan and action any interventions or responses accordingly. There is no 'magic wand'; this is about knowing individuals, and putting in place a range of strategies that will help children feel safe and secure. The question here is – is Observation, Assessment and Planning seen as a way of supporting brain development (and indeed helping children feel safe) – or just more 'paperwork we have to do'? (And we will explore this in more depth in Chapter 5.) Additionally, do we consider the 'unconscious' ways we react? The throw-away line, such as 'we do not run', or how we support the child who is desperately trying to stay so still and quiet as to not be noticed?

The world can be a scary place, whether you are a deer meeting a lion, a rabbit caught in the path of a fast car, a toddler trying to understand the world or, indeed, an adult worried about being late for work. In terms of the reptilian brain and PSED, our role is to support children to feel safe, in order that learning and development can take place. But before that can happen, we then also must navigate the emotional part of the brain.

The Mammalian Brain (Limbic Brain)

In this section, let us explore what we know about the importance of the limbic brain/mammalian brain in terms of the work we undertake in early childhood. Oxforddictionaries.com define a mammal as:

> A warm-blooded vertebrate animal of a class that is distinguished by the possession of hair or fur, females that secrete milk for the nourishment of the young, and (typically) the birth of live young.

Science tells us that the limbic area of the brain (in some form) is present in all mammals, hence the term mammalian brain. So, this links back to my experience with my two cats, who as mammals have some form of 'limbic brain'. As I discussed in the introduction I am fairly certain my two cats show emotion in some way, and there is research around this with other mammals too. Indeed, as mentioned previously, Charles Darwin's *The Expression of the Emotions in Man and Animals* from 1872 is a fascinating read. Additionally, the majority of the research we have and understand *is* from work based on medical research and observations on animal behaviour and animal brains. Whether we agree with this ethically, morally, personally, or not, is not a debate for here. Agreeable or not, the fact remains that this is where the basis of our knowledge comes from. Phelps and LeDoux (2005), in their article 'Contributions of the amygdala to emotion processing: from animal models to human behavior', offer a comprehensive overview on how this area of science has developed:

> Although studies in humans cannot explore the neural systems of behavior with the same level of specificity as research in nonhuman animals, identifying links in the neural representation of behavior across species results in a greater understanding of both the behavioral influence and neural representation of emotion in humans. (Phelps and LeDoux 2005, p.184)

In other words, science cannot (at least at the moment) fully explore functioning human brains, for obvious reasons. However, it is possible to use the research gathered elsewhere to develop our understanding of behaviours and emotions in humans. This, along with developing technology and new research with humans, is allowing us to learn more than ever before:

> Contemporary non-invasive neuroimaging methods have provided developmental scientists with the opportunity to track safely, cognitive and neural processes underlying human development. (Casey *et al.* 2005, p.104)

The mammalian brain is also known as the limbic area, and is in the very centre of the brain and cocooned or 'ringed' on all sides, and therefore difficult to access, in terms of research on 'live' subjects. As Goleman (1996, p.10) explains, it is 'called the limbic system from "limbus" the Latin word for ring'. And we know we still have much to learn. Rajmohan and Mohandas (2007) suggest:

> There is no universal agreement on the total list of structures, which comprise the limbic system. (Rajmohan and Mohandas 2007, p.132)

Whether the structure of the brain is universally agreed, or not, is not hugely important at this point. What is important, and is universally agreed, is the function that this part of the brain undertakes. The limbic system is the main area where emotion, memories, self-esteem, sense of identity and belief in ourselves are developed, and where the need for touch and affection is located. It is also widely acknowledged that the 'emotional mammalian brain' developed *before* the 'human thinking neocortex brain'. I particularly like Goleman's description of this. Perhaps this quote is one that should become as concrete and well known in PSED/human development as the nursery rhymes we sing from our own childhoods:

> The fact that the thinking brain grew from the emotional reveals much about the relationship of thought to feeling: there was an emotional brain long before there was a rational one. (Goleman 1996, p.10)

This knowledge of the interactional relationship between feelings/emotions and learning/thinking is well regarded in early childhood. We also know what happens when this relationship fails or is damaged. The damage caused by a range of factors and influences such as poverty, war, famine, abuse, discrimination, lack of interaction and attachment and so on, are ones that practitioners in early childhood ever strive to counteract. In ECCE, a great deal of emphasis is placed on strategies, activities, relationships, environments and so on, that support this area of the brain, and we recognise the importance of these areas of practice. In early childhood, these are often collectively highlighted under one category of PSED. Whilst it is acknowledged that PSED is not exclusively developed in the limbic brain, there is a direct correlation. In terms of early childhood, in recent years, this greater knowledge has resulted in elevating the status of PSED to a higher prominence than ever before, and rightly so. The importance of developing and supporting this middle part of the brain is well researched, documented and implemented into daily practice with young children. PSED is highly regarded as the key area that forms the foundations for all other areas of learning and development. In other words, the functions of the limbic brain are seen as hugely important in early childhood, but do we consistently put these understandings and beliefs into practice?

Let us consider this from an early childhood point of view: a child who has just turned three years old has been with you in your setting for a term. There is pressure to move the child into the preschool room, as there are more parents wanting places for their soon-to-be two-year-olds. The key person expresses concern that they have just started to build strong relationships with the parents, the child has only had one term to settle, and that the child is still struggling with understanding of the general routines, the environment and building friendships with peers.

Hopefully, in any effective setting, serious, thoughtful and compassionate conversations will take place, where the needs of the child will be considered. In other words, it will be the personal, social and emotional needs of the child that are at the forefront of any discussions. However, in some cases this will not happen. The business case will, understandably, have to be accounted for, parent pressure for the child to move up 'to be ready for school', etc. will all 'weigh in' to the argument, and in the middle of this, the child's voice can be lost. Once the move has taken place, will consideration be given to the various responses of the brain of the child, and therefore any reactions to the situation? Or once again, even unintentionally, will it be that the default 'blame' mode takes over? Let's consider how this could feel as an adult.

REFLECTIVE PRACTICE: CASE STUDY

Mammalian Brain Behaviours

After three months in a new job, you are told by your manager that you are moving areas at work. You are needed in another section and will be moving next week. You explain that you have just started to develop relationships, get used to the routine and have only really just settled in. Your manager downplays your concerns and says 'you'll be fine, just be a big girl/boy, you'll love it, they have so much fun in the other area'.

Consider the above scenario:

- How would you feel?

- How do you think your mammalian brain feels?

- How often do we do/say similar things to children?

- Considering this now – how does that make you feel?

Again, as in the Reptilian Brain Behaviours case study, this seems ridiculous when phrased like this, but this is often what happens to very young children. In terms of PSED, do we actively and consciously consider how our actions/words impact on children's feelings? Do we stop to consider the various areas and needs of the brain, and therefore the unconscious reactions we will then inevitably see in the child? On the whole, I am sure the child will be supported, but I also suspect that at times young children are told to be 'a big boy/big girl' and their emotions unintentionally dismissed, and we will explore this further throughout the book.

The mammalian part of the brain is the section of the brain that as adults we often find ourselves at a loss to describe, decipher and understand. For many humans, talking about emotions is, in and of itself, difficult. Our thinking brain struggles to find the appropriate words to describe how we feel, and equally we struggle to find words that will be acceptable to those we are talking to. In other words, we are worried that the words we use will cause an emotional reaction in others. For example, we struggle to discuss what we believe maybe contentious issues with our own friends, partners, family and the colleagues and families within our workplace. Additionally, we sometimes find our emotions taking over, and perhaps we behave in more impulsive ways than usual. Daniel Goleman describes this:

> In a very real sense we have two minds, one that thinks and one that feels... One, the rational mind, is the mode of comprehension... Thoughtful, able to ponder and reflect. But alongside that there is another system of knowing, impulsive and powerful, if sometimes illogical – the emotional mind. (Goleman 1996, p.8)

In essence, in ECCE, we praise the features of PSED, we shout loudly of the importance of children being supported, we explain to others why PSED is so important and then in the next breath complain that children are 'misbehaving', rather than referring back to our extensive knowledge and understanding of how brains work. In other words, we forget the emotional needs of the brain. Consider, then, the children and adults you know; are children and adults treated differently when they are experiencing emotions?

REFLECTIVE PRACTICE

Understanding Influences on Behaviours?

Consider your career history:

- Thinking about children, how are children supported with their emotions? How are children treated? Is this consistent – and if not, why not?

- How do adults usually react to children's emotions?

- What messages does that send to children?

- Now consider adults: how are adults supported with their emotions? How are adults treated?

- Are the adults and children treated differently – why do you think that is?

Hopefully, the mammalian brain is supported; however, I suspect that in the busyness of day-to-day practice, this is not always the case. I suspect that adults who are upset, for example, are often offered a listening ear and encouraged to talk, whereas, perhaps unintentionally, many young brains are left awash with emotions, confused by reactions to emotions and conflicted by what is acceptable, and what is not. Therefore, a brain that is awash with emotions will struggle to learn, develop, thrive and flourish.

The Neocortex

Now, let us contemplate the largest part of the brain, sitting on top, the neocortex. Depending on where you look, you may find words such as Cerebral Cortex, Cerebellum, Pre-frontal Cortex, the Frontal Lobe or Hemispheres and so on. These areas work together, connected through networks of neurons so that thinking, cognitive learning and development can happen, and for the purpose of this book, I am going to use the term 'neocortex', from neo (meaning new) and cortex (outer layer):

> The neocortex, as the name implies, is the newest addition to our brain and is considered to be the crowning achievement of evolution and the biological substrate [layer] of human mental prowess. (Rakic 2009)

The neocortex supports our ability to think, be creative and imaginative, develop language, have consciousness, pay attention, be involved and so on. For very young children, connections within the brain are being made at an astounding rate: currently there is some debate, but research seems to agree at somewhere between 700 and 1000 connections *per second* in the first few years of life. This is an astonishing figure, and shows clearly the importance of early childhood experiences. The more we can support the developing brain, the more connections are made, the more children can learn, develop, flourish and thrive. Sounds simple, doesn't it? However, a whole host of other factors also come into play.

As previously acknowledged, the areas of the brain do not operate in isolation, and in terms of the neocortex and the reptilian brain there is a need for the two to operate in harmony, in order for thinking and learning to occur. When discussing this, via email, with a colleague, the following sums this up:

> This functioning can be altered/switched off if the reptilian brain takes over. If neural connections between the limbic brain and the neocortex are not strongly myelinated, then thinking is also impaired. (S. Zeedyk, 2016, personal communication, 15 July)

Myelination within brains plays a very specific role; it allows messages to travel further and faster into the brain. Purves *et al.* (2007, p.57) describe this as: '...flows faster along the axon than it would in the absence of myelination'.

Our understanding of the importance of the myelin sheath and myelination is one that is continuing to grow as science progresses. Research by Deoni *et al.* (2015) showed how new magnetic resonance imaging (MRI) technologies, such as 'T1 relaxation time' and 'myelin water fraction (MWF)', are helping to shape our understanding, but not quite providing all the answers just yet:

> Results lay the foundation for future studies examining the relationship(s) between measures of cortical maturation and cognitive and behavioral functioning, deviations in atypical development or disease, or the relationship between cortical and white matter [nerve fibres and myelin] maturation. (Deoni *et al.* 2015, p.160)

It is generally accepted that myelination begins during pregnancy, develops rapidly during early childhood and then continues, as we learn new things, but slows at around the age of 30. This perhaps explains why it can be harder to learn new things as we get older. In a personal communication with Professor Lynda Erskine, Chair of Development Neurobiology at the University of Aberdeen, we had a conversation about the importance of myelination:

> Many nerves in the body do not become fully myelinated until well into childhood. So [myelination is] important in young children as information may not pass from brain to e.g. muscles as fast as in adults, so [children] will be less co-ordinated etc. (Professor L. Erskine, 2016, personal communication, 14 November)

This clearly shows that as adults, we have to give children time to process, consider and think about new information in order to learn. Whether, as Professor Erskine describes, this is information moving from 'brain to muscle' or information regarding emotions and responses to 'real or perceived' threats, children's brains need support and encouragement to help them understand their world. Is it any wonder that at times children go into meltdown? Think how your brain feels when you have worked hard to work out a problem, or read a difficult book, or had an emotional experience, for example; sometimes it takes a while for you to work out what to do next...but it does not stop there...there is still more for these little brains to contend with...

Additional to all the areas of the brain working in harmony and the levels of myelination, the brain also has a whole host of other factors to deal with, including everyday bumps and bruises, various foodstuffs and nutrition, disabilities and additional needs, other influences and so on, and we will consider some of these elsewhere in this book. For now, I want to concentrate on hormones. When we think of hormones, we tend to think of the 'raging' ones associated with teenagers, or the 'certain age' ones usually associated with later life. However, hormones play a much bigger role throughout our lives, and research is showing how this starts before birth and into early childhood. Sue Gerhardt discusses this very early on her book *Why Love Matters*:

> When a mother is very stressed during the last stage of pregnancy, her baby's own stress response can become more reactive (Oberlander *et al.* 2008)…her baby is likely to have higher than average cortisol levels at the age of four months (Kaplan *et al.* 2008). (Gerhardt 2015, p.21)

Designed to regulate and control various functions of the body, humans have around 50 hormones, and these are controlled by a group of glands. Hormones include cortisol, oxytocin, thyroxine, insulin, adrenaline, dopamine, serotonin, oestrogen and testosterone, to name just a few. Each of these hormones plays a specific role, and you may well have personal experiences of how the body reacts when they do not do the job they are designed for. In terms of PSED, I want to concentrate on the hormone cortisol, and the role of the RAS filter.

The RAS Filter
The Reticular Activating System (RAS) filter sits on top of the brainstem/reptilian brain. The word 'reticular' comes from the Latin for having a 'net-like' appearance, and meaning complex or intricate. In order for the brain to work correctly, the RAS filter deciphers information and allows that which is interesting and relevant through, and much like a 'gatekeeper' it protects the main part of the brain from being overloaded.

In humans (and indeed in mammals), when feeling stressed, frightened, worried or scared or similar (in other words, when feeling threatened), the hormone cortisol is released. A small amount of cortisol is good for the brain; it supports the effort needed to persevere and to reach goals and so on, such as when feeling slightly stressed/pressured to meet a tight deadline. However, in large quantities, cortisol is toxic to the human brain, and therefore in times of great stress, the RAS filter steps in to protect the rest of the brain from being overloaded with a toxic substance.

In effect, this means that the RAS filter shuts down access to the rest of the brain, acting as a gatekeeper or drawbridge, or imagine a net-like cluster that 'catches' useless or irrelevant information. This is an unconscious act, it is not thought about, and it enables the body, and indeed the brain, to concentrate on what is causing the threat. Only information in relation to the threat is allowed through. No other information is processed, and cortisol is prevented from poisoning the rest of the brain. This in turn allows the brain to concentrate and decide on a course of action – fight, flight or freeze.

It is very easy to see how a child (or indeed an adult) who is suffering stress, anxiety or fear, etc. whose RAS filter has come into play, will be unable to receive any further messages. You may well have experienced this in a simple way, for example, when that tight deadline becomes threateningly close, and you find that even reading/writing simple words becomes almost impossible. Additionally, as previously mentioned, this is an unconscious act. It is not intentional, deliberate or calculated. Sue Gerhardt describes this as:

> The higher part of the cortex cannot operate independently of the more primitive gut responses. (Gerhardt 2015, p.6)

Doesn't it sound simple when put this way?

- The reptilian brain is stressed/frightened.
- The RAS filter responds.
- Information cannot proceed.
- You must make a decision – fight, flight or freeze.

I know I have just used some of the estimated 86 billion neurons (Cherry 2017) in my brain to simplify years of research and effort into a few simple sentences. However, the point I am making is that we can use this wealth of neuroscience-based research, knowledge and understanding (albeit in a very, very simplified form) to great advantage when supporting very young children.

Early Childhood Scenario

Imagine the two-year-old, determined to reach the tin of biscuits/broken toy car/sharp knife on the work surface. After several minutes of trial, error and concerted effort, an adult will come along and remove the offending item further from the toddler's reach. The toddler, now deeply confused, will protest – and probably protest loudly!

The adult will try, with all available resources to explain, cajole and/or reason with the toddler as to why the toddler cannot have the 'offending' item at this moment in time (it is nearly lunchtime, it is broken, it is dangerous, etc.). The toddler, not fully understanding, or perhaps 'disagreeing' with the explanation, cajoling or reasoning, will protest louder and stronger, until eventually the fabulous meltdowns two-year-olds are so famous for will appear.

Alternatively, imagine the scenario with a slightly older child who constantly asks 'Why?' Often to the exasperation of the adult who is trying to explain the reasoning behind the child not being able to have the tin of biscuits, toy car or sharp knife.

Finally, imagine it with the older child/younger teenager, who not only asks 'Why', but offers alternative viewpoints, additional information and reasons as to why the 'offending' item should be allowed.

Now let us consider a more 'science-based' description, in a very simplified way.

The toddler trying to reach the work surface becomes stressed, angry, upset, frustrated and exasperated and so on, with the lack of progress in reaching the 'offending' item. The hormone cortisol is released; the reptilian brain starts to worry. The adult steps in, the situation is exacerbated, albeit unintentionally.

The limbic area of the toddler's brain is confused, so therefore emotions, neurons, pathways and so on are in chaos and turmoil. As more and more cortisol is released the RAS filter must step in to protect the rest of the brain. This ensures that cortisol cannot flood the rest of the brain, but also means that no further information can be processed either. Therefore, any intervention by an adult is completely unnoticed, no matter how well-meaning. This is a physical, chemical, but not intentional reaction: hence my wording of 'fabulous meltdown' rather than the use of the term 'temper tantrum'. I dislike intensely the term 'temper tantrum' when used to describe children. The term implies an intentional, deliberate and calculated response. Temper tantrums are misnomers: 'tantrum' means 'peevishness' or 'grumpiness', the toddler is not being peevish, or grumpy – they are reacting to the levels of cortisol in their brains, therefore, they have *no control* over their response. The cries and tears of a distressed child are very real:

> The full story of why our bab[ie]s cry is a bit more complicated. In Aletha Solter's book *The Aware Baby* [2001] she explains the science behind our tears, and why babies cry for two reasons, one is to get their needs met and two; to heal and recover from stress and tension.
>
> Dr William Frey is a biologist that investigated the chemical make-up of tears. He found that they actually contain cortisol, the stress hormone, so that when we cry we are literally releasing stress from our bodies. Tears also contain Manganese…important for balancing mood, and other toxins. (Orson 2016a)

If we refer back to our 'offending item' discussion, it is now very easy to see how the well-meaning interventions by the adult are so easily missed by the toddler. At such an early stage of PSED, the toddler is still trying to understand which situations might need a fight, flight or freeze response, still trying to understand their own emotions, as well as trying to see what their own bodies can and cannot do. Additionally, considering the slightly older child or young teenager, it is easy to see how they are beginning to understand, and constantly develop their understanding of, appropriate responses. In the simple scenario discussed earlier of an unsuitable 'offending' item, these older children are therefore less prone to fight, flight or freeze and are also beginning to use the rational area of their brains to negotiate, reason and understand. Therefore, the interventions of a well-meaning adult could either facilitate PSED, or unintentionally make matters worse.

It is easy to see how this would escalate quickly in a more serious situation. The toddler experiencing stress/anxiety, etc. is a 'fabulous' example of what too much cortisol can do to the human brain, and how any human (toddler, older child, teenager or indeed adult) would act if the situation caused further anxiety/stress, for example. Imagine the behaviours of a child, teenager (or adult), if the 'offending' item of a tin of biscuits was moved from reach after seven days of being shipwrecked on a desert island? The fight, flight or freeze mode would take over, and understandably so. It is therefore easy to see the importance of how some knowledge and understanding of neuroscience and brain development can be incredibly useful in terms of personal, social and emotional development.

Supporting PSED

This chapter is titled 'Brain Development, Neuroscience and Supporting PSED', so finally, let's have a look at what we mean by PSED It is truly wonderful that PSED has such a high profile in the ECCE field. However, one of the dangers of constantly referring to PSED as PSED is that it could potentially lose some of its power. PSED is *personal, social* and *emotional* development, and we forget this at our peril.

One of the reasons I will always shout loudly for, and advocate for, *Development Matters* (Early Education 2012) is because PSED is the first area of Learning and Development. By putting PSED first, *Development Matters* acknowledges that all other areas of learning and development are built on the foundations of *personal, social* **and** *emotional* development. Regardless of what documentation we may have, or indeed develop, in the future, there needs to be the understanding that without PSED, other areas of learning and development cannot happen. I often explain this on training programmes in the following way.

REFLECTIVE PRACTICE

PSED and Training

Consider how you feel attending a training course, then ask yourself the following questions:

1. How did/do you feel just before entering the training room?

2. What was/is the first thing you do when you walk in to a training room?

3. How did/didn't the trainer, or other delegates, react to you coming into the room?

4. How did/do you feel?

In all probability for most of us, and what most people say to me on training is:

1. They feel terrified, or at least slightly anxious, stressed or nervous just before entering a training room.

2. They usually look for a friend or someone they know.

3. If they get a smile or a welcome, or are offered a cup of coffee, etc. that helps.

4. How they feel – depends on the answers to questions number two and three!

In other words, attending a training course, walking into a room for the first time, it is our PSED that is most important! Not the learning and development… This very first experience of perhaps a new situation, or a new environment; it is not what we are about to learn that is at the forefront of our minds, it is our personal, social and emotional responses that have taken control. Therefore, this simple activity shows how even as adults, our PSED comes into play first. Imagine then how this feels for very young children. Imagine if children have had other stresses and strains *before* they enter the setting. Imagine if these very subtle signs are missed by the adults, who go about the day's business of 'teaching and learning', perhaps not realising the needs of the various sections of the brain are not being met.

On training programmes, when we talk about this we usually then go on to have a conversation looking at how you could be stressed about what has happened to you already that day, or stressed due to previous experiences, for example. We consider how your circumstances, health, family, etc. previous experiences of trainers who ignore you, or intimidate you, trainers who are too loud, or too quiet, other delegates who smile welcomingly, and those that don't – how all of these things (and more) have a direct influence on your ability to engage with the training and therefore learn and develop. Consider, then, how knowing this can influence your practice with young children.

PSED: The Sum and the Parts

As already acknowledged, it is truly brilliant that PSED has such a high standing in early childhood circles. However, it is worth consideration, that PSED is *also* split into three areas within *Development Matters* (Early Education 2012):

- Making Relationships [social]

- Self-confidence and Self-awareness [personal] and

- Managing Feelings and Behaviour [emotional].

I recognise there is cross-over in all of these, and they cannot be viewed in isolation, and there is also the acknowledgment that children may be developing in the different areas at different times. For example, some children may be able to 'play cooperatively with a familiar adult' (16–26 months), yet be struggling with the 'growing ability to soothe themselves' (8–20 months). In other words, a child could be developing socially, but struggling emotionally. I know that the world is not as clear cut as this and there will always be 'blurred edges', but I do think we need to remember that PSED is also about these three distinct areas of development.

If you think back to the reflective practice exercise and your experience on training, the chances are that you will, in that very early engagement at the point of arrival, have considered all three areas of your PSED:

- Personal: Do I feel confident, able to engage?

- Social: Do I know anyone? Is anyone smiling at me?

- Emotional: Do I feel safe and happy or scared and worried?

This will have all happened in the millionth of a second as you enter the room, and it is, on the whole, subconscious. And it is the same for children. There is a wealth of books and information out in the big wide world on how we can support these areas for young children, but for the purposes of this chapter, I want to concentrate on one document: SEAD.

SEAD: Social and Emotional Aspects of Development

In my opinion, one of the best PSED documents developed in recent years is the Social and Emotional Aspects of Development (SEAD) Practitioner Handbook, developed by the National Strategies as part of the then DCSF (Department for Children, Schools and Families) in 2008. The document drew on the extensive experiences of SEAL in schools (Social and Emotional Aspects of Learning). SEAD was developed by early years practitioners for early years practitioners – and it shows. It is very accessible, has case studies to consider and offers a range of research to reflect on. Although some of the language has changed slightly, the document, in my opinion, should be a must read for anyone in early childhood, and is still available online (see bibliography for more information).

SEAD (DCSF 2008, p.5) considers:

Personal, Social and Emotional Development (PSED) are three building blocks of future success in life. They are closely linked to each other and often bracketed together as one area of learning and development.

- Personal development (Being me) – how we come to understand who we are and what we can do, how we look after ourselves.

- Social development (Being social) – how we come to understand ourselves in relation to others, how we make friends, understand the rules of society and behave towards others.

- Emotional development (Having feelings) – how we come to understand our own and others' feelings and develop our ability to 'stand in someone else's shoes' and see things from their point of view, referred to as empathy.

Reading these through, it is perhaps easy for us to think of some adults who struggle with some of these areas, so imagine how difficult it must be for very young children in our world? SEAD (DCSF 2008, p.7) then goes on to discuss the idea of brain development and was one of the first widely available and accessible ECCE documents to consider neuroscience and the importance of this knowledge to early childhood:

Brain fact

Did you know…

Many things can interfere with the development of the brain while the baby is in the womb. One of these is the presence of high levels of the hormone cortisol in the mother's blood stream, which interferes with the development of the synapses. Cortisol is produced as a response to stress.

Babies and young children can themselves become stressed if their caregivers lack responsiveness to their emotional and physical needs. Their bodies will release cortisol at times of stress, affecting the brain by impeding the development of connections between brain cells. It is these connections that are needed for successful future development and learning.

In the intervening years since the publication of SEAD, our general understanding of brain development and the messages from neuroscience have developed exponentially. For example, it is now widely accepted that in terms of brain development and PSED, there is a huge correlation between personal, social and emotional development and the activities happening within the brain. In terms of adults, for example, imagine arriving for a job interview: your body is releasing small amounts of cortisol, which allows you to focus, but too much cortisol and your reptilian brain is tipped into fight, flight or freeze mode. An empathetic interviewer offers a smile and a warm welcome (in other words looks after your PSED), and your cortisol levels will lower. Or imagine you are asked a question that triggers a highly emotive memory; your reaction to the question will depend on the emotions involved and could perhaps be joyous, tearful or even aggressive. As adults, we find these and similar situations stressful, we are unsure what will happen, we perhaps don't know the people involved and we know we are being asked questions that maybe we are unsure about answering. In other words, our PSED is vulnerable. Now imagine how this feels for young children, perhaps arriving at a new setting or meeting an unfamiliar adult.

In conclusion, yes, I will always advocate for *Development Matters* (Early Education 2012), or any other similar material which supports PSED as the foundation for early childhood. Additionally, I will also always advocate that we remember that PSED is a collaboration of *personal, social* and *emotional* development. In order for children to flourish, thrive, learn and develop, we need to support and understand all three together, but we need to support and understand them individually too. In terms of PSED, we need to consider how knowledge of brain development and neuroscience relates to our understanding of early childhood. Knowledge and understanding of how the various elements of the brain all work in harmony (or not) is vital, and can help us understand, empathise and be compassionate when this harmony is uneasy, upset or disturbed.

Understanding how, if this is so difficult for us as adults, can support us to empathise with how it feels for children. If, as adults, we struggle to cope with, discuss and define emotions and emotional reactions, imagine how difficult it must be for a two-year-old or a four-year-old, for example. Imagine then, if you do manage to at least name an emotion, or explain your reaction, being told to 'be a big boy/girl' and to stop whatever emotion you are experiencing. In reality, as humans, we get the whole 'emotional reactions/responses' wrong in so many ways; either we are told to 'let everything out' or 'hold everything in' depending on who we are, where we are, who we are with and how old we are. This knowledge and understanding can, as will be explored throughout this book, help greatly in a move towards nurturing personal, social and emotional development in early childhood. Understanding the unique child, the environments we provide and the relationships and attachments we form, and how these influence the brain and behaviours, should be an integral part of early childhood:

> Babies and young children experience and express their emotions intensely and immediately; building close relationships with them means being able to provide effective emotional holding by developing a high level of empathic response. (Manning-Morton 2006, p.48)

Chapter 2

INFLUENCES ON PSED

As with my previous books, all the chapters, including the introduction, and in this case the foreword too, are always inextricably linked. That has never been more true than in this book and, in particular, this chapter.

This book draws on years of observation, reading, training, research and personal experience and practice. My understanding around neuroscience, brain development, personal, social and emotional development (PSED) and the other areas explored here has built on the collective efforts of many academics, researchers, writers and practitioners, and indeed on personal experience. It would be impossible to acknowledge every single piece of research, evidence, article, book, blog, or so on I have ever read or seen. Many of the areas covered are my understanding of 'generally accepted principles and practices'. Therefore, you may find that there are fewer quotes and references within this chapter itself. I have tried to include as many references as I can in the main text, and there is a comprehensive list of places for you to explore to further your own research in the bibliography section at the back of the book. Perhaps this will offer a useful starting point for further exploration. I do hope you will continue to develop your own repertoire of knowledge, understanding and opinion through your own research, reading and experience.

Additionally, it is fairly noticeable that this chapter is longer than the others. I must stress that it is not because I believe that this chapter is more important – it isn't. It is a longer chapter because I believe that the influences on PSED are the core of everything else that happens. If we get the 'influences' right, many other things fall into place. The influences on children's PSED are many and wide-ranging, and in some ways the book could have been just one long chapter. However, that would make it very difficult to read and navigate. This chapter, particularly, could become over-long and cumbersome, therefore for ease of reading it has been split into the following sections:

Part 1: Introduction

Part 2: Adults: Parents and Practitioners

Part 3: The Physical and Emotional Environment

Part 4: Managing Behaviours?

Part 5: Conclusion

Part 1 is self-explanatory and will be an introduction to the chapter. Part 2 will consider the role we as adults play and our influences on young children's PSED. Part 3 will look at environmental influences, both in terms of the emotional and physical environments. Part 4 is entitled 'Managing Behaviours?' and the question mark is important. What do we mean when we talk of managing behaviours? How do we (or how should we) consider the other influences of PSED and their effects on children's PSED, and therefore, in turn, children's behaviours? Part 5, the conclusion, will bring the chapter together and link into Chapter 3 on well-meaning.

PART 1: INTRODUCTION

Babies are born with some internal, as well as external, influences on their PSED already present. There is much research elsewhere that shows how their DNA, genes and chromosomes, experiences within the womb and during their birth, their place in the family, where they live (and in what conditions), and any disability or additional need could, and indeed in many cases does, have an impact and an influence on future lives, therefore I do not intend to repeat that here. Additionally, as we look wider, other children, adults, the environment, the community, socio-economic factors and so on, all come into play, and add to and influence PSED. It is widely agreed that how, when, where, who, what and why young children are interacted with all have an influence to some degree, and some of these influences are far reaching. Waldinger and Schulz (2016) consider early childhood experiences in their research accumulated over seven decades:

> Our study shows that the influences of childhood experiences can be demonstrated even when people reach their 80s, predicting how happy and secure they are in their marriages as octogenarians... We found that this link occurs in part because warmer childhoods promote better emotion management and interpersonal skills at midlife, and these skills predict more secure marriages in late life.

Before I started to write this book, or indeed any book, I usually sit down and plan what I think will go in each chapter; I have some ideas about the content, research, theory and reflective practice exercises that I want to include. Some things get moved about, but overall the plan I have is usually something like how the final book looks. This chapter was no exception. But, then something happened that made me think in a slightly different way, and I thought it would be useful to include it here, as we are looking at influences on PSED.

One Sunday, I fell and broke a bone in my foot. I would like to say I was doing something exciting such as skydiving or bare-back horse riding. Sadly, nothing as thrilling; I was simply vacuuming and fell off the bottom step! So, a fall of approximately 15 centimetres. This resulted in an enforced six weeks of reliance on other people for many tasks. Thankfully, many injuries such as these are not put into plaster casts these days, but the cast-replacement walking boot, whilst lighter and removable for bathing and sleeping, is intended to be just as restrictive. The boot is designed to ensure no weight or pressure is put onto the broken bone, and does its job very effectively. Additionally, it meant I did not need crutches. However, in terms of PSED, well, that's one thing the boot could not help with.

At differing points, I felt very vulnerable due to different tasks and activities I was unable to carry out on my own. Many people rallied around to support and for that I am ever grateful, but it was having to rely on this help that I struggled with most. And, it is this that has caused me to again reconsider how vulnerable young children are, as for many things they are reliant on our help. So, for example, as the cast-replacement boot is designed to be non-weight-bearing, I could still walk, and after a few days at home I was stir-crazy and desperately needed some fresh air. So, we went for a little wander around a local outdoor shopping centre. Not only was walking on uneven surfaces difficult, but other people just did not notice the boot, and therefore my difficulty in walking. I began to imagine how difficult it must be for small children walking around. Like my boot, small children are under most people's line of vision, and therefore not always noticed. Additionally, climbing up and down the smallest of steps, such as a kerb, was incredibly hard work. Again, I could empathise with how difficult this must be for toddlers.

Fairly quickly, I was completely exhausted, not only physically, but also emotionally, from simply trying to stay upright amongst people who, albeit unintentionally, did not see my poor foot. I could say easily and coherently that I had had enough and wanted to go home, but I was reliant on help to do so. In other words, I had to rely on my husband to take me away from this exhausting and quite honestly overwhelming situation, which, of course, he did without question. My feelings and exhaustion were acknowledged, and actions put in place to ensure my equilibrium returned.

As a confident and capable 'grownup', I had had enough, so imagine how this must feel for small children? I started to reflect on how children tell us these same messages and how we react. In the car coming back, I was thinking about how many times children find themselves in scary and overwhelming situations, and how perhaps, unlike me, they do not have either the language or the confidence to explain how they feel, or indeed, a trusting or caring adult who will listen and respond. Think of the toddlers new to the setting or the exhausted preschoolers after a busy day; it made me wonder how they feel, and how we, as adults, react?

Once home, I had other obstacles to overcome. I needed help to organise arrangements for meals, I could not carry more than one thing at once, as I needed a spare arm to balance, and I needed help getting in and out of the shower, as well as in and out of bed. I cannot stress enough how the support for these activities was given respectfully, compassionately, freely and willingly; however, I still felt vulnerable. The more activities I needed help with, the more vulnerable I felt, and the more I empathised with young children who are reliant on adults for their basic needs. Food, intimate care, such as nappy changing, dressing or bathing, for example, as well as opportunities for rest and sleep, are some of the most vital things that we, as adults, provide for children. My care was given with warmth and understanding. I was consulted on the food I would like; I was asked when I needed help and when I could manage. I was supported when I suddenly found myself unable to do something, such as bending down to pick something up. Importantly, I was treated with respect and understanding when I needed help with intimate care.

And, throughout all of this, I constantly had at the back of mind – I wonder how this feels for young children? I had a myriad of questions floating around my head. I wonder how young children feel when we bathe them, change them, feed them and when they need our help? I pondered how young children feel when they are rushed to do something because their carer is busy and needs to move on to the next thing. I considered how young children feel when they are not consulted about how they feel, or what help they might need. I wondered how young children feel when there is no-one who has the time to play with them, to talk to them, or listen to them…and more besides. It was almost as if I had been given a unique opportunity to experience life from a small child's perspective – and I must say I spent much of the time bored, worried, fed up, exhausted, frustrated, overwhelmed and/or lonely.

So, although I did not plan to put these thoughts in this book, as I did not plan to break a bone…I do think they are useful for 'framing' this chapter. This unique perspective of a child's eye view of the world brought into sharp relief the importance of being able to complete tasks for yourself, the inherent need to be independent and the in-built longing for companionship. In effect, I simply had a broken bone, and it should have been my physical development uppermost in my mind, but that was not the case. Again, I must stress that the support I received was given willingly and thoughtfully, but ultimately people have to return to work. My husband could not take several weeks off work to keep me company; additionally, as I was unable to drive, I could not visit anyone or anywhere either. Therefore, throughout all of this, it was my personal, social and emotional state that was at the forefront. In other words, it was my relationships and attachments that caused me the most concern, and the influence these have on the rest of my world.

The Importance of Attachment

Much has been written about the importance of attachment, particularly the work of John Bowlby and Mary Ainsworth. Their seminal work on the way that adults respond to children, and how this influences children's development, was and still is truly ground-breaking. Additionally, there were others who worked with either Bowlby and/or Ainsworth or who, influenced by their work, continued to research attachment and early relationships. Rudolph Schaffer, Peggy Emerson, Christoph Heinicke, Anna Freud and James Robertson are amongst some you might want to look into further. So, how can we, in early childhood, use this wealth of research to support children's PSED?

> ...the infant and young child should experience a warm, intimate, and continuous relationship with his mother (or permanent mother substitute) in which both find satisfaction and enjoyment. (Bowlby 1951, p.13)

It is interesting to re-read this from an ECCE practitioner point of view. The comment of 'permanent mother substitute', whilst perhaps a little sexist to our more modern understanding, could also be used to describe ECCE practitioners. Additionally, it talks of a 'continuous relationship...in which both find satisfaction and enjoyment'. Again, this is something I often talk about on training programmes; if we do not enjoy working with children – then why do it?

Mary Ainsworth is perhaps most famous for her development of the Strange Situation research (Ainsworth and Wittig 1969), which observed and recorded how babies reacted when their mothers left the room and a stranger entered. This study also looked at how the babies then reacted when their mother returned. This work formed the basis of what we now know as the different types of attachments experienced by young children (Ainsworth et al. 1978). Ainsworth, after many years of observation and research concluded that:

...an infant whose mother's responsiveness helps him to achieve his ends develops confidence in his own ability to control what happens to him. (Bell and Ainsworth 1972, p.1188).

In other words, the beginnings of self-resilience and self-regulation, but also the beginnings of PSED. Additionally, other research was, and still is, being conducted. For example, in a longitudinal study in Glasgow, Shaffer and Emerson (1964) observed 60 babies monthly for over 12 months. They discovered, that it was *not* the person who fed or changed the child that was the most important factor in the forming of attachments, but the *way* the adult responded to the child. In other words, the people who respond appropriately to eye contact, facial expressions, movements, sounds and so on.

In terms of early childhood, these and similar findings are hugely beneficial to know. I will always advocate that the role of the key person is vital, especially for intimate care, feeding, sleep routines and so on, but more importantly, it is not just the 'mechanics' of undertaking these tasks, it is *how* the key person responds that counts!

As with any research, there are people who are huge advocates and those who criticise, and the same is true of work on attachment. Like any research and theory, we must read and reflect and come to our conclusions. Page (2015a) offers suggestions of Dahlberg *et al.* (2007), Elfer (2014), Howes and Spieker (2008) and Schore and Schore (2008), as well as others, as places to go for further reading, and quotes:

> Rutter (1972) suggests that children experiencing high quality mothering can form multiple attachments with up to four or five caregivers without adverse effects. (Page 2015a, p.83)

Personally, I see any research, theory and opinion as a part of the learning journey we are experiencing in our quest to understand more of what happens in early childhood. Since the work of Bowlby, Ainsworth and Robinson, etc. the tireless work of many more people has added to our knowledge and understanding, and in turn this has developed the practices within early childhood, for example:

> ...there is a compelling argument for young children who attend day care to be given not only opportunity but time to become closely attached to one or two special adults – key person(s) rather than being indiscriminately cared for by a range of people. (Page *et al.* 2013, p.36)

If I go back to my broken bone, this is something I can very, very clearly identify with. The thought of indiscriminate people, whom I do not know, supporting me with some of the tasks I have discussed previously, fills me with terror! Similarly for it to be a range of random people, rather than one or two people to whom I have a connection, is as deeply disturbing. The more I reflect on this, the more I am convinced that PSED, relationships, attachments and connections should be at the heart of early childhood.

PSED from Pre-Birth

Bearing all the above in mind, let's consider briefly how babies' brains develop. As Suzanne talks of in the foreword:

> babies are born already able to communicate, and they engage socially with other people from the outset. Their brains are much more observant than our culture believes, and brains develop more rapidly within the first few years than they ever will again. The development of synapses between neurons in the brain is driven largely by a young child's experiences of their world, and the growth of those synapses happens a rate faster than anything we can realistically imagine.

As Suzanne so often brilliantly discusses, advocates and champions, babies are 'born connected'…but they need our help with the continuing building of their brains. Some scientists suggest that babies are born with under-developed brains, and therefore head size, so that they can fit through the birth canal, or that our ability to walk upright limits the size of the pelvis. Dunsworth and Eccleston (2015, p.58) consider:

> Regardless of whether selection for bipedalism [walk on two legs] (or some other unidentified reason) is limiting the expansion of the birth canal, other nonpelvic traits are contributing to the tight fit: Humans have relatively large and fat babies with large heads and broad shoulders that approach the capacity of the bony birth canal (Schultz 1949, Rosenberg and Trevathan 2002, Wells *et al.* 2012).

Whatever the reason, what is clear is that whilst some brain development has happened in the womb, much, much more still needs to happen. This means that babies' brains must continue to develop after their birth, and for that babies need our help. From a very young age, babies learn that we respond. If you have ever stuck your tongue out at a tiny baby, you will know that they respond and stick their tongue out at you. It is magical that such a tiny human being knows that an action they make will be replayed back to them by a caring adult. This is the 'science of connection' that Suzanne talks of with such energy and passion:

> …babies come into the world already connected – this means that the capacity to be an engaged, relational being doesn't happen sometime later in development, such as when children walk or talk or start school.

This capacity is present from birth. Babies share in mental and emotional experiences (the technical term for which is 'intersubjectivity'). This means that how we, as adults, relate to our babies matters. In fact, it matters not from birth but while babies are still in the womb. (Zeedyk 2012)

Additionally, Sue Gerhardt describes this as follows:

...what distinguishes humans from other new born mammals is the human baby's responsiveness to human interaction. Human beings are the most social of animals. (Gerhardt 2015, p.49)

So, just like me with my broken bone, babies are reliant on other people to help them in the world. A baby who learns that no-one responds to their cries will soon stop crying and learn that no-one is coming, whereas a baby who is comforted will learn that others are 'emotionally available to help notice and process feelings, to provide comfort when it is needed' (Gerhardt 2015, p.40). The soothing voice, the rocking arms, the soft touch, the calming and empathetic eye contact and facial expressions that adults display, all help to show babies that it is OK to be upset and that we are going to help. This could be by providing food, warmth, intimate care, reassurance or, quite simply, a cuddle (and we'll explore more on cuddles in Chapter 4). As babies grow, flourish and develop, their personal, social and emotional development is at the forefront.

REFLECTIVE PRACTICE

Early PSED (Part 1)

As we discussed in Chapter 1 on brain development, it is important that we remember that PSED is also three very distinct areas of development. Consider the babies and very young children you know/have known. Consider the things you have observed in their very early development. Then reflect on the following questions:

- What *personal* development are babies and very young children experiencing?
  - » What do we, as adults, do to support?
- What *social* development are babies and young children experiencing?
  - » What do we, as adults, do to support?
- What *emotional* development are babies and very young children experiencing?
  - » What do we, as adults, do to support?

I suspect that you will have many, many examples of babies' and very young children's personal, social and emotional development, and can easily undertake this reflective practice activity. However, as discussed in Chapter 1, the importance of personal, social and emotional development as a triumvirate is well recognised, but they are equally important as *individual* areas of development. Additionally, I suspect you will have many examples of babies and young children who struggle with one or more of these areas.

REFLECTIVE PRACTICE

Early PSED (Part 2)

Now consider babies and young children you know/have known who struggle with personal and/or social and/or emotional development. Reflect on the following questions:

- What *personal* development are babies and very young children struggling with?
  - » Why do you think that is?
- What *social* development are babies and young children struggling with?
  - » Why do you think that is?
- What *emotional* development are babies and very young children struggling with?
  - » Why do you think that is?

I suspect that it is the 'why do you think that is' questions that will have caused you the most concern. It may be that some babies and very young children are struggling with one or more areas of PSED due to personal circumstances such as illness, disabilities and/or additional needs, for example. However, I suspect that the majority of babies and very young children you are thinking about are struggling with one or more area of PSED due to *adults*. Whether it is something the adult(s) are saying (or not saying), doing (or not doing), my experiences, observations, research and exploration of theory usually all point to adults. It may well be that it is the environment that is causing the difficulties, but then as adults we have a responsibility to provide appropriate environments (whether at home or in ECCE), so even if environments are the issue, adults must shoulder the responsibility.

> The exceptionally strong influence of early experiences on brain architecture makes the early years a period of both great opportunity and great vulnerability for development. A growth-promoting environment that provides adequate nutrients, is free of toxins and is rich in social interactions with responsive caregivers prepares the developing brain to function well in a range of circumstances. An adverse environment in which young children are not well nourished, are exposed to toxic substances, and/or are deprived of appropriate sensory, emotional and social experiences is likely to disrupt the construction of important foundational capacities. (Center on the Developing Child at Harvard University 2016, p.7)

I feel quite sad writing this; in real terms, I am saying – adults cause babies and young children to struggle with PSED…and that is saddening. It also is likely to mean that you agree with me, otherwise you would not be reading this book. If you believed that the PSED of *all* babies and young children is tickety-boo and does not need any support, then why would you be reading this? So, then, that also means like me, that you think some things need changing – and therefore that this is able to be changed. This then also means we believe it *is* changeable, and if, as I suspect, adults are the root of much of this, then we, as adults, can change it…and that is heartening – and within our control. And that makes me very excited (and hopeful) – we can simply look at what we do, how we do it and why we do it, in terms of supporting, encouraging and empowering children's PSED.

> When we give children today what they need to learn, develop, and thrive, they give back to society in the future through a lifetime of productive citizenship. (Center on the Developing Child at Harvard University 2016, p.7)

Self-Soothe and Self-Settle

Whilst we are on the subject of early influences on PSED, you may have heard the terms 'self-soothe' or 'self-settle', particularly in relation to babies. Whilst the definitions of the terms self-soothe and self-settle are actually much wider, the terms themselves have been recently attributed to the specific area of 'teaching' babies to sleep through the night. I do not intend to go into this subject in too much depth, as there are not many settings that offer overnight care; however, you may be interested to look further into this. For ECCE, I feel it is useful for us as practitioners to have an awareness of these methods, and debates, in terms of supporting parents to understand how we as adults influence brain development, nurture PSED, and how this in turn influences behaviours. There is much research, information and comment around both sides of the 'sleep through the night' debate, and I would urge you to carry out your own research. Topics such as 'sleep training', the CIO (cry-it-out) technique, or gradual withdrawal are all terms you may come across. There are some further areas you might want to explore on this in the bibliography. In terms of reflective practice, considering the following questions may also help:

How do you feel when you wake through the night and experience one/some of the following?

- You are thirsty.

- You are too cold.

- You are too hot.

- You need to go to the toilet.

- You can hear music from a party in your street.

- You do not feel well.

- You have something on your mind.

- You hear a noise outside.

- You hear your neighbour's house/car alarm.

- You hear people outside shouting.

- You hear people next door shouting.

- You have had a nightmare.

Now imagine you are a young child, and these things happen. As I have said previously, there is much debate on this topic, and I would urge all readers to conduct their own research and come to their own conclusions.

PART 2: ADULTS: PARENTS AND PRACTITIONERS
The Adult Role in Personal, Social and Emotional Development

I think one of the major roles for practitioners in ECCE is to support parents and share with them our knowledge and understanding. *And* support parents to share their expertise and knowledge of their own children with us. There is a much-quoted line from the seminal EPPE

(Effective Pre-School and Primary Education) research that is a useful starting point for this section:

> For *all* children, the quality of the home learning environment is more important for intellectual and social development than parental occupation, education or income. *What parents do is more important than who parents are.* (Sylva *et al.* 2004, p.ii, emphasis added)

'What parents do is more important than who parents are' is a much-quoted, highly regarded, lauded and acclaimed statement. We know it, researchers know it – but do parents? And do we, in ECCE, do all we can to help parents know it? On training programmes, we sometimes have conversations about parents who appear to simply 'want to drop off/pick up their children and run'. It is very common for conversations to turn to parents who appear to be 'uninterested' or 'too pushy/anxious/clingy' or 'they talk to the manager, but not me, and I'm the child's key person' or 'they are too busy on their mobile phones', for example. My question, on training, and indeed here, is – but – do parents know what we know?

> But is this information about early, rapid brain growth – and how it is influenced by the quality of caregiving young children receive – reaching the people who need it most? If we care about babies and toddlers, we need to care about, listen to and meet the needs of their parents. Any effort to nurture and support young children, and to set them up for success in the long term, will be strengthened by helping their parents put this valuable brain science into action. (Zero to Three 2016, p.1)

I have never met a parent who is not interested in their child. I have worked with literally thousands of parents: I have met stressed parents, ill parents, worried parents, anxious parents, over-worked parents, vulnerable parents, misinformed parents, etc. but never a non-interested parent. Like us, parents are human – they have stresses, strains and complications in their lives which affect their behaviours. Similarly, parents can only process the available information they have at a point in time – we only know what we know. As many people, including Graham Allen, have said, 'babies do not come with a handbook' (Allen 2011, p.57), and nor should they. We do not want babies becoming robot replicas of each other. But that does not mean we cannot offer some sane and sound support to help parents.

So, in terms of ECCE, what do we do (or perhaps that should be, what *can* we do) to help parents? There is an overwhelming array of readily available information for parents, which includes in one, five-minute web search:

- 754,000,000 (million) hits on the term 'baby help'
- 220,000,000 (million) hits on the word 'parenting'
- 615,000,000 (million) hits on the term 'parent support'
- 74,000,000 (million) hits on 'parent magazine'
- 170,000 (thousand) books with the word 'parent/ing'.

Add to this the attention-grabbing, often derogatory or misleading headlines from the media and elsewhere regarding parents and parenting, and is it any wonder parents are confused? As I say elsewhere, much of this so-called 'information' will be unhelpful, and possibly even downright dangerous – but how to tell, how to work out, let alone find, in this vast behemoth of information overload, the bits that are actually useful?

> 58% [of parents] say there is so much parenting information available that it's hard to know whom to trust.

> 63% of parents say 'I am skeptical of people who give parenting advice and recommendations if they don't know my child and my situation specifically.' (Zero to Three 2016, p.21)

Perhaps, therefore then our first role in supporting babies and young children's PSED is in simply developing a two-way sharing of knowledge? After all, if 63 per cent of parents would prefer support from someone who knows their child and circumstances, then we, in ECCE, are ideally placed to offer that support.

In my opinion, some of the best training and research in this area is PEAL (Parents Early Years and Learning), and the work undertaken through the Early Childhood Unit (ECU) of the National Children's Bureau's (NCB). Built on a very solid foundation of accumulated research, theory and good practice, the PEAL approach champions true and authentic partnerships between parents and ECCE practitioners. PEAL underpinning values include:

- Children learn best in the context of warm, loving relationships.
- Parents play a key role in children's learning. They are experts on their own children and are their child's first and enduring educators.
- Parents want the best for their children and want to be involved in their children's learning.

(Wheeler and Connor 2006, p.10)

Having been an associate trainer for NCB for many years, I have seen the real difference PEAL makes (and continues to make) to early childhood practice. The PEAL approach, of true and authentic partnerships, acknowledges that both parents and practitioners have a role to play. The PEAL principles include:

- Practitioners need to acknowledge, value and support the role parents play in their children's learning.

- Parenting is complex and families have to cope with a wide range of pressures. Practitioners need to ensure that they are creating opportunities for all parents to be involved and to acknowledge that if parents don't respond to invitations this does not mean they are not interested in their children's education.

(Wheeler and Connor 2006, p.11)

Any search around the topic of 'parent partnership' will offer a range of ways we could encourage parents to be involved in the children's learning and development. Some work and some do not. Some work with some parents but not with others. Some work one year and not the next. I have worked in, and with, many ECCE settings and with many parents, and have never yet met a parent who has said 'I'm not interested in my child', but perhaps they need a range of more creative, more personalised ways to be involved. So, if we are agreeing that it is true that parents are interested in their own children, then this leads me to think that perhaps what we need to consider is what engages us, and how we can use this knowledge to our advantage in our efforts to engage others. Let's consider some of the reasons why we personally might not get involved in particular events/activities.

If you consider the reasons why you did, or did not, attend certain events, and how you felt about each event, the chances are that parents are thinking along similar lines. There will be a multitude of reasons why you did not attend or accept some of the invitations; some reasons you will have shared openly and honestly, such as illness or prior engagements, for instance. However, other reasons you will have very quietly kept to yourself. There will be some events/activities that you, for whatever reason, felt you simply could not attend.

REFLECTIVE PRACTICE

Encouraging Involvement

Consider your life, both professionally and personally. Think back over the last few years, reflect on when you have been invited to any/all of the following (a couple of blank rows have been included for you to add your own events):

Event	Did you attend? Yes/No	Then consider: The ones you *did* attend and why. The ones you *did not* attend and why.
A formal interview for a new job		
A meeting with a senior manager		
A party in another part of the country		
A wedding		
A Christmas/Eid or other festival event		
A get together at a friend's house		
A theatre trip/play/ cinema outing, etc.		
A fundraising event		

Now consider how parents feel when they are 'invited' to events and activities within your setting. Could some of those reasons you had for not attending an event be the same reasons parents have? Are the very same reasons you have considered personally here, the same ones that prevent some parents from accepting the invites you so enthusiastically offer? Could it be that those same concerns you have are shared by parents? Perhaps previous detrimental experiences, worries of what might be said (or not said), worries about expectations (such as what to wear or how to behave), concerns about potential pressure from others attending, pressure from partners/others not to attend, clash of personalities, worries about what will/might happen at the event, lack of money, lack of confidence and so on, are all considerations we in ECCE have to take into account when developing parent partnership.

In terms of future practice, therefore, how can you use this knowledge to cultivate more of the things that did engage and encourage you to attend, and mitigate some of the things that disengaged you? So, for example, if you did not attend something just because it was at the wrong time for you, then maybe something as simple as considering times and dates more carefully might be a useful way forward.

The key here is, it is not a one size fits all. What works for some parents will not work for others, what works in summer might not work in winter, what worked last year with last year's group of parents might not work this year with the current group of parents, or conversely, just because it did not work last time that does not mean it will not work if you tried again. We all get invites to attend different things, some we choose to go to willingly, excitedly even, others we go to because we feel a duty to attend, some leave us feeling terrified and vulnerable, and some we flatly refuse to attend – and for all kinds of reasons – it is no different for parents.

Developing Partnerships?

On NCB's PEAL Training, one activity, similar to this discussion, asks practitioners to consider how a range of circumstances can influence parental involvement. Reflect on the events mentioned above; now imagine you have received the invite, and consider you could be affected by one (or more) of the following statements:

- You have a young baby

- You have mobility impairments

- You have a child to take somewhere who has mobility impairments

- You have three children under seven, two to get to different places
- You have difficulty reading written information
- Your first language is not English
- You have mental health issues
- You are living in poor housing conditions
- You have a very low income
- You have been racially or otherwise abused.

(Connor and Wheeler 2006, p.13)

Now consider the parents you work with; many of them will be dealing with possibly several of these issues on a daily basis. Is it any wonder that parents may appear to be reluctant to be involved? Add to this parents' own experiences of education, time and work commitments and pressures, elderly relative care or illness, for example, and we have a set of very valid explanations for parents appearing to be uninterested. And…that is before we add into this mix the difficult realities faced by families around issues such as domestic abuse, family member in prison, substance abuse, severe debt, discrimination or terminal illness, for example.

Additionally, I often have conversations with practitioners regarding parents who appear too 'pushy', too 'clingy' or anxious, etc. But surely the discussions throughout this chapter still apply? Many of the discussions within this book, and indeed my other books, are not about being a child or an adult, they are about being *human*. We all have basic similar needs, no matter how tall or small we are. So, yes, parents have PSED needs too…and, no, I am not saying we should all turn into counsellors, but I am saying we need to read the signals parents are sending…and that goes for *all* parents.

What about Daddies?

I cannot write a section on partnership with parents without a specific mention on the role of men in their children's lives. There is a wonderful article on the Huffington Post website, by writer and mother Ashley Miller (2016), entitled *Dumb-Ass Stuff We Need to Stop Saying to Dads*. Miller considers how society portrays fathers as 'inept babysitters' merely 'holding the fort' until Mum comes to the rescue. I know there are many ways that settings try to involve dads and, like the discussion regarding general parental involvement earlier, some will work, some of the time, with some of the dads. However, I do agree with Miller, that this is about needing more generic, wider, general understanding around the issues for men in early childhood.

Daddies Day

Oliver arrives one morning, desperately pulling a tall man behind him. 'Good morning Oliver, how are you today?' asks Sadie, Oliver's key person. Oliver beams with excitement. 'I'm going to show Daddy the buckets, we are going to make a sandcastle,' says Oliver, practically heaving off his coat at the same time as pulling his daddy into the room. Daddy smiles at Sadie, before being dragged by his now squirming son across the room. Sadie knows it is unusual for Daddy to bring Oliver, and is not sure what, if anything, to do.

Sadie quietly consults with Helen, one of her colleagues, and asks Helen what her thoughts are. Helen says that she thinks Sadie should go speak to Dad, and say to Oliver what a special treat it is for Daddy to bring him today. Helen also says that it might be useful to ask where Mummy is. Helen goes on to say that it would be a good opportunity to find out if Daddy is likely to be coming again, and if he could maybe stay longer and do something with the children, as it is so difficult trying to get dads involved. Helen says that maybe Daddy could do something with the wooden bricks and tyres outside as the boys love that kind of thing.

Now consider the following questions:

- What would you do in this situation?
- What do you think of Helen's advice? Why?

OK, so first a disclaimer... On the surface, Helen, is trying to be helpful, and I acknowledge that. So, if anyone out there has been in Helen's shoes, then *please, please* don't take this personally. The whole point of reading a book such as this one and reflecting on our practice is to help us to consider how we might do things differently in the future... We have all (me included) done things that later, on reflection, we could, should or would have done differently.

This book is about PSED in very young children, and part of that is about the messages that children, and their parents, hear. The case study above is played out in many settings, with or without the advice or actions indicated. However, my concern is that it is very easy to inadvertently and unintentionally send messages that conflict with our usual PSED practice. So, whilst I acknowledge the advice given is with the best intentions, here are some thoughts that you might want to consider...

Is it really a special treat for Daddy to bring his own child?

- Should it be? Or perhaps should it just be that one parent has simply dropped off today?

- Does the idea that it is a special treat make Daddy feel less of a parent because for whatever reasons he does not drop off more often?

- Does this add to the societal understanding discussed earlier that daddies are mainly 'inept babysitters'?

- How could Mummy feel when her days are not seen as a special treat?

- What messages does this give to the children? Is Daddy more special than Mummy?

- What about the children who do not have a 'special Daddy' to bring them; what messages are they hearing?

Asking where Mummy is:

- Why? Do we ask where Daddy is every other day?

- What messages does asking where Mummy is send to Daddy? How do you think that would make Daddy feel?

- Does asking where Mummy is add to the 'inept babysitter' construct?

- How does Daddy feel walking in to what is likely to be a predominately female environment? Does this and similar questions make those feelings worse?

Asking Daddy if he is likely to be coming again/if he can stay longer:

- Why? Do we ask Mummy to stay longer?

- How do you think Daddy would feel if asked these types of questions?

- What messages do you think this would send to children?

- Is it appropriate to have these conversations in front of children? Why do you think that?

Suggesting bricks and tyres outside as an activity:

- Why? Is it because this would be seen as a way to engage dads? What if some dads prefer cooking or storytelling, for example?

- What messages does this send to dads?

- What messages does this send to children?

Hopefully, after reflecting on these questions, you can see why I believe that involving dads in their children's lives needs wider, more general consideration. I am not saying that dad-only days or special dad-focused events aren't useful; they are, and can be a good place to start, and many dads and their children benefit greatly from them. However, what I am saying is that as the ECCE field, we need to consider how our resources, environments, words, deeds, actions and so on, albeit unintentionally, can add to the gender stereotyping and 'inept babysitter' understanding that sadly so many people accept as true.

There is a growing body of research which clearly shows the positive impact of the involvement of dads. The Canadian organisation FIRA (Father Involvement Research Alliance) undertook a research summary, which found many benefits, but in terms of PSED and wellbeing specifically, there are clear correlations:

> Infants whose fathers are involved in their care are more likely to be securely attached to them (Cox, Owen, Henderson, and Margand, 1992), be better able to handle strange situations, be more resilient in the face of stressful situations (Kotelchuck, 1976; Parke and Swain, 1975), be more curious and eager to explore the environment, relate more maturely to strangers, react more competently to complex and novel stimuli, and be more trusting in branching out in their explorations (Biller, 1993; Parke and Swain, 1975; Pruett, 1997). (Allen and Daly 2007, p.3)

They go on to say:

> Children of involved fathers are more likely to demonstrate a greater tolerance for stress and frustration (Mischel, Shoda, and Peake, 1988), have superior problem solving and adaptive skills (Biller, 1993), be more playful, resourceful, skilful, and attentive when presented with a problem (Mischel et al., 1988), and are better able to manage their emotions and impulses in an appropriate manner.

In terms of social development specifically, for example, the findings indicate:

> Children of involved fathers are more likely to have positive peer relations and be popular and well liked. Their peer relations are typified by less negativity, less aggression, less conflict, more reciprocity, more generosity,

and more positive friendship qualities (Hooven, Gottman, and Katz, 1995; Lieberman, Doyle, and Markiewicz, 1999; Lindsey, Moffett, Clawson, and Mize, 1994; Macdonald and Parke, 1984; Rutherford and Mussen, 1968; Youngblade and Belsky, 1992). (Allen and Daly 2007, p.4)

I'm sure you can see, from the huge number of names and dates in the above quotes, that more and more research is saying the same thing: having dads involved is good for children. However, it is also worth noting that being involved with their children is good for dads too. The FIRA research summary also found that:

Fathers who are involved in their children's lives are more likely to exhibit greater psychosocial maturity (Pleck, 1997; Snarey, 1993), be more satisfied with their lives (Eggebean and Knoester, 2001), feel less psychological distress (Barnett, Marshall, and Pleck, 1992b; Gove and Mongione, 1983; Ozer, Barnett, Brennan, and Sperling, 1998), and be more able to understand themselves, empathically understand others, and integrate their feelings in an ongoing way (Heath, 1994).

Involved fathers report fewer accidental and premature deaths, less than average contact with the law, less substance abuse, fewer hospital admissions, and a greater sense of well being overall (Pleck, 1997). (Allen and Daly 2007, p.12)

Therefore, if we want to challenge the stereotype of 'inept-daddy-babysitters', and reflect in terms of wider PSED and involving dads, it might be useful to consider the following:

- Why do we need to consider the language we use when trying to encourage dads in to settings?

- How can the resources that we have in settings help (or indeed hinder)?

- Do the images we have in settings support dads to be involved, and support children to see positive male role models? And if not – why not?

- How do we challenge gender stereotyping (such as boys can't push prams, or blue/boys' toys and pink/girls' toys, etc.)?

- How do we support the growing number of same-sex families? How do some of the issues discussed here affect these families?

- What else could we do?

There is much information available to help with reflecting on practice in this area (please also see bibliography), and it is a start, but unfortunately, despite the best intentions, information produced doesn't always have the desired effect. For example, Clapton (2013) considers the language we use:

> In the most studiously neutral examples aimed at mothers and fathers, in an effort not to identify only mothers with child-care, the words 'parent' or 'parents' is used as in 'parent and toddler group'. However very few people read or hear 'mother' *or* 'father' in this and other examples because of the societal default understanding that parent equals mother. (Clapton 2013, p.8)

Therefore, if we are to truly address the issues discussed in this section, we need to consider how we – as parents, aunties, uncles, grandparents – as predominantly female ECCE practitioners, and as society as a whole tackle the wider issue of men in early childhood. For example, Clapton (2013, p.7) goes on to consider how in many examples of literature, publicity materials, photographs, and so on, as well as the words and phrases used, there is often a message that 'fathers are either non-existent or to be treated with suspicion'. The wider debate needed here is that is not just fathers who are treated with suspicion.

Men and Early Childhood: The Bigger Debate?

We cannot consider the involvement of dads, and other male relatives, and indeed men in general, in early childhood without considering the 'elephant in the room': society's view of men and young children. Sadly, in the media, in society and, let's be perfectly frank, in some cases, directly within ECCE, there is a perceived mistrust of men who want to be around young children. If we are honest, we know women hurt and abuse children too, indeed many of the recent high-profile ECCE-related cases have involved women, and yet women are not generally treated with the same mistrust as men. Whilst it is acknowledged that we need to ensure we keep children safe, we also need to acknowledge the flip side of this debate. Research asking men about working in the ECCE sector found that:

> 50% were worried what other people would think. This included peer pressure and men's fears of being accused of inappropriate behaviour. They also voiced concerns about parental attitudes to men carrying out intimate care of young children... Concerns were expressed that there may be deep-rooted prejudices from women opposed to men working in childcare or the expectation that they would be expected to do stereotypical activities like football and lifting heavy objects... (O'Sullivan and Chambers 2012, p.4)

Similarly, I have had dads and male friends who are dads, granddads and uncles say that they are fearful of playing with children or taking children to the park alone; they are unsure if they are allowed to bathe or cuddle young children or change nappies (especially if the child is a little girl). I have had men say to me that when they witness a child fall, they want to help, but feel unable to due to what other bystanders may say. This breaks my heart. What are we doing to the caring, gentle, wonderful men in our world that they feel this way – and importantly, what messages does this send to children, who are the parents of the future?

Additionally, within the ECCE field I have had male practitioners tell me that they have been told not to comfort children, change nappies, undress children who are wet from playing in water, sit children on their knee for a story, or play rough and tumble games with children, for example, because of how these activities may be viewed. Furthermore, there is the whole debate around touch, cuddles and hugs in the ECCE sector generally, and we will explore this further later in the book. If we are to truly support men in early childhood, regardless of the role of parent or practitioner, we need to do some serious reflecting on our own and society's thoughts and feelings. A good place to start might be to reflect on and understand the reasons behind *why* we want/need more men involved in early childhood. This is not a reflective practice exercise, but if you are interested in this topic, here are some questions you might want to consider as a starting point:

- Why is it important for men to be involved in early childhood?

- Why is involving men in early childhood seen as difficult?

- Why is early childhood mainly seen as a 'women's domain', and what can we do to challenge that?

- Do we understand the benefits and the barriers?

  - How can we develop more of the benefits?

  - How can we help colleagues/society, etc. to understand more of the benefits?

  - How can we help colleagues/society, etc. to understand the barriers?

  - What can we do to address some of the barriers?

- Are the issues the same or different for male ECCE practitioners and dads?

- What steps can you personally take to help involve men in your own area of practice?

This is a huge and ongoing debate, for which, sadly, there is not enough room in this book; however, it is something I wanted to highlight. Men's involvement in early childhood is something we need to continue to encourage and value if we have any chance of nurturing all aspects of PSED in early childhood. There are a number of items in the bibliography which you may also wish to consider in terms of your own practice; additionally, David Wright, who supported me with this section, has a forthcoming book on the wider subject of men in early years, due to be published in 2018. In order to address this debate, we need to continue to reflect on, examine and consider our own and society's thoughts, feelings and, importantly, misconceptions.

> Much more worrying is evidence from Blount 2005, Fifield and Swain 2002 and Weems 1999, who concluded that women are seen as nurturers: there is an assumption that men wishing to work in this context are often effeminate, homosexual and/or paedophiles. The consequence Farquhar *et al.* 2006 and King 1998 asserted is that this position discourages both homosexual and heterosexual men from wanting to work with young children – further reducing the presence of men in early childhood education. (O'Sullivan and Chambers 2012, p.6)

For now, I would like the final word to go to a group of dads who are trying to change some of the issues discussed in this section: the Scottish organisation Dads Rock, who have been invaluable in their support with this section of the book. Dads Rock offer the following on their website, which would be useful for practice everywhere:

> **Our Vision:** For a Scotland where dads are seen as being equally valuable and vital.

> **Our beliefs:** We believe children need a diverse mix of parenting and that dads can and do play a vital role in the upbringing of their children.

> Children have better outcomes when they have involvement from their dads, research backs this up. We are the rock for dads, but know that irrespective of gender all parents/carers rock! (Dads Rock 2017)

Let's Talk?

More and more research is showing us the importance of practitioners and parents working together to support children. Bearing in mind the definition of 'parents' as defined in the preface as 'any adult carer', we need to consider mums, dads, grandparents, aunties, uncles, foster carers, and anyone else who is involved in the child's life. If then, we also agree that PSED is the bedrock of child development, then this means that the relationships we form with *all* adults involved in the wider role of 'parental care' are crucial to ensure a stable foundation on which PSED can develop. Mums and/or dads who are stressed, worried, anxious or vulnerable, and so on, will find it all the more difficult to support their children. In turn, children of parents who are worried, anxious, vulnerable, and so on, often show signs of being worried, anxious, stressed or vulnerable themselves.

> Parents' life circumstances and socioeconomic contexts have a fundamental bearing on the early years and children's outcomes... These factors are also critically related to parents' health and wellbeing, which in turn impact on early years and childhood outcomes. Hence, the health and wellbeing of children cannot be addressed in isolation from the health and wellbeing of parents. (Dodds 2016, p.6)

In other words, we cannot address the PSED of children without taking into account the PSED of parents. Therefore, as ECCE professionals, we have to use our skills, knowledge and understanding to support, empower and encourage parents in any way we can. Research undertaken by Zero to Three found that:

73% of parents feel 'parenting' is their biggest challenge

8 in 10 parents agree that good parenting can be learned

69% of parents say that if they knew more positive parenting strategies, they would use them

54% of parents wish they had more information about how to be a better parent

55% of parents wanted to know more about children's emotional development

51% of parents wanted to know more about early brain development.

(Zero to Three 2016, pp.3, 6, 8, 21)

This, and the Zero to Three quote from earlier, regarding 'people who give parenting advice and recommendations if they don't know my child and my situation' (2016, p.21) as well as other research clearly shows that parents worry about being parents, and that we, as ECCE practitioners, are ideally placed to help. We see parents, and their children, almost daily, we have the research readily available, and we know what makes a difference in early childhood.

Children develop within an environment of relationships that begins in the family but also involves other adults who play important roles in their lives. This can include extended family members, providers of early care and education, nurses, social workers, coaches, and neighbors.

These relationships affect virtually all aspects of development – intellectual, social, emotional, physical, and behavioural – and their quality and stability in the early years lay the foundation that supports a wide range of later outcomes. (Center on the Developing Child at Harvard University 2016, p.8)

Sometimes, it is as simple as just listening, sharing stories and sharing the ups and downs of being around small children. Yes, I am sure parents need to know what their children have eaten, and what fluids and solids have entered (and indeed exited) their children – but surely there is more to life than poo? Tell mums and dads the fun and exciting things their children have been doing, help them to smile and be enthusiastic about, and with, their children. Help mums and dads be involved in their children's learning in simple, easy and cost-free ways, such as talking about how you have been using the colour red, and suggesting they look for red things on the way home. You might also want to consider the section in Chapter 5 on Observation, Assessment and Planning in relation to this. Additionally, practitioners need to be able to signpost parents to other professionals and organisations that can offer further help and support if needed. After all, if we are putting children and their PSED at the heart of practice, the relationships between parents and practitioners are vital:

- Children learn to be strong and independent through *positive relationships.*

- Children learn and develop well in *enabling environments,* in which their experiences respond to their individual needs and there is a strong partnership between practitioners and parents and/or carers.

(DfE 2017, p.6, emphasis added)

So, why do we find developing partnerships with others so difficult? One of the things I hear regularly on training programmes is that practitioners are worried about speaking to parents. However, I also hear regularly that parents appear worried, or hesitant, about speaking with practitioners… so it almost seems like we simply have trouble talking to each other? Let's consider this in a slightly different context.

REFLECTIVE PRACTICE

Conversations and Communications

Scenario 1

You and your partner/mum/grandfather/friend/colleague arrive at your local supermarket to pick up some groceries. You wander around the shop and collect the necessary items. As you approach the checkouts your companion says 'Oh, look, that checkout does not have a queue, let's go there, we'll be quicker.' You turn and give a wry smile and reply, 'Oh yes, there is never a queue at that checkout, the assistant is miserable, never smiles, never talks and does not even look at you when giving you your change. Most people would rather queue than go there.'

Scenario 2

You and your partner/mum/grandfather/friend/colleague arrive at your local supermarket to pick up some groceries. You wander around the shop and collect the necessary items. As you approach the checkouts your companion says 'Oh, look, that checkout does not have a queue, let's go there, we'll be quicker.' You turn to your companion and nod your head and reply, 'Oh yes, I feel really sorry for that assistant. She always looks so unhappy, like she has the weight of the world on her shoulders. Lots of people avoid her checkout. I always go and try and smile and wish her a good day. Sometimes it works and she smiles back, sometimes she doesn't.'

Scenario 3

You and your partner/mum/grandfather/friend/colleague arrive at your local supermarket to pick up some groceries. You wander around the shop and collect the necessary items. As you approach the checkouts your companion says 'Oh, look, that checkout does not have a queue, let's go there, we'll be quicker.' You turn to your companion and say, 'Oh no we wouldn't. That assistant never stops talking, she asks what you've done today, what you are having for tea. And, she examines your shopping all the time, commenting on things that look lovely, what she does like and what she doesn't like. It takes forever at that checkout.'

Scenario 4

You arrive at the local supermarket to pick up some groceries. You wander around the shop and collect the necessary items. As you approach the checkouts, you scan the queues and look at which assistants are having conversations with customers. Your partner/parents/flat-mates are away, so you are going home to an empty house and to be honest you've had a difficult day. It would be lovely to have a conversation with someone, that is not work related and would just help to clear your head a little, and make you smile before you head to the empty house.

Scenario 5

You arrive at your local supermarket to pick up some groceries. You wander around the shop and collect the necessary items. As you approach the checkouts you notice a checkout without a queue. You head straight to it, and beginning unpacking your items. The assistant starts talking to you and asks if you need any help, if you've had a good day and if there is anything else you needed. You respond briefly, but in all honesty, you just wanted to get your shopping over and done with and head home. It has been a difficult day and you still have a thousand and one things to deal with.

I am sure you can see the analogies here. Change these scenarios to an ECCE environment and these, and similar, situations happen in many, many settings every day. The reluctance to approach particular people, the attempt to support someone having difficulties, choosing who to speak to (and when), or simply the lack of communication due to a pre-occupied brain. These and other situations like them will be very familiar, to parents and to practitioners. None of them are intentional, none of them are intended to hurt or distress, and all of them are so, so easily misunderstood. Sadly, misunderstandings happen all too frequently and all too easily, even when we actually do want to speak to someone, it can still all go unintentionally, but horribly, wrong…

In my opinion, one of the most diabolically misused and misunderstood sentences in the English language is 'can I have a word?' In my book, *Performance Management in Early Years Settings*, I offered:

> I would *ban* 'can I have a word' in all forms, in all contexts and in any version. I often discuss this on training, and I have never met anyone who disagrees with my theory; 'can I have a word' is never followed by 'you've won the lottery' or 'you are going to get a pay rise' or 'thanks for doing a wonderful job' or indeed, any form of praise whatsoever. Whether a child in school, parents at the school gates, an employee, a friend, a relative or a partner, etc. hearing the term 'can I have a word', makes most of us anxious. In fact, what I hear most from people is 'can I have a word' makes most of us feel sick! (Garvey 2017, p.206)

So, yes, it is a simple misunderstanding. 'Can I have a word?' is just five simple little words, just 13 letters. It might just mean you want to talk to someone more privately, or simply that you have just remembered something you wanted to tell the person about... But the sentence 'can I have a word?' is now virtually unanimously seen as negative, and causes huge, unnecessary anxiety. So, if you also agree with this, perhaps next time you need to speak to someone, you consider how you approach the conversation; after all, causing people to feel anxious is never a good place for a conversation to start.

Bearing all of this discussion in mind, and if we now perhaps have a little more understanding of maybe why parents and practitioners sometimes find it difficult to have conversations, then perhaps we can use this information to develop relationships between the adults in a child's life and therefore support this area of influence on children's PSED, and their behaviours, as well as learning and development in general:

> Using an ecological framework, Bronfenbrenner (1979) suggested that not only do single settings contribute to a child's development, most importantly it is the nature of the relationships *between* adults in those settings that plays a critical role in development and learning. Bronfenbrenner also suggested the critical piece in building a *bridge* between home and school [setting] is when families are involved in their children's education. (Cardona 2008, p.1)

Practitioner Role

So, in the previous section we looked in some detail about the role of parents (mums, dads, grandparents, indeed all adults in whichever 'parental care' role); however, this section of the chapter is entitled 'Adults: Parents and Practitioners', and we have also covered some aspects of the role of the practitioner. To finish off this section, I would just like to explore one further aspect of the practitioner role in nurturing children's PSED: the influences we have directly on children's PSED whilst they are with us in professional ECCE settings. We will also explore this further in later chapters.

From the moment children enter an ECCE setting, the adults who work there will have some influence on the child's PSED. From the person who greets them as they arrive, to the person who waves them goodbye as they leave, all adults within the setting will have some influence. The person who brings the food at lunch and snack times, the person who cuts the grass, the person who works in the office, as well as the ECCE practitioners, all have a direct influence on how children feel, in terms of PSED. As discussed previously, young children rely on us as adults for help and support in so many of their daily needs. What that support is, why it is needed, how it is supplied, who supplies the support, where it is supplied and when it is supplied are vitally important questions in relation to children's PSED. Help and support can be given freely, respectfully, generously, sensitively, willingly, thoughtfully, sincerely and appropriately, or not...and this will have an influence on all children's PSED. Whether this is done intentionally or not, we will explore later in the book. For now, let's consider this from a different angle.

REFLECTIVE PRACTICE

Practitioner Influence on PSED (Part 1)

Imagine you need a minor operation. It is nothing serious, but will require you to be admitted to hospital for a couple of nights. Additionally, as the operation includes medication which could make you drowsy, you will be confined to bed for the duration of the stay.

You arrive on the morning, and are told by Cherelle, a member of staff, which will be your bed. Cherelle begins to take your coat off you and, when you protest, says in a cheerful voice, 'Stop being silly, we need to get you ready, sit there and we'll get you sorted.' Cherelle takes your bag and puts it in the locker saying, 'You will not be needing this, so we will put it in here for safe keeping.' Once you are in your nightwear, you say to Cherelle that you have a few questions. Cherelle tells you to get into bed and stay there; someone will be along later to explain the operation.

There are a few magazines on the bedside table; you pick them up, but they are all tatty and torn, and all the crosswords have been completed. You consider getting off the bed and bending down to the locker and getting your phone from your bag, but you are not sure if you are allowed out of bed. There is a small TV on the wall, it is playing a local news channel, the volume is turned up high, you guess that is so everyone in the room can hear it, but it does seem a little loud.

After a few minutes, someone arrives with a clip board. 'You have not filled all the paperwork in yet. Please fill this in fully and I'll pick it up later. If you cannot fill it in yourself, ask one of the staff for some help.' The clip board is thrust into your hand, and the person leaves.

You look around the ward. There are three other people, two are sitting in chairs next to their beds, and you immediately feel jealous and cross. Hmmph, you think to yourself, how come they can sit in the chair and I can't? One person suddenly looks up and makes eye contact, you look away, suddenly shy and embarrassed, you do not want them to think you were staring. The third person is laid flat on their bed so you cannot see their face, they have lots of machines around their bed. The machines are making strange noises and you are not sure what they are all for, the machines look a bit worrying and you can feel yourself becoming anxious and stressed. 'I hope I don't have all those machines' you think to yourself.

After what seems like an eternity, a Doctor approaches your bed. You are glad the Doctor is here; you have some questions, such as when your visitors can come, what, and when, you can eat, and what to do about going to the loo after the operation. You smile warmly, but the Doctor is too busy reading notes and doesn't look up. The Doctor does not tell you her name, she is wearing a name badge, but you cannot read it clearly. The Doctor says that the operation is simple, is easy to do and tells you not to worry, 'Ask the ward staff if you have any questions,' says the Doctor, and then walks away. You lay back on the pillows, and stare at the ceiling.

A little while later, another member of staff approaches your bed: 'Hi, I'm Stevie, time for a loo trip, you have been here a while.' You start to explain that you do not need the loo, but Stevie cuts you off. 'Come on now, don't fuss, let's try, you might need one when we get there.' You say to Stevie that you do not really want to leave your bag in the bedside locker, and that you have a few questions and ask who should you speak to. Stevie says the ward is short staffed but that someone will be along later to explain the operation and answer any questions.

After a couple of hours, you have read the tatty magazines, examined every inch of the ceiling and have seen the same news stories about ten times, plus the noise of the TV is now starting to give you a headache. Suddenly, you hear a clattering out in the corridor. The clattering gets nearer and after a while, a shiny metal trolley arrives in the doorway. 'Lunch time,' shouts a man in a white overall. The man approaches your bed and puts a plate of food down on your bedside table. You look at the food and try to explain that you do not like half of what is on the plate, you are hoping you can swap it for something else. 'Excuse me,' you say and try to catch his attention, but he has already moved to the next bed and does not hear you. You push the food around on your plate with a fork but none of it reaches your mouth, and after a while you put the fork down on the plate and lay back against the pillows.

There is only question for this reflective practice exercise:

- At each point, how do you think you would feel?

First, I want to make something very clear, this is *not* intended in any way to be an attack on hospital staff. This is just another way of considering how if we, as adults, were treated in a particular way, we might feel, and I am sure you can see the analogies here. All the staff discussed here are trying to do their jobs, and probably trying to do the jobs well. However, in a busy day, so many seemingly minor details can be overlooked. If this scenario happened to us, as adults, many of us would be at the point of firmly demanding answers, perhaps even shouting loudly, or at the very least demanding someone listened. Some of us would retreat into our inner worlds and hope quietly that someone who could listen and answer questions would come soon. Most of us would be counting down the hours until we could leave and go home. In other words, our behaviours would clearly show how we were feeling. So, imagine how young children must feel if some of these types of things happen to them…and the reactions we might then see.

The influences practitioners have on young children are huge, they can be supportive, encouraging and empowering, but sadly, they can also be detrimental, demoralising and disheartening. The staff in this reflective practice exercise are not aware of each other's actions, so unintentionally add to the stress, confusion, anxiety and worry. The overwhelming noise levels, the fear of what might happen next, and having personal items removed from arm's reach ratchet up the tension further. This would be a difficult scenario for any adult, so how does it feel for young children?

REFLECTIVE PRACTICE

Practitioner Influence on PSED (Part 2)

Let's consider some of the analogies in the scenario. Imagine the same/similar types of situations, activities or issues happening to a young child:

Personal Belongings and Personal Space

- When children arrive, do we immediately begin to take off their coats? Why?

- Are all children comfortable with this?

  » How do you know?

  » What signs/symptoms/indicators, etc. do you see?

- Do some children need to keep their coats on for a little while?

  » Why do you think that is?

  » What about children who need clothes or nappies changing, etc. – how might they feel?

- Why do you think children have comforters (dummies, toys, blankets, etc.)?

- How do you think comforters support children's PSED? Why do you think that is?

- Do children have somewhere to store their personal belongings, that they can return to again and again, and whenever they wish?

  » If not, why not?

- Why/how do you think this supports their PSED?

- What else might you need to consider?

Environment

- How can equipment, resources and noise levels influence children's PSED?

  » How can you help with this?

- How can equipment or resources that maybe children have not seen before influence PSED?

» What strategies could you put in place to help children new to ECCE?

» What strategies could you put in place to help when introducing new equipment or resources, for example?

- What else might you need to consider?

Interactions

- What influence might new members of staff, 'non-ECCE staff', or visitors, for example, have on children's PSED?

» How can you support staff who are leaving and new staff arriving to consider their influences on children's PSED?

- How can children influence each other's PSED?

» What makes you think that?

» How could you help?

- How could lack of reassurance or interaction from adults influence children's PSED? Why do you think that?

» What could you do to help?

- What else might you need to consider?

Routines

- How do routines support children's PSED?

» What makes you think that?

» How could you help?

- How could routines adversely affect children's PSED?

» What makes you think that?

» How could you help?

- Are there some routines that children find difficult?

» Why do you think that?

» What could help with this?

- What else might you need to consider?

These are just some questions for you to consider to reflect on practice, and I am sure you can come up with many more. The point here is that everything we do, everything we say and everything we provide has the potential to influence children's PSED in a positive way, or even unintentionally have a detrimental and adverse effect. Whilst we cannot always change everything about the physical environment, nor can we be responsible for other's actions, we can be responsible for, and change if necessary, our personal influences on children's PSED. Whether the physical or emotional environment, there are things that we can influence. If we consider some of the concerns in the reflective practice exercise there are numerous incidences that we can control. For example, we can influence noise levels, we can listen, we can answer questions, we can reassure, we can support making choices and decision making, we can support links between colleagues, and also support links with home, we can remove broken equipment, and we can provide flexible routines which offer the feelings of security and safety without stifling and constricting.

In other words, we can ensure that those all-important, seemingly minor but actually hugely important details are not missed. All of these influences are within our personal control, all of these influences require no additional funding, all of these influences simply require us to use our personal experiences, knowledge, skills and understanding to support and nurture very young children.

PART 3: THE PHYSICAL AND EMOTIONAL ENVIRONMENT

Additional to the adult role in supporting children's PSED, the physical environment can have a huge influence on how children feel, behave and act. Thankfully, many settings now understand the importance of natural light, ventilation and neutral colours and the over-stimulation of having too many bright walls, decorations and displays, for example. If you are still unsure of this argument, I would urge you to look at the book *The Importance of Being Little: What Preschoolers Really Need from Grownups* by Erika Christakis (2016), or indeed the growing evidence of research around 'sick building syndrome (SBS)', which the UK's NHS (National Health Service) Choices website describes as follows:

Since the 1970s, researchers have tried to identify the cause of SBS. As yet, no single cause has been identified. Most experts believe that it may be the result of a combination of things.

Possible risk factors for SBS may include:

- poor ventilation
- low humidity
- high temperature or changes in temperature throughout the day
- airborne particles, such as dust, carpet fibres or fungal spores
- airborne chemical pollutants, such as those from cleaning materials or furniture, or ozone produced by photocopiers and printers
- physical factors, such as electrostatic charges
- poor standards of cleanliness in the working environment
- inadequate ventilation when using chemical cleaning products
- poor lighting that causes glare or flicker on visual display units
- improper use of display screen equipment
- psychological factors, such as stress or low staff morale.

(NHS Choices 2017)

Alternatively, consider from a personal perspective how you would feel if every room in your home had walls painted lime green, luminous yellow, pillar-box red and electric blue, you could not open the windows, or had poor lighting, for example – I'm pretty sure that after a while you'd have a headache, feel a tad overwrought and desperately want a calmer place to be, and this is exactly what happens with children.

> Therefore, maintaining focused attention in classroom environments that contain extraneous [unimportant] visual displays may be particularly challenging for young children because visual features in the classroom may tax their still developing and fragile ability to actively maintain task goals and ignore distractions. (Fisher *et al.* 2014, p.1363)

I do not want to go into too much detail in regards to what constitutes a quality physical environment in ECCE settings, as there is a wealth of useful information readily available on this topic. Therefore, I would urge you to undertake your own research in this area. However, just to put this into context for this chapter, there follows a (very) brief discussion on the physical environment: both regarding indoor and outdoor ECCE provision.

In 2015, research based on the results of the HEAD Project (Holistic Evidence and Design), funded by the Engineering and Physical Sciences Research Council, was published by the University of Salford. 'Three types of physical characteristic of classrooms were assessed: Stimulation, Individualisation and Naturalness, or more memorably the SIN design principles.' Carried out over three years, the research team found that:

The factors found to be particularly influential are, in order of influence:

- Naturalness: light, temperature and air quality – accounting for half the learning impact [influence of 50%]

- Individualisation: ownership and flexibility – accounting for about a quarter [influence of 25%]

- Stimulation (appropriate level of): complexity and colour – again about a quarter [influence of 25%]

(Barrett, Zhang, Davies and Barrett 2015b, p.119)

They go on to say:

A very positive finding is that users (teachers) can readily action many of the factors. The suggestions included show that small changes, costing very little or nothing, can make a real difference. For example, changing the layout of the room, the choices of display, or colour of the walls. (Barrett *et al.* 2015a, p.3)

The physical environment, of course, is not just about buildings, walls, displays and so on. The importance of equipment, continuous provision and enhancements, as well as the indoor and outdoor environment in ECCE will all have a role to play. For example, we provide 'child-sized' furniture so that young children can choose, self-select and be independent within their environment. Additionally, we add what are known as enhancements, to 'enhance' or develop an area, usually based on developing interests – the aim being to enhance each area with a range of resources that develop children's ideas and thinking. The enhancements may be developed from a child's interest (i.e. an interest in new babies), the weather (such as snow) or to generate interest and exploration (i.e. heuristic play or treasure baskets).

As for indoors and outdoors, much is written elsewhere. Again, I would urge you to undertake your own research. An excellent and easily accessible starting point would be anything by Jan White. For example, in her book, *Playing and Learning Outdoors: Making Provision for High Quality Experiences in The Outdoor Environment with Children 3–7*, Jan expertly, and concisely, sums up the importance of outdoor play:

Young children need outdoor play. When given the choice, the outdoors is where most children want to be and play outdoors is what they most want. (White 2013, p.2)

Of course, additional to the physical environment, the emotional environment needs consideration, and in some ways, this whole book is about children's experiences of the emotional environment. If we consider this from an adult perspective for a moment, I am sure you will have walked into meetings, events or buildings where you felt anxious, stressed, apprehensive or unsure. How you were treated on arrival, and throughout the duration, will have added to, or calmed, your stress levels.

Add to this the experiences discussed earlier in this chapter that you have had, or are having personally, such as illness, disability or personal worries, and we can see how easy it is to feel completely overwrought. As adults, we have developed ways of dealing with situations that make us feel uncomfortable; we can ask for support, we can remove ourselves from the situation or we can tackle the reasons and attempt to change the situation, for example, and even then, we do not always react appropriately!

Again, these exact same experiences happen to children. Young children are aware of how the physical and emotional environments feel to them. Think how sometimes children react to the slightest change in the environment, or how children seem to 'know' if there is excitement or tension amongst the adults. Young children still have to learn the skills to cope with, or understand how to remove themselves from, situations where they are uncomfortable or over-excited, for example. Additionally, they may not have the language necessary, or indeed the confidence needed to use the skills or language, so the approach children take is often very different.

REFLECTIVE PRACTICE

Behaviours/Misbehaviours (Part 1)

Think of a situation where your day has not gone the way you had hoped. Perhaps the heating or hot water was not working, or maybe you did not get something you were hoping for (such as a promotion), or maybe an outing/event did not turn out the way you expected, for example. Perhaps a friend/partner/colleague did not support you in the way you had hoped. Now consider the following questions:

- How did you feel?
- How did you express those feelings?
  - » If you did not express your feelings – why not?
- How did your behaviours change?
- Who (if anyone) helped you?
- What did that person do/say that helped you?

Leave these thoughts to one side for a moment, and consider Part 2.

REFLECTIVE PRACTICE

Behaviours/Misbehaviours (Part 2)

Now consider a situation that surprised you, excited you or exceeded your expectations. Perhaps you did get that promotion, or someone organised a special trip or surprise for you, or maybe, simply, someone said thank you and made you feel appreciated, for example. Now consider the following questions:

- How did you feel?

- How did you express those feelings?

  » If you did not express your feelings – why not?

- How did your behaviours change?

- Who (if anyone) helped you?

- What did that person do/say that helped you?

I am sure you can see where this is going. As adults, we learn (hopefully) how to deal with disappointment, frustration, anger, jealousy and other emotional reactions. Also, we learn how to deal with being excited, surprised or proud, for example... But, we do not remember learning these skills, or the journeys we went on to learn them. We also learn how to acknowledge our own needs and take appropriate action, and we learn how to find people to help us with our experiences. Additionally, you can also probably think of adults you know who still struggle with dealing with, and expressing appropriately, their emotions, or who struggle with their reactions to certain situations or experiences.

Now, let's add some everyday occurrences into the mix. Consider the two situations above separately, the one that did not go as you expected, and the one that surprised/excited you. How would the following have affected your feelings, actions and behaviours? Imagine you were feeling, needing or experiencing, one or more of the following 'physical or emotional environmental factors':

Happy	Sad	Frustrated	Cold
Excited	Tired	Interested	Cuddle/hug
Worried	Interaction	Valued	Illness
Hot	Hungry	Frightened	Routine/Change

Angry	Security	Knowledge	Scared
Loved	Motivated	Environment	Equipment
Relationships	Respected	Safety	Bored

It is easy to see how the addition of feeling too hot or too cold and hungry to an already emotionally charged situation can feel overwhelming... I often say I can cope with being hot or cold *and* hungry, but add in tired, and I am awash. I personally cannot deal with tiredness. I know I have had enough and have to remove myself from the situation in order to deal with the (sometimes conflicting) demands of my body *and* importantly my brain. But, I don't always listen to my brain – and then become overtired and I am truly overwrought – I am grumpy, cross, bad-tempered, irritable, and I'm sure my lovely friends and family could add a few more choice words here! So, as I've said – I am absolutely certain you can see where this is going – if as adults we sometimes find it difficult to deal with what life is throwing our way, is it any wonder young children struggle with their behaviours sometimes too?

I use the word behaviours purposefully. I hope you will notice it has the letter 's' on the end. Behaviour is often used as a plural, but that is not actually accurate. We tend to say 'children's behaviour' meaning all-encompassing, everything, rather than the more linguistically correct 'behaviours'. Additionally, the word 'behaviours' encompasses our words, actions, deeds, manner and conduct – in all its possible permutations. Yet, oddly, the word 'behaviour' (minus the 's') has come to have a definite and definitive, negative undertone. When we say 'we want to talk about children's behaviour', we usually assume, usually correctly, that this is behaviour that is unacceptable or 'misaligned'. In other words, we use the word 'behaviour' as an all-encompassing term for any so-called 'negative' behaviour, perhaps in an unhelpful way of trying to avoid using the word naughty?

PART 4: MANAGING BEHAVIOURS?

This section of Chapter 2 will specifically concentrate on a few select topics that come up regularly when talking about young children and their behaviours. This is not a book about *behaviour management*. This is a book about *nurturing* children's *PSED* and *understanding brain development and children's behaviour*. Therefore, in this section the discussion will concentrate on how children's personal, social and emotional development influences their behaviours. Additionally, we will look at how we, as adults, can help, or indeed hinder, children's understanding of their own behaviours, and how this also influences children's PSED. There are many places we could start this section, but let's be radical – let's start with the word 'naughty'.

Let's Look at Naughty!

On many training programmes, and talking to many practitioners, I often hear people say 'oh, we are not allowed to use the word naughty', or 'we do not use the word naughty'. In most information available the word 'behaviour' is now more commonly used, so why then is naughty still so prevalent? When I ask delegates on my training programmes, answers such as 'oh, but the children use it', or 'the parents use it' are common. It is still used occasionally in some children's books, and on children's TV, but if it is not used in ECCE circles, and most information now uses the word behaviour, that would suggest we, in ECCE, do not like the word itself. Therefore, if that is the case, it would seem 'naughty' is only lingering on as a purely historical word, handed down through generations, and like other long-gone outdated terms, perhaps the word 'naughty' needs relegating to the annals of history.

When I am tired and grumpy no-one would ever say I am being naughty. Yes, I might be 'misbehaving' in the truest sense of the word, in that my behaviour is misaligned with a particular situation – but I am absolutely, categorically, positively not being naughty. I dislike the word naughty intensely, and there is a very good reason. Over the years, I have done much research and reading around the word naughty, and its origins may come as a surprise. The original meaning of the word naughty seems to come from the 14th century and means to be 'needy', or have 'naught' (or nothing). This makes perfect sense – nought, as in the numerical spelling, is the written version of the number zero, or nil – so nothing, or naught/nought.

However, around the 1800s the meaning of the word started to change. One theory could be that this is perhaps as those who had 'naught' turned to prostitution in order to survive. Therefore, the word naught developed into naughty, and became associated with being sexually promiscuous. I think it is truly horrific to contemplate that a word used perhaps many times a day to some children, has its origins in an area that is as far removed from early childhood as we could ever hope it to be.

Sadly, more modern meanings of the word naughty are not much better, and include:

Evil	Wicked	Unpleasant
Disobedient	Bad	Malicious
Badly behaved	Ill disciplined	Wayward
Rude or indecent	Unhealthy	Vicious

I am going to ask the same questions here as I do on training programmes:

- Are these words that describe the children you know?

- How would you feel if a child you love was described like this?

Whenever, and wherever, I share this information – people are horrified. Whether they work in early childhood, or not, whether they are parents or not is irrelevant – everyone I have ever had a conversation with around the word 'naughty' is as horrified as I am. They all, without exception, vow to never use the word 'naughty' again, and to tell all their friends and family too. Therefore, yes, I believe the word 'naughty' is outdated and inappropriate – but the word behaviour(s) needs help too. The word behaviour(s) is about *all* behaviours, the words we use, our actions, manner, conduct and deeds and not just so-called negative or misaligned ones. So maybe another part of our role in supporting children's PSED is supporting others to understand the wider meaning of the word behaviours too?

Behaviour Management or Self-Regulation?

This section of Chapter 2 is called 'Managing Behaviours?', and the important part of this title is the question mark at the end. Here's a question:

- Who is trying to manage the behaviours – adults or children?

I suspect in the majority of cases, the answers will be 'well of course, it's adults'. Hmmm…now, let's consider this a minute, do we really want children who only know how to act in a range of situations because they have adults on hand to manage their behaviours for them? Shouldn't the case be that we are supporting children to manage their own behaviours? What do we actually mean by 'managing behaviour', and does that essentially translate as:

- getting children to behave…or

- do what we want them to do…or

- obey our instructions…or

- to stop children hurting themselves…or

- to stop children hurting someone else…or

- to stop children breaking something…or

- to show children that they cannot always get what they want…or

- so they do not question your authority…or

- because 'it' (whatever 'it' is) will be good for them…or

- …more you could add?

However we word it, this list still feels ever so slightly uncomfortable to write… Again, how would we feel as adults, if other people tried to 'manage' our behaviours for these reasons? Additionally, I can't help thinking about 'wet paint' signs… What happens when you see a wet paint sign, or a 'do not touch' sign in a gallery or museum? Oh, come on, admit it, be honest – you want to touch, don't you? And many of us indeed do just that. Just to check, of course, but we touch just the same. It works for 'keep off the grass' signs too… Would we class our grownup selves as being 'naughty'? Or, how would we respond if some other well-meaning person told us we were indeed being naughty? Based on my research, observations, personal experience and conversations with thousands of parents and practitioners, when young children's behaviour is misaligned with a particular situation – there is *always* a reason for it. Or let me put it another way: young children are *never* simply being 'naughty'.

Oh horror, I hear you cry, yes, they sometimes are…they are being naughty for attention, or because they want a particular toy, or they do not want to share, for example… And, therefore, yes, I agree, the behaviour is perhaps misaligned with the situation – but the behaviours always have a very valid reason behind them. Exhibiting behaviours for attention, for example, is common, and could be about simply needing a reassuring hug. If you think about young babies for a moment, what do they do when they need a hug? Of course, they put out their arms and we oblige, pick them up and give them a hug. As children grow they try other ways to get hugs, some of which work, and some, depending on the circumstances, don't work. When their limited strategies fail to work, these very young children start to worry, their bodies start to release more cortisol (see Chapter 1), they worry a bit more, and then they absolutely *have* to find some way of gaining our attention. So, attention-seeking behaviours work, children get our attention, and often in dramatic ways, but not because they are being naughty.

If we refer back to the list of why we might 'manage behaviours', I acknowledge that sometimes it is about keeping children safe – but if you think about it, how do children actually learn that it helps to hold onto something when walking up or down stairs, or that an egg breaks when you drop it, for example? Do they learn from the numerous, repeated and well-meaning instructions and directions from an adult? I would say, rarely. Of course, we have to keep children safe, and I am not suggesting children should be allowed to race up and down staircases, or juggle eggs, for example, but I suspect that no matter how many times they are told 'to hold on' or 'carry the egg carefully', they only truly learn these and similar lessons through personal experience. In other words, as part of development, and as part of growing up – again, not because they are being naughty. However, children sometimes seem to push adults to the limits and exhibit a range of behaviours, which seem purely to have the aim of 'testing' the grownups. Therefore, as adults, we need to look at the reasons behind the behaviours being presented and how we can support children to learn the skills necessarily to realign and manage their own behaviours appropriately, rather than simply step in and manage behaviours and situations for them.

> We want our children to learn that all emotions are normal and (eventually) in their control. (Harris 2013)

REFLECTIVE PRACTICE

Behaviour Management or Self-Regulation

Imagine you go to visit a friend. You are looking forward to seeing them, as you have been having a few difficulties at work and need someone to talk through the situation with. You arrive at your friend's house and are welcomed warmly with a smile. Then your friend turns to you and says:

'Oh, good morning, it is so lovely to see you, come on in. I am very pleased you are here. Come in and sit at the dining room table, I have made you a coffee, but we cannot have biscuits as it is too close to lunchtime. Now come on and sit down.'

You sit at the table, and your friend returns with the coffee (but no biscuits), and then smiles and says 'OK, so what's on your mind?' You tell the story, and after a while realise that you are more upset about this than you thought, a single tear drips on to your cheek, and you can feel the flood ready to erupt.

'Oh, no come on, we don't cry,' says your friend, 'big girls/boys don't cry. Now come on sit up and stop shuffling.' You take a deep breath and continue with your story. After a while, your friend interrupts and says, 'Now, come on, you are being very silly. I think this is something you are blowing out of proportion. You just need to go in to work and be a big girl/ boy, and stop being silly.'

You friend pats your arm, and says, 'I am sure whoever is doing this does not mean it. You just need to go in and say sorry, it will all be sorted out. Now come on, dry your eyes, let's go look at the garden.'

Again, I'm sure you can see the analogies here, I could go on, using other similar things that are said to children (I acknowledge, often with the best intentions)…but doesn't it look ridiculous when put into adult context like this? However, the message is clear: shouldn't we be supporting children to name and express emotions, be able to express concerns consider a range of options and so on, and in other words, develop self-regulation skills? How we express our feelings, thoughts and concerns is part of our self-regulation, so how would we feel if someone told us how we should and should not behave? (Imagine not being 'allowed' to have a good cry at a soppy movie.) Or, if someone simply ignored how we were feeling and either disregarded, dismissed or belittled our feelings, or tried to distract us from those feelings? Yes, we may need help and support to internalise, understand and possibly even translate verbally how we are feeling, but, and it is a big but, that is not the same as someone managing our behaviours for us.

REFLECTIVE PRACTICE

Supporting Self-Regulation

In terms of future practice, the following questions might help you decide where practice is going well, and what needs further development.

By simply managing children's behaviours for them, do we:

- Take out completely the need for them to learn and understand the reasonings behind why their behaviour is misaligned to a particular situation?

  » Why do you think that?

- Take away the opportunity for children to learn how to name and express feelings appropriately, develop language, communication and negotiation skills?

  » Why do you think that?

- Potentially influence friendship and relationship building?

  » Why do you think that?

- Send messages that it is inappropriate to feel unhappy, sad, jealous, angry or simply need a hug or a cuddle?

  » Why do you think that?

- Nurture children to understand and manage their own behaviours?

  » Why do you think that?

How can/do we support children to:

- learn and understand the reasonings behind why their behaviour is misaligned to a particular situation

- learn how to name and express feelings appropriately, develop language, communication and negotiation skills

- learn about and understand friendships and relationships

- understand that it is OK to feel unhappy, sad, jealous, angry or simply need a hug or a cuddle

- understand and manage their own behaviours?

And…what else might we need to consider?

'Sit up. Sit straight. Sit still. Look at me. Don't do that. Do it this way. Stop that. Do this. Play nicely. Share. Say sorry. No fighting' and so on, are all sayings I am sure many of us have heard said (or indeed said ourselves) to children, many times. Whilst they were probably said with the best intentions, or in the heat of the moment, at the time, they do not give children the opportunity to understand their own range of feelings, emotions, behaviours and reactions, develop their own behaviour management skills or develop self-regulation, or as Dr Suzanne Zeedyk suggests the language of 'helping children take care of their emotional needs' (Twitter, 09/04/2017). Equally, children need support to understand how all of these things influence other people, and how other people influence them. I suspect you will all be able to think of adults who have difficulty expressing their feelings and emotions. Similarly, you will have been in situations where another adult has responded inappropriately, or seemed unsure of how to behave, in a particular situation. I acknowledge that sometimes we all make mistakes and misread signs, but on the whole, these lessons are learnt in early childhood. Furthermore, they are learnt with help and support from interested adults.

In order for us to nurture children's PSED, we first have to understand that there are a range of behaviours, and *why* we see the range of behaviours we do (in all humans, and indeed in many mammals, and not just young children).

A Range of Behaviours?

From birth, humans show a range of behaviours, and for our very youngest children these behaviours are mainly vocal. Parents will often say how they learn to distinguish their new baby's range of cries depending on the need at the time (such as cold, hungry, tired, wet/soiled). This also works in mammals too, for example research led by Dr Karen McComb (2008), a specialist in mammal vocal communication at the University of Sussex, found that cats raised in houses where there is only one human have developed a specific cry that is 'hidden within the purrs' (McComb *et al.* 2009). The hidden cry is similar in tone and pitch to that of human babies. The high-frequency cry triggers a sense of urgency in the human brain, and results in the cat being fed.

Additionally, footage on the BBC TV series *Animal Planet II*: Episode 3, Jungles (2016), showed a female baby Spider Monkey exploring higher than she ever had before. High up in the Guatemalan Rainforest, the young Spider Monkey is filmed sneaking off when her parents are not looking to explore the highest, and therefore thinnest, branches. Suddenly a branch breaks, and she is saved only by her prehensile tail which is tightly wrapped around a very thin, precarious looking, spindly branch. Her screams, even to human ears, are easily recognisable as ones of terror and fear, and they ring out across the rainforest canopy. Clearly frightened, she dangles upside down, held only by her tail, on a perilously thin branch that swings terrifyingly with even her light weight. The wonderful voice of Sir David Attenborough informs us that a fall from this height would mean certain death.

Then, just as we are all gripping the edge of our seats, Daddy Spider Monkey, hearing her cries, shows up, and using his much bigger, stronger body, easily makes a bridge between two branches, so his inquisitive offspring can use his body to climb down safely. Sighs of relief all round… Watching this footage reminded me of many scenarios with human children. Just like a parent helping a human child learn how to climb down from a height in a playground, the male Spider Monkey supports and encourages his little one to use her own skills, rather than taking over and simply lifting her to safety. By acting in this way, Daddy Spider Monkey supports the infant to learn from her experience. After all, if she is to survive hundreds of feet off the ground, the baby Spider Monkey needs to learn to overcome the obstacles that she will meet in daily life. Once safely down from the branch, and no longer in mortal danger, the baby Spider Monkey's first action? To cuddle straight into Daddy, and bury her head in his chest…

> Less maternal [*adult?*] anger, negative affect, and hostility during play at 24-months was associated with more optimal effortful control skills and cognitive skills at 24-months and fewer...behavior problems, attention problems, and ADHD symptoms. Similarly, in Kochanska *et al.*'s (2000) sample, children whose mothers [*adults?*] were more responsive (e.g., more sensitive, accepting, cooperative, and emotionally available) had children who exhibited better effortful control skills by age three. Positive parenting [*adult?*] interactions may facilitate the development of effortful control and other cognitive and behavioral competences in children born preterm and full-term, whereas angry, critical interactions may interfere with this process. (Poehlmann, *et al.* 2010, p.14, emphasis added)

Just as an aside, it is also interesting to note that at no point do any adult Spider Monkeys step in, take over or admonish or reprimand either! In other words, it is *how* we, as adults, react that is important. At the very basic level, all babies use a range of cries and behaviours to ensure their needs are met, they stay safe, and therefore they can grow, develop and flourish.

> The toddler who has learned that the people she depends on for comfort will help her when she is distressed is more likely to approach others with empathy and trust than the toddler whose worries and fears have been dismissed or belittled. (Shonkoff and Phillips 2000, p.90)

What all of these writers, authors and researchers are saying, we can relate to the baby Spider Monkey too. Monkeys, like humans, are social animals and being part of the troupe helps with built-in needs such as survival, having play-mates and breeding and so on. If baby Spider Monkeys were punished and not comforted by the adults, they would then, over time, develop mistrust, and be less likely to develop self-regulation. In any social group, being constantly mistrustful and unable to regulate your emotions is never going to be helpful. Shonkoff and Phillips 2000 (p.121) go on to explore this further:

> Stated simply, early development [of self-regulation] entails the gradual transition from extreme dependency on others to manage the world for us, to acquiring the competencies needed to manage the world for oneself.

Or, to put it another way, young children whose distressed behaviours are supported appropriately are more likely to be confident, and therefore more likely to be able to self-regulate and trust, and therefore, in turn, empathise with, and support others. As children grow and develop, they will learn a range of new behaviours and will learn to compromise, debate, negotiate, care for each other, and use vocabulary and other skills to behave in certain ways in certain situations. In other words, learn to manage their own behaviours, These, and similar abilities, of course are the foundations to living in any social group, and therefore forming friendships and relationships, and so on. But not if adults continuously only offer instructions and directions, or simply step in and manage all situations and behaviours for them. I am not saying that children should simply be 'left to their own devices', but I am saying that we perhaps need to consider the ways in which we support young children, and our approaches to so-called 'behaviour management'. Learning about their own behaviours, learning through making mistakes, learning though trial and error, for example, and building on these experiences, will help children to form friendships and relationships, soothe the feelings of themselves and others, and make it easier in a whole range of ways for children to negotiate their way through the world. This is never truer than for two-year-olds...

Not So Terrible Twos!

There are a whole host of angles I could cover in this book, but there is only ever so much room, and somehow, as a writer, you have to decide which things are the most interesting, important or useful. So, just for now, I want to concentrate on the much-maligned toddler. Terrible twos, temper tantrums, biter, screamer, naughty, attention seeking, playing up – you name it, the toddler has been labelled with all of these, and more.

I would like to offer it a different way... These wonderful, animated and gregarious little humans, usually with very little verbal language, manage to show us big humans exactly what is happening in their brains, with barely 24 months' experience of the big wide world... Think what you have done in the last two years. You might have got married, had a child, got a new job, passed your driving test, qualified as an early childhood practitioner, and a whole host of other things beside...but...think how fast that time has gone.

In this incredibly short timeframe, a child who is now about two years (or just 24 months) old has perhaps learnt amongst other things to: sit up, crawl, walk, bend, stretch, hold things in both hands or one hand then the other hand, get up and down stairs (often in unique ways), speak a few words, eat, swallow, chew, feed themselves, read facial expressions, laugh when things are funny, cry when they are hurt or wet or frightened, give cuddles (and kisses), clap, smile, frown, point to their eyes, nose, mouth and so on, make some animal noises, make a pretend cup of tea, build with bricks, hold a book, push toy cars, select, recognise and keep a favourite comforter, make a mark with a crayon, press buttons, put their arms out when dressing, go rigid (or floppy) when they do not want to go into the car seat/pushchair, make choices about food (for example), understand routines such as mornings or bedtimes, splash, pour and squirt water in the bath, recognise household equipment and what it is used for, know that some things are hot and dangerous, express their thoughts such as by saying 'no' (often clearly and very insistently), recognise noises such as fire engine sirens and recognise characters from books...

Very young children of around this age have also probably learnt what happens when you: pull the paper on a toilet roll, turn on a tap, flush a toilet, quickly turn over mid-nappy change, empty a cupboard, empty the cat dish, climb on a chair, fall off a chair, stand up under a table, splash in the bath, slip in the bath, throw toys from a cot, turn a full bowl of breakfast upside down, drop a plate or empty a cup of juice, touch something hot, breathe on glass, put your fingers in cereal/pasta or the toilet, touch the table with sticky fingers, splash in a puddle, squash a banana...

...do I need to go on? The difference between these two lists – and many, many more things I am sure you could add – is how we as adults see them. If I go back to the BBC *Animal Planet II* (2016), there was a wonderful description of baby orangutans, which offered 'young orangutans learn about their world by constantly interrogating it'. And this is exactly what human children do too. I have to say, I could identify with the word 'interrogation', and I'm sure if you have ever spent any length of time with inquisitive toddlers, I am sure you will too:

> Play is highly vulnerable for a reason. We were judged, we were condemned, we were punished, sometimes harshly, for simply being our innocent curious selves. (Gowman 2015)

If we reconsider the two lists of all the things a toddler can do, I wonder how many were punished for 'interrogating their world'? However, as far as the toddler is concerned, both lists belong together, they are inseparable, the toddler is simply learning about the interesting, amazing and sometimes topsy-turvy world we live in...and, what happens when they interact with the world around them...and that is why I think, when looked at like this – toddlers are truly amazing...and their behaviours, and how they learn to understand their behaviours, are amazing too!

REFLECTIVE PRACTICE

Understanding Toddler Behaviours

Consider the following points:

- A toddler wants to have a toy that someone else already has.

- A toddler is left at the setting for the first time, after a two-week break due to illness or a holiday.

- A toddler sees a new member of staff for the first time.

- A toddler arrives at the setting to find that their key person is away that day.

- A toddler watches another child who is distressed due to an accident outside.

- A toddler whose parents have not arrived yet watches other children being collected.

Now consider how you feel in these, or similar situations:

- A friend has the new latest gadget, phone, car, handbag, shoes or similar.

- You return to work for the first time, after two-week sickness or holiday.

- You meet a new manager for the first time.

- You arrive at a party just as a friend texts/calls to say they cannot make it.

- You see a friend who has hurt themselves in a fall.

- You wait for your lift home on a dark night when everyone else has left.

I am sure you can see the analogies here, and perhaps understand how overwhelming some experiences are for very young children. The young child who is perhaps, as far as they are concerned, simply exploring, does not yet understand why it is OK to explore some things, but not others, and their hormones take over. The chemical reaction in our brains is exactly the same, but as adults we have developed skills to understand and regulate our thoughts and feelings; toddlers on the other hand still have a way to go. As adults, we sometimes struggle to explain our thoughts and feelings in some situations. Yet here we see, in very small children, with limited experiences of, and in, the world, the ability to express feelings in very honest and upfront ways. What young children need is our help to identify, name and understand these emotions. As they mature, and appropriate to their development, children can then be supported to understand and be in control of their emotions and the associated behaviours, in other words self-regulation. Shonkoff and Phillips (2000) quote a range of research, including Eisenberg, Cumberland and Spinrad (1998) and Valiente, Lemery-Chalfant and Reiser (2007), who consider how when adults respond appropriately to children's emotions, what we are doing is offering effective strategies for self-regulation. They go on to explore how high levels of appropriate reactions to children's emotions and low levels of negative reaction are associated with higher levels of self-regulation.

Therefore, as adults, our ability to empathise is crucial when we are nurturing young children and their PSED, and helping children to understand their behaviours. Understanding how it perhaps might feel for us as adults, maybe returning to work after a two-week break, for example, can go a long way in understanding how this might then feel for young children, in a similar situation. Similarly, understanding that toddlers put their fingers in food in order to explore what it feels like, and not because they are being 'naughty' or trying to be difficult, is helpful too. So yes, I do think toddlers are wonderful, gregarious and inquisitive and therefore their behaviours are truly amazing. The key here is the adult, who, hopefully, recognises the signs and symptoms, supports the development of language, empathises, nurtures, comforts and cares, and provides the assistance needed so that young children can understand, learn, develop, flourish and thrive.

As we discussed in Chapter 1, the toddler experiencing a cortisol meltdown is a reaction to the hormones being released, and is no different to an adult involved in a full-blown row with a partner. Yet, our behaviour is not seen as 'naughty' or as a 'tantrum'. We calm down, hopefully, we talk (and listen) more clearly, hopefully, we compromise, hopefully, and reach an amicable solution, hopefully...

Additionally, when we are excited about something, perhaps getting louder, waving our arms around and becoming more and more animated by the minute, hopefully, we do not collapse in a heap of emotional exhaustion...

Furthermore, hopefully, when we are jealous, frightened, stressed, scared, anxious or worried and so on, we have the skills needed to cope. When we are faced with a new situation, an unfamiliar environment or meeting new people and so on, hopefully we can draw on previous experiences, where hopefully we were supported to overcame the obstacles...

Because, *hopefully*, some wonderful, understanding adult way back in our past helped us to name, recognise, organise and control the dizzying array of emotions that as humans, we have to deal with. Because, *hopefully*, the adults in our lives helped us to (and continue to help us to), overcome situations and experiences that frightened us, supported us to try new experiences and allowed us to feel those emotions and understand why they are there. In other words, because, *hopefully*, somewhere in our past we had adults that cared, and *hopefully* we still do!

Tots, Toddlers and Teeth!

One of the most common discussions I have on behaviour, brain development, self-regulation and resilience, or child development training with practitioners, goes something like this:

Delegates: How do we deal with biting?

Me: Why do some children bite?

Delegates: Frustration, anger, overtired, lack of language, testing/ mouthing, attention seeking, boredom, inappropriate environment, lack of adult support, lack of understanding of 'social rules' (such as sharing), it is part of development, etc...

Me: OK, so if we agree biting is part of normal development and we know why some children bite, why is biting an issue?

Delegates: Errm... It's hard to explain to, and discuss with, parents?

Me: Why is discussing biting any harder than all the other difficult conversations you have to have with parents?

Delegates: Errm...well... Parents go ballistic about biting?

Me: Why biting? I do not understand why biting is such an issue.

By now some delegates are usually looking a little puzzled too. I can see people thinking – 'yes, why is biting such an issue?' Then, there is usually someone who says 'ah, but biting leaves such a nasty mark'.

Me: If I hit you with a wooden block, or knock you off the top of the climbing frame, that would leave a nasty mark too. I am really not trying to be difficult – I genuinely still do not understand why biting is such an issue.

Delegates: [looking more puzzled, I can see them thinking 'hmm, maybe Debbie has a point – why is biting such an issue?']

By this point, I can see people thinking, really, really, thinking hard – why is biting such an issue? Let's have a look at a typical scenario.

REFLECTIVE PRACTICE: CASE STUDY

Bob the Biter

Bob is 22 months old and is a typically active and energetic toddler. One day Bob is playing with the water wheel in the water tray. As Bob's key person, you have noticed Bob playing with the water wheel a lot recently and you know he loves it. You have been adding other elements to the water tray to help Bob use differing sizes and shapes of containers to pour the water into the wheel.

You are at the other side of the room and can see Bob happily splashing about in the water tray. Bob's friend Sam goes over to the water tray and tries to take the water wheel from Bob's hand. Bob shrieks loudly at Sam in protest and hangs onto the water wheel. Sam pulls harder and starts to pull the water wheel away from Bob. You start to walk over to try to help, but as you get to less than a metre from the boys, Bob sinks his teeth into Sam's arm, and bites down – hard. Sam releases the water wheel and bursts into uncontrollable sobs, with huge tears falling down his cheeks.

Some questions to consider:

- Why did Bob bite (hurt) Sam?
- What (if anything) could you have done to prevent the situation?
- What are you going to say to Bob's parents?
- What are you going to say to Sam's parents?

So, I suspect this is a normal, maybe not everyday, but fairly usual, situation in many ECCE settings. The questions above are fairly straightforward, and ones I suspect you would go through after any incident, not just a biting one. However, on my training programmes, there are other questions I ask practitioners to consider:

- What does it say in your behaviour/biting policy?
- Who do you think 'suffers' the most in a biting situation, so in our scenario:
  - Sam?

- – Sam's parents?

- – Bob?

- – Bob's parents?

- What are you going to do if it happens again?

In my opinion, these questions often trigger deeper reflection, and the first question will often clarify the other points. I believe that all settings should have something about biting in their behaviour policies. If all parents understood from day one, that for some children, biting is a *normal part of development*, the reasons behind why children bite and your procedures for supporting everyone concerned in a biting situation, I believe there would be less concern generally.

Invariably on training programmes, when we discuss the bullet points, there is initially some disagreement on who 'suffers' the most. If we take each of the 'characters' in turn, my opinion is:

- Sam – will be upset initially, but will in all probability be back playing with Bob later in the day (as is often the case with toddlers).

- Sam's parents – their reaction will depend on their previous experiences, how the situation is handled and if/when it happens again.

- Bob – will be fine, he is oblivious of the distress caused, too young to understand how much biting (or indeed any other retaliation) hurts… And anyway, Bob has his water wheel back, so has achieved his desired result.

- Bob's parents – in my opinion and experience, it is often the parents of the child who has bitten that are often the most traumatised by a biting scenario.

Throughout the whole situation, the practitioner's reaction and handling of this is crucial. *If* when we see the biting occur, we react in shock, outrage or horror, for example, and then there is a huge fuss created by other children, staff and parents, then I can see why toddlers look and think 'oh, wow, what a reaction, I'm going to do that again and see what happens'. Additionally, they often bite the same child again and again, and I think this is perhaps related to testing to see if the reaction is the same (remember we are talking about the logic in a developing, curious, inquisitive toddler mind, not a fully grown adult). Or, the toddler might see that biting has the desired effect, 'I got what I wanted', so use it as a successful way of gaining the upper hand in other situations.

But in all of this, it is the parents of the child who has bitten that I have most concern, empathy and compassion for. For some bizarre, inexplicable and seemingly unexplainable reason, biting is seen as the most horrific situation and almost deemed to be 'the crime of all crimes' in early childhood. The parents of the child who has bitten have to look on whilst their child is labelled 'the biter', their child is ostracised from games and not invited to parties, other parents hurriedly move their own children away and look at the floor, or call for the child who has bitten to be excluded... I know we never name the child in these situations, but usually, within a matter of hours, everyone knows. And everyone talks about 'the biter'.

What does this message convoy to everyone concerned? Imagine you have habit of biting your fingernails. Imagine you hear people talking about you in hushed tones. They call you 'the biter', in fact it becomes so intertwined with you as a person, that no-one actually uses your name anymore. You don't get invited to nights out, no-one will talk to you at lunch time, and if anyone does talk to you, their friends pull them away quickly. Imagine also if people called for you to be dismissed. It sounds ludicrous when put into an adult context this way. If we treated adults in this way, this could very well be seen as tantamount to bullying, yet this is what actually happens to children who bite. And it is their parents who notice these things, and have to cope with watching their little one be treated in this way...

How do you feel reading that last couple of paragraphs? Because I feel sick just writing them...but this is the reality, and this is why I think it is the parents of the child who bites that need the most support, understanding and compassion in these situations. The children will, of course get through this, they will (on the whole) grow out of this stage. The parents of the child who has been bitten will calm down or, worst case scenario, take their child elsewhere, where this could all still happen again anyway. But, the parents of the child who bites will never, ever forget how they, or more importantly their little one, was treated for what *we* actually know is a part of normal development! There is a quote that could be useful here, by perhaps Maya Angelou, Carl W. Buehner or Carol Bucher, depending on where you look, which states:

I've learnt that:

People *will* forget what you said,

People *will* forget what you did, *but...*

People will *never* forget how you made them feel.

Mammals and Teeth?

Let's explore this a little further. If we reconsider Chapter 1, we are all mammals. Mammals usually start life suckling their mother's milk. Then as baby mammals grow, they develop teeth in order to chew and eat more grownup, non-liquid diets. Therefore, we need teeth to grow and develop. In humans, for example, we have a range of different teeth to perform different jobs: incisors for biting, canines for ripping and tearing and premolars and molars for chewing and grinding – each type of tooth perfectly formed and perfectly placed to do the job it is needed to do. Young mammals however, do not always have the understanding that teeth are not for biting each other.

For example, a friend of ours has recently acquired three young kittens; they play wonderfully together, rough and tumbling across the floor and up and down the staircase. We sit spellbound, watching their amazing antics and energy and empathising when one of them accidently bites a little too hard on one of their siblings. Additionally, *we* play with them; imagine four adults on the floor with balls of fur, claws and teeth whizzing around at light speed and you are somewhere near the picture. And, sometimes they play with us too. They play with toys, and love to jump out of play-tunnels and from under chairs on to unsuspecting feet. More than anything they love to roll over on to their backs, and have an accommodating human tickle their tummies...

And then, and then...they get over excited and they bite us, and claw and scratch, all the while purring away at such a fun game, oblivious to our whines of pain and blood speckled hands and arms. What do we do? Do we 'bite them back', or lock them out of the room, exclude them, until they 'learn their lesson'? Force them to say sorry? No, of course we do not! Over time, like our toddlers, they will learn that biting is for food and not humans (or indeed each other). However, the point I am trying to make here is that why are kitten (or puppy, for that matter) behaviours seen as perfectly normal and yet in a toddler seen as the crime of the century? The fact is, mammals, and therefore kittens, puppies and indeed young humans, have teeth. Teeth are there for biting, and young mammals need help to learn when, and when not, to use teeth. So therefore, the upshot of this is – using your teeth is a normal part of normal mammals' development – and therefore a normal part of development for young children.

I acknowledge that not all children bite, and that if biting is still occurring in older children then it may well need further investigation. But for the purposes of this section, biting in toddlers does not need to be, and should not be, treated with such horror, with calls for the child to be immediately excluded and ostracised, or labelled as 'the biter' to anyone who will listen. My question is simple – what messages does this give to the children, parents, colleagues and wider society? And again, back to the question about naughty – how would you feel if this happened to a child you love?

And...so, after all that, despite all the research, reading, experience, conversations, etc. I have undertaken, I *still* do not understand why biting is seen as such a major issue. I do however think it is time for serious, cross-sector, cross-society reflection and for consideration on some actions and steps we can put in place to decriminalise, demystify and help mitigate the tensions surrounding biting situations.

REFLECTIVE PRACTICE

Reflections on Biting

Consider the following questions; how could the discussions we have had here help you in your practice, and help to support toddler development?

- What does your Behaviour Policy say about biting? Do you need to add additional information, or perhaps develop a separate biting policy?

- What information do you have for potential or new parents regarding possible biting incidents?

- What information do you have for existing parents regarding biting incidents?

- How do you support the children to understand what is, and what isn't acceptable uses for their teeth?

- How can you support colleagues, parents and the wider community to have a greater understanding of the wider issues regarding biting?

- How can you ensure that you, your colleagues and parents do not inadvertently overreact to a biting incident?

- What simple strategies can you put in place if you have multiple biting incidents?

- What is your procedure for supporting children who bite?

- How are you going to support everyone concerned if there are calls for the child who has bitten to be excluded, or for comments such as 'bite them back'?

In terms of research to support this area of child development, whilst there are many blogs and individual papers available, there is little empirical examination and evidence. In my opinion, one of the best pieces of research available is *Dealing with Biting Behaviours in Young Children*, by Ron Banks and Sojin Yi, from the Early Childhood and Parenting (ECAP) Collaborative, College of Education at the University of Illinois. They offer the following:

> The National Association for the Education of Young Children (1996) estimates that 1 out of 10 toddlers/2-year-olds engages in biting behaviours. (Banks and Yi 2002)

This estimation is helpful in ECCE as it helps us to see how common biting actually is. If we imagine an 'average' toddler room, filled with, let's say, 24 available places. With perhaps up to 40 children on roll, as some children will only be accessing the setting part-time, or for a set number of hours, we potentially have four children developmentally engaging in biting behaviours *at any one time*. Additionally, and importantly, Banks and Yi (2002) looked at data gathered in relation to quite a large study of children:

> Garrard, Leland, and Smith (1988) examined the injury log of one large (224 children) early childhood centre. They also studied the biographical information about each child filled out by the parent at the time of admission and financial records to document enrollment. They determined that 347 bites occurred during the study year.

If we consider the number of biting incidents of 347 in one year, this is also helpful. If we surmise that most settings are closed for, let's say, 10 days over the Christmas period, plus 8 Bank Holiday days, plus weekends – then an average full day care setting is open approximately 242 days a year. Then we divide 242 days by 347 biting incidents, that equates to 1.4 biting incidents every day! Knowing this can be reassuring when trying to support other adults to understand and empathise in a biting scenario. Banks and Yi (2002) go on to explore how the study by Garrard *et al.* (1988) found that boys were more likely to bite than girls, and the newest children were most likely to get bitten. Again, we can use this information to help plan how to deal with biting scenarios, and importantly how to support parents and children in these situations.

One further thought when biting situations escalate, 'official complaints' are often used as a threat in endeavours to push settings to deal more severely with the situation, such as by excluding the child committing this 'heinous' deed. For example, it may be that settings are told that the incident will be referred to a greater power, or to the Local Authority. However, in my experience, as long as you have correct ratios in place, have appropriately recorded the incident and your intended actions, for example, incidents such as these are rarely given much credence, are regarded as part of normal childhood, and usually, as children are supported to learn and develop, biting is something that most children grow out of.

Much of the discussion in this section, is, as mentioned, directly about toddlers; however, much of this is also useful when looking at other age groups. Good practice regarding young children is good practice, regardless of their ages. Children might react or behave in slightly different ways, how we respond might be slightly different, but ultimately good practice when nurturing PSED is good practice. Children need adults who, for example, listen, respond, acknowledge, take notice and empathise, regardless of their ages. The examples we have considered can cause anxiety across the age ranges: older children may be anxious after a break due to illness, babies might be worried about a new member of staff, teenagers may struggle with feelings regarding the latest gadget their friends have, elderly relatives may be worried about being picked up from an appointment. How we support these differing age groups might be slightly different, but ultimately this isn't about the age on your birth certificate; this is about being human and understanding humans, and the wider influence of PSED on our lives.

PART 5: CONCLUSION

So, in conclusion, what influences children's PSED, indeed all humans' PSED? One simple answer – *everything*! Everything we have covered so far, brain development and the various influences we have covered in this chapter, as well as everything we will cover in the rest of the book has some influence on children's PSED and behaviours…

> This evidence review emphasises the importance of emotional attachments and relationships and highlights the need to both prevent Adverse Childhood Experiences (ACEs) and to ameliorate the impacts where these have occurred. We can build on learning to date and continue to seek to shift from historical 'shame and blame' approaches to those that are focused on 'understanding and nurturing'… (Dodds 2016, p.54)

> Early childhood is a time of great promise and rapid change, when the architecture of the developing brain is most open to the influence of relationships and experiences. Yet, at the same time, significant disadvantages in the life circumstances of young children can undermine their development, limit their future economic and social mobility, and thus threaten the vitality, productivity, and sustainability of an entire country. (Center on the Developing Child at Harvard University 2016, p.4)

Children's own experiences, skills, knowledge and understanding, their place in the family, illness and poverty, for example, can influence their PSED. The physical environment, the social environment and the emotional environment individually, and collectively, have roles to play, and these can be helped or hindered by adults. As adults, whoever we are, our thoughts, words, deeds, actions, facial expressions, body language, what we do say, what we don't say, and so on – all have a part to play. After all, I am sure we will have all had the sometimes hilarious, or even perhaps uncomfortable, but always highly accurate, experience of witnessing a small child mimic something we have done or said! As adults, we need to be aware of the huge influence we have on young children, how we nurture PSED, and understand behaviours. Additionally, as adults, we need to consider how the things we do don't always have the positive influences on PSED that we hope, however unintentional and well-meaning, and we will explore this in more detail in the next chapter.

Chapter 3

WELL-MEANING?

On the whole, the things that we, as adults, do for children are intended to support, nurture, benefit, entertain, and so on. The things we do and say are all intended to help children, amongst other things, feel safe, grow, have fun, develop, learn, thrive and flourish. At differing times, as adults, the majority of us see roles such as protector, teacher, carer, entertainer or provider as intrinsic to having small children in our lives. To paraphrase *Development Matters* (Early Education 2012), we see each child as unique, we develop positive relationships and provide enabling environments. The words may change slightly depending on the situation, but I am sure you can see my point:

> This is a highly skilled role; practitioners need to differentiate, to understand each child as an individual as well as part of a family, community, society and culture and personalise the curriculum content to reflect and build on their needs and interests. (Duffy 2014, p.122)

We generally carry out these responsibilities with love, care, enthusiasm and attention and in return see children who flourish and thrive, and grow and develop a range of skills, knowledge and abilities. I know there is a lot more to it than this, but I hope you can see the general point. We, on the whole, aim to do the best we can for the children in our lives. Occasionally, though, it sometimes feels as if some of the things we do are not as helpful as they originally might seem.

I believe there are a range of situations, circumstances, communications, and so on, that are 'presented' to children by well-meaning adults, that perhaps cause more stress, distress and anxiety than is ever anticipated. I am not saying that any of the things discussed in this chapter are 'mortal sins', and should never, ever be 'presented' to, or for, children, but I am saying perhaps they need a little more thought and consideration. I am saying that maybe we need more reflection on some of these issues in terms of nurturing personal, social and emotional development (PSED) and understanding children's behaviours. I too have been involved in some of the situations discussed here, and was, of course, involved with the best intentions at the time. However, the more I research, the more I go around the country talking to other practitioners, and families, the more I am convinced that some further reflection is perhaps needed. Additionally, we need to bear in mind we are talking about children, on the whole who are just four years old, or 48 months, or under.

The chapter comes with a health warning, that should be considered at all points:

I am not saying that we should *never* have celebrations and events. I am not saying that children cannot cope with change, or difference in routine or transitions, for example. What I am saying, is, that for some children events such as the ones discussed in this chapter, as well as others you may be aware of, perhaps need further consideration... And, I am saying that this chapter needs to be considered, in context, alongside everything else in this book. Neuroscience and the effects of hormones, the myriad of influences in children's lives, the importance of wellbeing and listening, for example – will all have a direct result on the situations we will be considering in this chapter. Additionally, you will know your children and families best, and that too will need adding to the mix. Therefore, all of this will need taking into account when reflecting on your own current, and indeed future, practice.

This chapter is entitled 'Well-Meaning?' Acknowledging the question mark as you proceed through this chapter is vital. The chapter title is a question, and the question is there to aid reflection. This chapter offers an opportunity for adults to consider their role, the situation concerned, and whether the well-meaning intent is, in real terms, actually a benefit for children or not. I acknowledge that this chapter may well be a little controversial, contentious and provocative, but isn't that the whole point of reflection? An opportunity to consider a differing viewpoint, an alternative, or to consider things from another angle? So, if we are going to have a discussion that may be a little challenging, let's kick this off with what is perhaps the biggest event in the UK calendar – Christmas.

Early Years Author Cancels Christmas...

Or perhaps...early years author says 'Bah Humbug to Christmas'? However, no, I am *not* cancelling Christmas, but I can see this as a headline in the media if this chapter is misinterpreted. So, let me repeat that – I am *not* cancelling Christmas – and nor am I suggesting you should either. Why then, in a chapter entitled 'Well-Meaning?', am I talking about Christmas? Let's explore this a little.

REFLECTIVE PRACTICE

Changing Rooms?

You are going to stay with a friend for the weekend, and while you are away, your lovely partner/parents/friends decide to surprise you by decorating your home. In order to achieve the desired results, your thoughtful loved ones:

- remove half of your clothes from your wardrobe

- remove half of your furniture

- take several of your potions and lotions out of the bathroom

- swap your living room and dining room spaces

- put strings of lights in all the rooms, and remove all the ceiling light fittings

- change all your crockery and cutlery for ones that have red and green stripes

- fill your cupboards with one particular style of food

- remove all your music and replace it with one genre

- change the décor in every room to silver and gold

- remove all your ornaments and photos and replace them with new ones

- fill your home with huge plants.

Now, consider the following questions:

- How do you think you would feel on your return?
  - » Why do you think you would feel that way?
- How do you think you would react?
  - » What might you say?
  - » What might you do?
- Why do you think these people would change things without asking you?

Before we go any further I need to make it absolutely clear: I love Christmas, my friends and family call me Mrs Christmas, I do *not* want to ban Christmas...but, I guess you can see where this is going? I do worry about how very young children see Christmas. Often, for young children, Christmas appears overnight – pow! Suddenly the world is red and green, with fluffy white thrown in, and then covered in sparkly glitter for good measure...which is great, if you are resilient, emotionally secure and able to talk about it coherently...but...maybe not so great if your little world is already slightly chaotic and this is the one place where you feel safe.

Suddenly, the world you know and feel safe in does not look the same. The toys that you like so much are not where they usually are, the lights look different, and there are these huge trees everywhere, for example. Consider the very young brain as we discussed in Chapter 1, or some of the influences we discussed in Chapter 2, and suddenly all the glitter, cotton wool and tinsel can seem a little scary. In effect, we are actually talking about change, and the impact change has on very young children.

If you think back over your career, consider the times you have made changes to a room or building. How did the children react? I recognise that many, many children will love the pizzazz of the excitement and build up to a revamped room, new building, special event or celebration, but many children will not. I suspect we can all recall children who were worried, anxious, tearful, stressed or nervous, just because the furniture had been moved into a slightly different place. We will all be able to recall the preschool child who would only ride the red bike, the toddler who insisted on the same story or the baby who would only use one type of cup, all probably for reasons only known to them at the time. And, I am sure we can all recall the heart-rending cries of very real distress when the red bike, specific story book or special cup disappeared. Neuroscience tells us that this is because routine and familiarity make the reptilian brain feel safe. If we reconsider Chapter 1:

> The reptilian brain needs food, warmth, sleep, routine and people who help it to feel safe, and once all these things are in place the reptilian section of the brain feels secure.

In terms of change, it is the routine bit here that is important. The routine of furniture and equipment being in the same place, for example, helps children (and indeed adults) to feel safe. This is one of the reasons why in ECCE, we have the 'continuous provision' of equipment and resources, so that children know they can return to them again and again. Of course, feeling safe enables children to develop understanding of the equipment and resources, and enables children to be able to explore, learn, develop and thrive:

> My definition of continuous provision is not the provision that is continuously out. It is far more rich and complex that that...should continue the provision for learning in the absence of an adult...is challenge and support in all areas for *all* children...[should include] a measure of ambiguity and

open-ended experience. Children need to have the freedom to interpret the environment... We want children to be 'explorers'...use their own interest, curiosity and creativity to interpret, use and apply what they see around them in ways that are individual to their own needs and experiences. That is when the fun really starts! (Bryce-Clegg 2015, p.4)

Additionally, also worth considering is the 'people' element of the quote from Chapter 1. If those same people who usually help us feel safe are suddenly acting very oddly, more excited than usual, or appearing more stressed than normal, then the child's intuitive brain will pick up on this. We are then back to the levels of cortisol increasing and rising stress levels. Definitely not what we as adults envisaged when we strung lights, sprinkled glitter and hung decorations everywhere. So, let's explore what change means for us as humans in a little more detail.

Personal Transition Curve

John Fisher originally developed the 'Personal Transition Curve' in the late 1990s. Since then he has adapted and developed it; it is widely available and well respected. One of my favourite explanations is on the businessballs. com website. Fisher discusses how change brings about various reactions in humans:

Any change, no matter how small, has the potential to impact on an individual... I would argue that we transit through all stages (although the old caveat of some of these stages may be extremely quickly traversed and not consciously recognisable applies). In the main we will progress through all the phases in a linear or sequential way (although we may move in either direction as circumstances change throughout.) Each stage builds on the last stage and incorporates any learning (positive and negative) from our experience. (Fisher 2012)

REFLECTIVE PRACTICE

Personal Approach to Change

Consider the grid, adapted from the Personal Transition Curve (Fisher 2012), on the following pages. Think about times when you have gone through a process of change; some change you will have welcomed, other change may have caused anxiety or fear. Considering each of the stages, can you think of how you exhibited your feelings – in other words, how did you behave?

Additionally, can you consider, for future episodes of change, strategies that you could use to help you at each stage?

Stage	Sample Statements	Personal Thoughts/Feelings/Strategies
Anxiety	Feel out of control Cannot picture the future Do not have enough information Cannot see my role in the future	
Happiness	Feel views are recognised and shared by others Relieved that something is going to change Anticipation/excitement at the possibility of improvement Expecting the best and anticipating a bright future Feel lucky/involved and able to contribute	
Fear/threat	Worried will need to act in a different way Worried it will have a fundamental impact on who we are Unsure as to how we will be able to act/react Worried how will it affect me Worried about new/alien environment Worried 'old rules' no longer apply or what 'new rules' will be	
Guilt	Worried about the inappropriateness of previous actions Reflecting on my previous reactions Worried about impact of my behaviours Considering how I will react in the future	
Depression	Lack of motivation Confused – how do I fit into the future world? Uncertain as to what the future holds No clear vision	
Gradual Acceptance	Beginning to make sense of the change Can see my place within the change Can see that where we are going is right Seeing some successes Feel good that we are doing the right things in the right way	

Stage	Sample Statements	Personal Thoughts/Explanations
Moving Forward	Starting to feel I have more control Can make more things happen in a positive sense Feel comfortable Making the right choices Feel we are experimenting within our environment more actively and effectively	
Disillusionment	Feel my values, beliefs/goals are incompatible with those of the organisation Feel unmotivated/unfocused Feel increasingly dissatisfied Feel ready to leave	
Hostility	Tried new ways before, it never works Cannot see point of new ways of working Cannot see how it will work with my role	
Denial	I do not want the change to happen I cannot see how it will affect my role Current way of working works – why change it	
Anger	Feel change is 'forced' on me Am angry at myself Feel the situation has escalated outside my control	
Complacency	Have survived change before Not really interested – it'll be fine Can't see what all the fuss is about	

(adapted from the Personal Transition Curve; Fisher 2012)

I am sure you can see how this can be difficult for adults, so imagine how change must feel for very young children. Add to these changes some of the other potential influences or impacts on the child's life we have discussed elsewhere, and we have a potentially explosive mix:

> if someone is going through multiple transitions at the same time; these could have a cumulative impact on them as individuals. As people could be going through all the different transitions almost simultaneously – it then becomes a case of more and more 'evidence' all of which is supporting previous negative, a rapidly dropping self confidence and increasingly negative self image which just compounds the problem. We end up similar to the 'frozen rabbit in the headlights not knowing which way to turn'! (Fisher 2012)

So bearing all this in mind, perhaps Christmas, or indeed any other changes, need a little more thought. I know we do these types of 'activities' with the best intentions, our actions are well-meaning, but my question is, how do these types of activities nurture children's PSED, do they acknowledge what science is telling us and do they help/hinder children's behaviours? For future practice, you might want to consider the following questions as a starting point:

- Why might you need to consider how you approach changes in the future?
- Why could change be difficult for some children?
- How could the children be involved in the changes?
- Who might you need help/support from?
- What else might you need to consider?

If we reconsider the earlier reflective practice example ('Changing Rooms?'), if we returned home to a house we did not recognise, we would feel uncertain, perhaps anxious and maybe even worried or scared, and rightly so. We certainly would not be called naughty. Additionally, we like to know where things are, so to find our favourite plates missing, for example, could cause anxiety. In addition, depending on other influences and circumstances at the time, the anxiety could be much greater and cause further unintended stress for the brain. As Fisher (2012) goes on to say:

> Much of the speed of transition will depend on the individual's self perception, locus of control, and other past experiences, and how these all combine to create their anticipation of future events. The more positive you see the outcome, the more control you have (or believe you have) over both the process and the final result the less difficult and negative a journey you have.

So, perhaps we need to reflect on the amount of control very young children have on changes in their lives. How do we involve children more in the preparations for Christmas, for example? How do we help children to see Christmas as a magical time, whilst being aware of other 'multiple transitions', or changes that may also be happening? And, how do we help young children to build on previous experiences so that their journeys through change are 'less difficult and negative'? Whilst we are on the subject of Christmas, let's just consider the Christmas stalwarts, the 'Christmas Concert' or 'Nativity Play'.

REFLECTIVE PRACTICE

Carols, Concerts and Nativity Plays

Scenario 1

It is early October and at a staff meeting, the team decide which songs are going to be sung at the Christmas Concert. There will be several songs to sing, and the team agree the children will need a few weeks to learn them. It is agreed that the new songs will be introduced a couple at a time, from next week.

Additionally, there will be a nativity play, so the team decide which children could play the key roles, with all the other children playing various animals or stars. A couple of staff members volunteer to take the children for a couple of sessions a week to learn some simple lines.

The manager agrees to send out a letter asking parents for costumes, and explaining the policy of not using mobile phones or taking photographs or videos, etc. A local media student has volunteered to film the whole event and parents can purchase a DVD, with any funds raised going towards a day out for the children in the spring.

After several weeks, and much practising, the children can now sing many of the songs with gusto, the younger ones joining in with the actions where they can. The day of the event arrives, the staff are excited; indeed, many are wearing 'festive jumpers' to mark the occasion.

Once lunch is over, one room is emptied of all equipment, and the little chairs are laid out in rows for the guests to sit on when they arrive. The children are shepherded into another room to get ready for their big moments. After 40 minutes, most of the children are in their correct costumes. There have been several altercations with children not wanting to get changed, some children are still a little tearful, a few children are looking flushed, red and hot, and the staff are frazzled and anxious. The tension is mounting.

After a little while the children are brought into the room in a wavy, snake-like line and sat in rows facing the rows of chairs, and their parents, grandparents and loved ones. The manager stands up and welcomes the parents, who clap enthusiastically, and then wait expectantly as the opening bars of the music introduce the first song...

And then...

And then...

OK, so do I *really* need to ask the question – What happens next?

Anyone who has ever been in the above situation will know that sometimes exactly what happens next...is...

Nothing!

Nada!

Zilch!

The children do not sing with gusto, the younger ones do not join in with the actions... it is the *staff* who perform. Grinning wildly, frantically trying to encourage some enthusiasm amongst the children and desperately trying not to look too embarrassed. Meanwhile, the children sit frozen, staring at this room full of strangers, one or two realise the music has started and frantically join in, desperately trying to sing quickly to catch up with the music. The ones with more lung power sing loudly, whilst others barely whisper the words.

Meanwhile, little James starts to suck his fingers. Salima waves at her mummy. Harry says in a very loud voice that he needs a wee! In the audience, Grandad Joe pulls funny faces, making his granddaughter keel over in peals of laughter. Meanwhile, Isabella starts to cry, and several others join in to keep her company... And the staff keeping on singing, getting hotter and redder as the session continues.

The nativity play is usually a very similar story. Mary drops the baby-doll-Jesus, which the adults find endearing, smiling indulgently and giggling softly. Mary, however, is distraught and sobs uncontrollably. The adults had said she must hold the baby carefully. Now Mary thinks she has made a terrible mistake, but is not sure why, and she is not sure why the grownups are laughing at her either. The child playing the role of Joseph refuses to say anything, and stands looking at his feet, his face crumpled in terror: a caring member of staff jumps in and holds his hand, whilst saying his lines for him. The innkeeper is an energetic child who shouts every line as if his life depends on it, and in the middle of it, someone invariably falls of the makeshift stage, or wets themselves.

The parents, grandparents and other relatives love it (as long as it wasn't their child who cried or froze or weed), and look forward to the DVD, and showing it to their little cherubs' future partner in 25 years time. By the time the afternoon is over, the staff are hot, embarrassed, sticky, sweaty, exhausted or frazzled, and incredibly stressed.

But my question is…what about the children? Some, I acknowledge, will have loved it, but my experience, and what others tell me, is that the majority of the children are traumatised. The children are upset, anxious, stressed, teary, frightened, fearful and perhaps even self-admonishing, because they didn't 'get it right'. I wonder how many of you will identify with the concerts and plays as described here, either in your professional life, or indeed with children you love, or may be even your own childhood? Were you James or Isabella or the Mary who dropped the baby? And…if so, do you still carry those memories and feelings with you many years later? Oh, I know some readers will be thinking I am over-emphasising this, and this is not like some of the huge childhood traumas children face… And I agree – but I still think it is a trauma for many children involved. Let's consider this from a different perspective…

REFLECTIVE PRACTICE

Carols, Concerts and Nativity Plays

Scenario 2

At the staff meeting in early October the manager announces that the team will be putting on a show for parents and guests. The show will be performed twice, once in the afternoon, and once in the evening so that as many visitors as possible can attend. Everyone will be expected to take part, and no-one is allowed to take holidays on the day of the event. The manager has identified several songs, and says that the team are expected to learn them all, and the actions, by heart, in time for the big event. Additional to this the manager says the team will be performing the traditional nativity play. The manager distributes a sheet naming the key roles, with extra staff being identified as various animals or stars. The manager asks that everyone provides themselves with an appropriate costume.

Finally, the manager says that members of staff are welcome to invite their own parents, partners or friends to attend. The manager explains that a letter will be sent to everyone detailing the policy on mobile phones and taking photographs or videos, etc. A local media student has volunteered to film the whole event and people will be able to purchase a DVD, with any funds raised going towards a day out for the children in the spring…

Do I need to go on? I don't know about you – but I think it sounds ridiculous when put like this. When we put this, and similar celebratory events, into an adult focus, it often highlights in sharp relief the issues that children face. If you still aren't sure, think of how you feel when asked to participate in a role-play activity on a training course. Just like children, some of us would be delighted at being put 'centre stage', quite literally. Others, however, would be traumatised. So, therefore, if Christmas is meant to be such a special, exciting, magical time, is this really how we want children (or adults, for that matter) to feel? In reality, there are a range of issues around events such as these that may need consideration. Some are subtler than others, but the effects could be lasting and far reaching. Consider how you would feel being forced to participate in a concert or play:

- What if you do not want to be involved?
  - » How would you make your thoughts and feelings known?
- What if you have difficulty remembering things?
  - » What if you are having difficulty reading?
- What if buying a costume is an additional, difficult expense?
  - » What if buying a DVD is an additional, difficult expense?
- How would you feel being offered a seemingly 'minor' role?
  - » How would your loved ones feel seeing you in a seemingly 'minor role'?
- What if your loved ones cannot attend (for whatever reasons)?
  - » What if you have lost a loved one recently, for example?
- What if people around you have unrealistic expectations (too high or too low)?
- What if you have other issues, influences or concerns in your life?
- What if you have low self-esteem, low confidence or image anxiety?

So, yes, I think the word 'trauma' is appropriate. For some of us, the thought of being involved in this kind of event would be a trauma. The word 'trauma' means shock, upset, ordeal and so on, and so yes, for us as adults having to perform in front of a group of strangers would be a trauma. Our reptilian brains would be starting to worry, and therefore we would start to have heightened cortisol levels from the moment this is announced – and there are still many, many weeks to go. And, if the thought of this sends us, as adults, into 'fight, flight or freeze' mode, then imagine how it feels for very young children. Maybe Christmas events suddenly do not feel so glittery and sparkly?

Another angle to consider is the pressure events such as these put onto parents. A simple example is costumes. Gone are the days when a stripy tea towel and piece of string on a child's head served its purpose for a shepherd's headdress. Nowadays, immediately following Halloween, stores are awash with a dizzying array of pre-made nativity, as well as other Christmas-themed, child-sized costumes. At an already expensive, busy and stressful time of year, this could simply increase the pressure on already possibly frazzled parents to produce the 'ultimate' costume. Add to this the potential competitiveness to ensure your little star 'shines' and we have yet more stress added to the situation. For future practice, it might also be useful to re-look at the more in-depth discussions in Chapter 2 around parental involvement, and you may want to reconsider these two sections together.

An alternative?

OK, so if I love Christmas, if I am not trying to be 'Humbug!' and not trying to spoil everyone's fun, is there an alternative? Well, let's have a think... How about this...

REFLECTIVE PRACTICE

Carols, Concerts and Nativity Plays

Scenario 3

In early October, the manager brings up the subject of the Christmas celebration event. Everyone will be invited along to a Christmas sing-song. The team pick about eight songs, that the children will be supported to join in with from the beginning of December.

The event will be held twice, once in the afternoon and once in the early evening, to enable as many people as possible to attend. All staff are asked to attend if possible, especially to support children whose loved ones cannot attend for whatever reason.

The manager asks if anyone is willing to lead the singing and stories. Stacey works part-time at the local youth club, and regularly joins in the karaoke with the kids, and happily volunteers to lead the singing. Tasha is of Russian heritage and volunteers to lead a few short stories, including one from her own childhood.

On the day of the event, the children have the opportunity to make simple props of the songs and story characters, to use at the Christmas sing-a-long. The staff help too, and make a few extra, so there are plenty of props for anyone who might want to join in later.

At the event, the lights are turned lower, and the Christmas tree lights twinkle. Children, families and staff sit as a group, and join in with the songs, led expertly by Stacey and the other staff who enjoy singing. The children sit snuggled with whoever they choose, with the laps of the extra staff offering safe spaces for children whose grownups are not there. Everyone has a song sheet and is encouraged to join in if they want to, or to just simply clap along. At the end of the singing, Tasha tells a short version of the traditional Nativity story, as well as a traditional Russian story about Babushka who visits local children and delivers presents. Afterwards, everyone tucks in to mince pies, mini chocolate rolls and warm cocoa.

OK, so I recognise that this would not work for everyone – but it is meant to be *one* alternative. Just one way that a Christmas celebration could happen, could still be magical and with a lot less stress, anxiety and panic for everyone involved. It would take a lot less planning too.

The aim of the alternative is to offer an opportunity for you to consider which you would prefer, as a practitioner, as a parent, as a grandparent, etc. In addition, for you to consider which you think the children you care for, professionally or personally, would prefer. Reading through these scenarios, I know which one I would rather attend, and I also know which one the children I love would rather attend too.

To finish off this section, there are just a few other thoughts that you might want to consider:

- When is Christmas introduced in your setting?
  - Why is that? Is it very early? Do some children struggle with the fact that Christmas is still well over a month away?
  - Does introducing Christmas take into consideration families who may be facing financial difficulties?
- Are children encouraged to be involved in the preparation and planning for Christmas? And if not – why not?
- Are other major festivals and celebrations giving as much credence as Christmas?
  - Why do you think that is?
- What about children and families who do not celebrate Christmas, for whatever reason?
- How do we introduce Christmas to very young children and babies in a way that is meaningful to them?

- What other Christmas events are usually held?

  – Do they also need further thought and consideration?

One final thought: I am not going to 'fully' open the whole 'can of worms' of strange men in children's houses in the middle of the night (or even the tooth-fairy for that matter), or how 'good' children receive gifts. I really would be accused of not just being anti-Christmas, but anti-childhood…but I do feel it needs some thought. And the research base for this is growing too.

Anecdotally, we will all know some children for whom this is this more than they can handle. We will all know toddlers who screamed hysterically at the man in the red suit. We will all know children who refused to smile or sit on the jolly chap's knee. The emerging research is, in part, questioning if we need to consider the mixed messages this gives children, and what will happen when they find out the truth? I am not saying we should *not* have the jolly chap in red, I am simply offering this as yet another angle for you to consider:

> For psychologist Christopher Boyle, a professor at the University of Exeter in the UK, one of the authors of the paper, the 'morality of making children believe in such myths has to be questioned.' All children will eventually find out they've been consistently lied to for years, and this might make them wonder what other lies they've been told,' he said in a statement. 'Whether it's right to make children believe in Father Christmas is an interesting question, and it's also interesting to ask whether lying in this way will affect children in ways that have not been considered. (Welch 2016)

Deborah Best, PhD, a professor of psychology at Wake Forest University, offers a slightly different perspective:

> 'I think most children are disappointed when they find out that their parents are Santa Claus,' she said. 'They're disappointed in the magic going away, but I'm not so sure that they're angry at their parents about lying. I don't think I've ever heard that. It's more of a loss of that magical part of childhood.' (Welch 2016)

As I said earlier, I love Christmas. Our wedding was as close to Christmas as it could be. I love the magic. I love the fairy-tale. I love the build-up. I love the excitement, the music, the food. I love the family traditions. I love shopping for little personal presents that I know will make people smile. I love the smell of cinnamon, mince pies and fir trees. I love the twinkling lights, the TV specials, and writing notes in cards to far-away family and friends. I know by heart just about every line in every Christmas carol and song. I love watching (and quoting) the old traditional Christmas movies, especially the ones that make me cry even after the thirtieth time. What I love about Christmas is the feeling. It is the whole.

I think perhaps what I am trying to say is, do we as adults need to take more responsibility for our words, roles, actions and deeds in nurturing PSED experiences that do help to create magical, memorable childhoods? Rather than unintentionally creating more stress… And this goes for other events and celebrations that children are involved in, that potentially have similar impacts too, and we will explore some of these further into this chapter.

Hopefully, this discussion has put into some context the aim of this chapter: the many well-meaning things that we, as adults, do, that unintentionally have an impact on children's PSED. I started with Christmas as I acknowledge that not only is this subject likely to be contentious, but also not everyone celebrates Christmas; however, I do suspect that for the majority of settings Christmas is the biggest celebration of the calendar. The wider debate around the multicultural nature of the world today is for elsewhere, but as we are talking festivals, let's consider one that many settings do celebrate, Chinese New Year.

Festivals and Celebrations

One January, I was lucky enough to be in London with my 14-year-old niece on *the* day when Chinese New Year fell. We finished the work we had originally been in London for, and with a couple of hours to spare before the train home, headed to China Town. We arrived to a heaving, teeming, buzzing crowd, just as the dragon dance started. It was magical. We watched the dancers, went into a couple of Chinese supermarkets, bought some Chinese pastries from a patisserie, bought some traditional souvenirs and brought back some traditional sweets and fortune cookies to share with our family. We saw the traditional Chinese way of handling money (with two hands), we saw traditional fruits (such as longan and durian) and we saw crispy duck, roasting on spits. And, I was struck by seeing so many people, from so many cultures, joining in with the celebrations.

On the train journey home, I sat reflecting on the experience, thinking about why I felt it had been so magical. I have been to London's China Town many times, but this visit seemed particularly special. I know partly it was because I had my niece with me for her first experience of this wonderful part of London, and partly because it was the actual day of the New Year celebrations. What made it so special, though, was the fact that it was 'real'. It was bustling, busy, cultural, noisy, fun, exciting and *real*. I was not imagining what it might be like to celebrate the New Year. I was not just ordering Chinese food, and enjoying using chopsticks. I was there, I was in the middle of it – living it for real. This started me thinking about how we celebrate festivals and encourage an understanding of multiculturalism with children.

This is not the book for a whole debate on the approaches of the ECCE sector to multiculturalism. However, in a chapter about well-meaning and in a book about nurturing PSED, understanding other cultures deserves a mention. In terms of practice, there are a wealth of books, articles and information available around developing understanding in this area. I would just like to ask one little question:

• Do festivals and celebrations feel 'real' for children?

Of course, I am not saying we should take all children to China Town, for example, no more than it would be appropriate to celebrate and recognise every festival. But, additionally, simply having every child make identical cards for Diwali/Divali/Deepawali, or having a party for Eid, does not help children develop empathy, compassion and understanding around culture and difference or individuality. So, maybe, if we are looking at the well-meaning and well-intentioned things we do with and for children, perhaps festivals and other celebrations also need some further thought? In terms of other celebrations, there is one event that seems to be gaining popularity across the ECCE sector, and in terms of well-meaning, perhaps this is another area that needs further reflection – graduations.

Graduations

If we consider the word 'graduation', most dictionaries, including Merriam-Webster, offer the meaning of 'the award or acceptance of an academic degree or diploma', or similar. But, here's the thing, graduation ceremonies for preschoolers are becoming more and more popular in the UK, and I am not so sure that this is a good thing. As I have said previously, please, please do not be offended if this type of event happens at the ECCE setting you work at, or even the setting your children attend. I just want to offer the opportunity to reflect on this for a moment, and then it is up to others to decide if it still feels like a good thing for young children to be involved in.

Most ceremonies seem to follow a similar pattern. A zigzagging-line of four-year-olds, walking across a makeshift stage, each resplendent in child-sized cap and gown, to receive a 'scroll', from a visiting dignitary (I have seen firemen and even a Mayor in some photographs). A speech from someone in a managerial position, or perhaps a slideshow/presentation of children's photographs set to music, or children reciting poems or singing appropriate songs, or US army drill-style chants are all suggested in various websites. All accompanied by a dizzying array of what is deemed 'appropriate music' (S Club 7's 'Reach for the Stars', Heather Small's 'Proud' or Take That's 'Never Forget', to name a few). Then into another room for the quintessential 'Graduation Photograph', which parents and other doting family members can purchase at a later date.

Is this not similar to the tension-laden moment just before the Christmas concert, as discussed earlier? ECCE internet chat rooms, forums, social media and indeed it seems also staff rooms, around the country are awash with comments about a 'pointless event', filled with 'anxious, tearful children' not wanting to 'put on a cap and gown' and 'walk across a stage' in front of a group of clapping, teary parents and loved ones. Concerns are also raised about explaining to younger children why they too do not have a cap and gown, and being reassured that 'it'll be your turn next year'. (Isn't a year a long time when you are three? Just a thought...)

When challenged by other professionals as to, 'why bother then?', the response is often 'oh, but the parents love it...'. My own online research suggests otherwise, with many parents calling graduation ceremonies 'ridiculous', asking concerned questions about what their children should wear, and saying that they feel the ceremonies are 'superficial' and that they do not think their children understand the relevance. Many also clearly feel that graduation ceremonies are not child-focused; 'this is for the adults, let's be honest' is a regular statement. Parents also express concern at their child being the one 'who did not behave' or 'do what they were supposed to', so this would indicate parents too feel the pressure to conform to this increasingly popular event.

My question then is – who are we doing graduation ceremonies for – and why? I also think that many of the issues discussed in the Christmas section of this chapter fit equally here too. Change is difficult for young children, so for children perhaps already anxious or stressed about the impending 'big school', a 'graduation' event may add to the already stressed reptilian brain. I would also question whether some children actually understand that they will not be returning to the setting ever again, and so therefore understand the significance imparted to a graduation ceremony.

In terms of reflective practice, this is a difficult one. Many readers will personally have attended leavers events and graduation ceremonies and such like, and will indeed have fond memories of these special rituals. Events such as these are often a 'rite of passage', or mark a significant event in our lives. Celebrating a programme of study, achievements, or the leaving of one place to move on to a new one, for example, are important, but *we* are adults: we know *why* we are attending. We understand that the colours on the ceremonial hoods and stoles are linked to a specific area of knowledge, we know that the 'tossing of the mortar board' during photographs is a symbolic gesture, but we also know the stress these events sometimes cause. We understand the effort that has gone before, the trials and tribulations to reach this point, and mostly, we are excited about the new step... And we understand the significance of the event, as does the wider community and society as a whole. We are applauded for our achievements, our learning and our academic success, and here perhaps lies another angle for reflection.

Schoolification?

One perspective uncovered during my research on this, is how events like graduation ceremonies perhaps add to the 'schoolification' of children. By putting very young children in 'cap and gown' and presenting 'scrolls' do we imply that early childhood care and education is about academic success? Brogaard Clausen (2015, p.356) quotes works such as Jensen *et al.* (2010) as defining schoolification as

> a term used when the early years are understood as preschooling and not achieving legitimacy on their own terms.

Note the use of the term 'preschooling' not 'preschool' in the way we would use 'preschool'. This is about the idea that ECCE is simply a preparation for school, rather than valid in its own right. And it is causing a huge national and international debate. At a time when many, many professionals and experts are calling into question the push to make early years more formal, are events such as graduations simply adding to the idea that early years is only about academic learning and preparation for school?

> Despite a mountain of scientific evidence about the long-term social importance of early childhood education and care, the voice of the experts in early years education is rarely heard... This is particularly the case in countries with an early school starting age...their voices are increasingly drowned out by advocates of early 'schoolification'. (Palmer 2016, p.166)

And, interestingly, this debate is also happening across the world. In the USA, for example, in an interview with Erika Christakis, Turner (2016) paraphrased Christakis's book, *The Importance of Being Little* (2016):

> '...the distinction between early education and official school seems to be disappearing.' If kindergarten [age 5] is the new first grade [age 6], Christakis argues, preschool [under age 5, sometimes referred to as Pre-K] is quickly becoming the new kindergarten. And that is 'a real threat to our society's future.'

Additionally, Katz and Chard (2000, p.54, original emphasis) offer:

> It is reasonably clear to us that formal instruction in the early years may serve the normative ends at the expense of the dynamic long-term aims of education. Given what is being learned about the nature and acquisition of knowledge, we suggest the principle *that the younger the children, the more informal and integrated the curriculum should be.*

So, the question perhaps is do events such as graduations weaken further the importance of early childhood, especially at a time when funding for ECCE seems to be going against all the research? In *Early Childhood Development: Economic Development with a High Public Return*, Art Rolnick and Rob Grunewald (2003) of the Minneapolis Federal Reserve Bank found that:

> Early education investments yield a return that far exceeds the return on most public projects that are considered economic development...yielding more than $8 for every $1 invested. (Clothier and Poppe 2004)

In other words, the growing research clearly shows that *quality* early childhood experiences make a difference long term. In monetary value terms, it is widely accepted that for every $1/£1 invested in early years, there is an eight-fold return, for example on savings made on not needing later, more intensive (and therefore, usually, more expensive), health, social, education or other interventions. Therefore, my question is, are we actually making this worse for the wider understanding of the importance of play, PSED, outdoors, paint, glue, sticky fingers and all the other wonderful early childhood experiences we celebrate and enthusiastically champion? By using a highly regarded ceremony which is recognised as an adult way of celebrating academic achievements do we add to the confusion around the importance of early childhood? Unintentionally, are we as an ECCE sector saying, look, we are celebrating academic success – so it must be important? Or, are we saying – look our children are 'ready for school', and therefore inadvertently saying that their time in early childhood has come to an end, and is therefore not as important as school?

> 'School readiness' implies, for me, that children are essentially imperfect and need to be standardised to fit the system. It seems that the child is not at the centre of this thinking – probably nowhere in it at all. It is as if we are preparing children to fit into a system which isn't designed to nurture and support them as individuals to reach their chosen goals, but to make them passive receivers of facts, be good at sitting still, to know how to queue up quietly and, above all, pass assessments so the school meets its targets – the school, not the children! (Gladstone 2016)

Or, as the Organisation for Economic Co-operation and Development (OECD) document, *Starting Strong II – Early Childhood Education and Care*, pointed out:

> to some extent, this 'schoolifying' of the early childhood years is reinforced by the current focus on 'readiness for school' and learning standards. (OECD 2006, p.3)

I am not suggesting that the significant events in children's lives should not be acknowledged, it is *how* they are acknowledged that I think needs further thought. It is interesting to note, that for the writers of the many, many forums, blogs, articles and posts on graduation in ECCE, it is not the idea of celebrating leaving preschool/nursery that is uncomfortable, but the 'graduation' part. It is the idea of very young children taking part in events designed for much older children, young people and adults, that the writers struggle with. It is the young child's understanding of the event which many caring adults question.

Alternatively, many, many people tell heart-warming stories of children, parents and staff celebrating a young child's time at a setting, in meaningful, fun and fitting ways. Parents discuss being delighted with treasured 'natural' photographs of children covered in paint, and having fun, or children's artwork, framed as a keepsake, and children stress-free and playing with their friends. They discuss the 'leaving' itself, often accompanied by, and celebrated with, relaxed parties or picnics, where everyone can comfortably join in, or sit back, as they wish. I don't know about you, but this sounds like a party most children would want to be at.

> He's not yet five. Yesterday he was messing about..., building a 'dinosaur trap' from sticks and mud. Today he's scrubbed and shining...in his new school uniform but unnaturally subdued in this strange new environment... welcomed into the classroom along with twenty-odd other little boys and girls...wide-eyed, wondering, trusting, hopeful...and so, so young! (Palmer 2016, p.11)

Body Image, Body Consciousness, Self-Confidence and Self-Esteem?

I acknowledge that there are two sides to every debate, and the discussions here are no exception. However, I cannot find any grounded research or theory that says that these types of events are a good thing for young children. The positive comments around graduations, for example, tend to be around the topics of 'what harm does it do?' or 'they look very cute' or 'the children were so proud' or 'I love looking back at the photos'. However, put these into the context of nurturing PSED, as well as understanding neuroscience and behaviours, and do these comments still ring true? In terms of does it do any harm, well, maybe not 'actual harm', but children who have other influences going on in their lives may well find these situations very difficult.

The comments of 'looking cute' is a personal opinion, what one person finds cute another may not. The concern is that confidence and esteem issues are affecting children at a younger and younger age. So, the questions perhaps need to be, what messages does implying that 'being cute' is important, send to children? Are these the messages we would want for children? Do events such as these help, or indeed hinder, children's self-confidence and self-esteem?

There is much elsewhere about how to support areas such as children's body image and self-confidence, as well as the impact made by TV, media, magazines, books and so on. The general rule is around focusing on *who children are*, rather than *how they look*. The summer of 2016 saw a new report publish alarming findings. The whole platform of media and social media outlets was horrified, the 31 August 2016 saw collectively outraged headlines from around the world:

> Children as young as three have body image issues, while four-year-olds know how to lose weight. (*Telegraph*)

> The children as young as THREE with body issues: Nearly a third of nursery staff have heard youngsters describe themselves as fat or ugly. (*Daily Mail*)

> Well Here's the Most Depressing Possible Study About Body Image. (*New York Magazine*, The Cut)

These, and other headlines, and the debates on social media, arose from research conducted by PACEY (Professional Association for Childcare and Early Years). Dr Jacqueline Harding, an Advisor to PACEY highlighted:

> 'By the age of three or four some children have already pretty much begun to make up their minds (and even hold strong views) about how bodies should look,' she said. 'There is also research evidence to suggest that some 4-year-olds are aware of strategies as to how to lose weight.' (PACEY 2016b)

I am not *simply* saying that events such as a graduation ceremony will affect every child's self-confidence and body image. What I am saying is that some children are already worried about how they look, are already constantly told that 'being cute, pretty or handsome' is important, and are already under pressure to always look 'neat, tidy and perfect' and so on. Therefore, maybe we need to consider, do these types of events strengthen those messages? I am sure you have friends, family or colleagues who, as adults, struggle with esteem and confidence, and have negative body issues, and I am sure that many of them will be able to state how these issues go back to childhood.

Finally, the comments of the various writers regarding graduation ceremonies, of 'the children were so proud', is one that could also be questioned. *Development Matters*, Characteristics of Effective Learning (Early Education 2012, p.6) talks of:

Being proud of how they accomplished something – not just the end result.

Perhaps this is in direct conflict with a 'Graduation Ceremony'. Does an event of this type support children to be proud of 'how they accomplished something'? What are we actually celebrating? What has been accomplished? Are we celebrating the journey – or is it just about the end result (the ceremony)? Additionally, does this support children to develop self-confidence and self-esteem, or resilience or empathy, or kindness, or indeed any of the other abilities that sound, grounded, well-respected and widely researched early childhood practice advocates for young children? I'm not so sure it does.

As I have said elsewhere in this book, you do not have to agree with everything I say. In the end, you need to consider your own experience, consider the research and theory and make your own mind up regarding how you feel. Your thoughts on this topic, how you feel about this discussion and your own research will all influence your practice. All I ask is that we remember that very young children are in the middle of all of this, and how they feel about this may not be how we feel. In terms of the above discussions, there are also a range of other celebrations and events, that are often held with all well-meaning intentions. It may well be that as a result of your reflections here, you may decide to consider some of the other events in your calendar.

The reasons mentioned for liking graduation ceremonies also included the keepsake photograph. However, there is also another 'event' linked to capturing a moment in a child's journey: photograph day. Intended to be a reminder of a child's journey through their childhood years, but in reality, often a day filled with tears, anxiety, apprehension and panics about paint, food, clothes, hair, smiles and so on. 'Oh no,' I hear you say, 'now Debbie is going to say we shouldn't do a photograph day either'. No, I am not… As elsewhere in this book, I am simply going to ask you to consider a few questions, to help you reflect on your practice, and then make your own decisions.

REFLECTIVE PRACTICE

Photograph Day

- What are the stresses and pressures:
  - » for you?
    - – Why do you think that is?
  - » for parents?
    - – Why do you think that is?
  - » for children?
    - – Why do you think that is?
- Are there some parents who do not buy the photographs?
  - » Why do you think that is?
- Why do you hold photograph days? What are the reasons?
- Who enjoys photograph days?
- What are the benefits of the day:
  - » for you?
  - » for parents?
  - » for children?

In all honesty, capturing moments of any description, whether photos of graduation ceremonies or otherwise, can be a fraught business, but surely in any quality setting there would be a myriad of photographs which could be used more appropriately as keepsakes for parents and loved ones? Do these more natural 'snapshots' more realistically and honestly reflect the child's true personality? In addition, wouldn't these types of photographs truly show a child's confidence, esteem and character? Think about children you know and love, would you rather see natural shots, full of laughter and fun, that truly reflect the children, or 'staged' 'controlled' photographs, with forced un-natural smiles?

This, then, is my worry about Christmas, performances, graduations, cultural and festival celebrations and indeed all other 'events' of a similar nature...much of it is outside of children's control. We, as adults decide what happens, where and when, and who does what, and how. We, as adults, decide what is included and why… Yes, it is well-meaning, yes, it is well-intentioned and, yes, it is all done with the genuinely caring goal of creating an amazing time for children. In reality, it is often the exact opposite that happens, and then we question the behaviours that we see emerge… Imagine how that would feel as an adult if your world was suddenly turned upside down. Imagine if suddenly everything was different, the building, the routines, or even that you were asked to do something you did not really understand. I don't think we would allow it to happen to us for very long before we would clearly, unequivocally and loudly, make our feelings known.

I believe that many of these celebratory events end up being hugely stressful for everyone concerned. The staff are stressed organising the events, the parents are stressed getting their children or themselves to the events and the children themselves are often left confused, stressed and tearful in the middle. I wonder if the messages that events such as these send out to the wider world are appropriate. When we look at them this way, are these the messages we would really want parents, other adults, the wider community, and the big wide world, to think about early childhood? Additionally, are these the messages we want for very young children?

Please don't think I am a kill-joy; I love a party, a celebration or an event – but it should be fun and exciting. Not everyone running around stressed, anxious, worried or tearful. Your setting, your colleagues, your parents and your children may well have different experiences to the ones I am describing here – and if so – brilliant. However, my suggestion would be, talk to your parents and colleagues, have a look at some of the online forums and blogs and see what parents and staff are really saying about events such as these – you might find yourself more than a little surprised. And, importantly, talk to the children: what would they really like to see happen, what would they like to be involved in, what would they like to do – after all, very young children are usually pretty good at giving you an opinion!

(Note: there are several articles and blogs in the bibliography that may help with your own research and reflections.)

Food Glorious Food?

So, in terms of well-meaning, let's explore another area of early childhood, usually 'presented' with the best intentions – food and snack times. Food is a huge part of a children's lives. Some children will try anything and everything. Some children seem resolute in their determination to live their lives eating only two or three absolute favourite foods. Some children seem to barely ever have an appetite, and some children eat with great enthusiasm. Some children eat one thing one day, and then scream as if being poisoned when offered the very same a couple of days later. A bit like adults really (OK, maybe not the screaming, but I am sure you get my point). And we as adults try ever more well intentioned, ingenious ways to tempt these fickle eaters to eat their five-a-day, get enough vitamins and minerals, get the right balance of fruit, vegetables, proteins, dairy, fat, salt and sugar and so on. Is it any wonder that food sometimes seems one long battle?

> Around 31% of the mothers questioned admitted to feeling tense, anxious and stressed during meal times. This can negatively affect the child's eating behaviour. It is therefore important to recognise that meal times are not just about eating, but also about having good quality family time together. Modelling good eating in social groups, as well as praising toddlers when they eat well, will encourage them to enjoy their meals. (Venterand and Harris 2009, p.393)

I am sure this rings true, not just with mothers, but also with fathers, grandparents, aunties and uncles, and indeed early childhood practitioners. Whenever I speak to adults (practitioners or parents), food is always high on the list of areas causing the most amount of stress. Breakfast battles, lunchtime overloads, teatime troubles and screaming hysteria over snacks are common everyday occurrences for many small children, and indeed the adults around them. Let's look at this from a slightly different angle.

REFLECTIVE PRACTICE

Good Enough to Eat?

Sally and her friends are very excited, it is Sally's birthday and they are all going to their favourite restaurant for a meal to celebrate. An hour before meeting at the restaurant, text messages whizz between the friends as they compare outfits, excitement and travel arrangements. Alice, Sally's best friend, arrives to pick Sally up, and is munching on a bag of crisps. Sally gasps in horror, 'Alice, what are you doing, we are eating soon, you will spoil your appetite.' Alice sticks her tongue out at her friend, grabs Sally's hand and bundles them both out of the house.

The friends meet at the restaurant, and are greeted by a beaming waiter. He is new to the restaurant. 'Ah, good evening, Sally's party I suspect. Come in, come in. Please, follow me, this way. I am Alfred, and I will be your waiter for this evening.' The friends follow Alfred to their table, and start to sit down. 'Wait a moment,' says Alfred suddenly. 'Have you all been to the toilet, have you all washed your hands? I don't want anyone having to get up in the middle of the middle of the meal.' Everyone nods, slightly puzzled. 'Fantastic,' grins Alfred, 'now we can sit down. Sally, you sit here please. You are such a clever girl, and it is your special day. Alice,' he says turning to Sally's friend, 'you sit there please, we know you get silly if you sit with Darcy. OK, thank you everyone, sit down please and I will get you some menus.'

Once everyone has had time to look at the menus, Alfred returns, and begins taking orders. Jackson asks for his meal to be served without salad as he does not like it. Madison asks for her sauce on the side, as she likes to dip her food. Aaliyah asks for a smaller portion as she is not feeling particularly hungry. Mateo orders three small tapas bowls, as he likes his food separated rather than all on one plate. Darcy orders just a starter as she is much more excited about dessert. Finally, Farran orders a vegetarian meal.

Alfred collects up the menus and hurries off to the kitchen. Alice stands up and says to Sally that she is just nipping to the loo. Suddenly Alfred appears, asks her where she is going and tells her to hurry up before the food arrives. As she walks towards the toilet, Alfred shouts after her 'and don't forget to flush, and wash your hands'.

When the meals arrive, Alfred stands at the head of the table, and says 'OK, so here are your meals, but please eat quickly as we need to wash up and clear away.' Alfred then informs the other waiters who has ordered which meal:

- Jackson's plate arrives with salad and he is told 'try a little, you might like it'.

- Madison's food is covered in sauce and she is told 'that is how the kitchen make it'.

- Aaliyah's plate is a full-sized one, and she is told 'you don't have to eat it all, but try'.

- Mateo's food arrives all on one plate and he is told 'stop being silly, everyone else has one plate'.

- Darcy is told she must eat everything otherwise she cannot have a dessert.

OK, do I need to go on? Let's consider a few questions:

- How do you think Alice feels?

- How do you think Jackson feels?

- How do you think Madison feels?

- How do you think Aaliyah feels?

- How do you think Mateo feels?

- How do you think Darcy feels?

Just imagine if this happened in your favourite restaurant, or your elderly relatives were treated this way in a care home. There would be outrage – and rightly so! So why does this all seem acceptable for young children? I know this is perhaps over-exaggerated, but writing it, I do not know whether to find it hysterically funny or deeply saddening. If this happened to adults, at first it probably would be hysterically funny, but I am pretty sure that would soon change. I recognise that many of the approaches to food are well-meaning and well-intentioned and intended to support healthy eating and so on, but do the approaches we use nurture and support PSED, and actually encourage a range of 'appropriate' behaviours?

> We have a positive and welcoming eating environment, to encourage children to eat well, and develop good eating habits and social skills. I/We use the whole day, as well as meals and snacks, to teach children about healthy eating and encourage a positive attitude towards mealtimes. (Children's Food Trust 2012, p.58)

In early childhood, we recognise the importance of meal and snack times as a social and positive experience too. As adults, we know the importance of food in our social lives, and how a difficult experience can take away the enjoyment and fun aspect of meal times. If we reconsider the previous reflective practice exercise, there are then other questions that might also be useful:

- Would the feelings of the characters be different for an adult or a child?

  - Why do you think that?

- Would being treated in this way encourage children (or indeed adults) to try new foods, eat more healthily and so on?

  - And if not – why not?

  - What would help?

- What messages does this type of situation give to children?
  - Why do you think that?
- Does this type of situation help children to truly understand appropriate behaviours?
  - And if not – why not?
  - What could help?
- How could mealtimes be better facilitated to support children?
- Are mealtimes an enjoyable, sociable time for children?
  - And if not – why not?
- What else might you need to consider?

If we, as adults, felt rushed, controlled, not listened to and so on, we too would soon start to exhibit behaviours that clearly showed our feelings. In terms of neuroscience and behaviours, there is a whole body of evidence around the importance of food and healthy eating and how what we put into our bodies, influences our brains and behaviours. Tom Kerridge, the popular TV and Michelin-starred chef, has even produced a cookbook, *The Dopamine Diet: My Low-Carb, Stay-Happy Way to Lose Weight*. The recipes are based on neuroscience, and the book explains how Tom has lost an incredible 11 stone in three years, by eating foods intended to be healthy and, importantly, keep him happy. In other words, foods high in dopamine:

> When you experience a pleasurable sensation…dopamine is released in your brain…low dopamine levels can lead to decreased motivation and make us feel lethargic and apathetic and even depressed… Our bodies create it [dopamine] by breaking down an amino acid called tyrosine, which can be obtained from lots and lots of different – and fortunately, delicious – foods. (Kerridge 2017, p.14)

In many cultures, and around the world, much importance is placed on food, and particularly the relaxed, social aspect of food and sharing food. Different cultures have different food traditions, different ways of eating and even different tools to eat with and as we become a more multicultural, globalised world, we embrace these differences. As adults, when we get the chance, the majority of us appreciate meals that are relaxed, un-rushed and enjoyable. In general, as adults, we choose where we eat, where we sit, we choose the foods we like, and who we are prepared to share with (or not) as the case may be. We may have friends who always order the same thing, or friends who are adventurous with food (personally, I can think of one friend in particular who gets me to try all kinds of foods I would not normally try). We like our surroundings to be pleasant, the lighting and furniture are important too, we may have music, a choice of beverages and we chatter away, laughing, relaxing and simply enjoy the moment.

Isn't this what we should be aiming for, for children? Happy relaxed mealtimes, filled with foods that are nutritious, exciting and make us feel happy as well as full? In my experience, on training programmes and speaking to practitioners and parents, mealtimes are often seen as the most stressful points in the day. If, however, we take into account the discussions within this chapter, and other chapters, perhaps we can begin to see why? If in early childhood we want to nurture children's PSED and use our knowledge of neuroscience to develop practice, and support understanding of behaviours, then food-associated times maybe need to be given greater credence, thought and consideration? Maybe then, children would enjoy food and mealtimes, rather than seeing them as a battle, or an opportunity for reward?

Rewards and Incentives

I'd just like to explore one final area of well-meaning, well-intended practice: rewards and incentives. Star charts, stickers, smiley faces and other incentives are often used as a way of developing appropriate behaviours in young children, often accompanied by the ability to 'collect' up smaller incentives for an ultimate bigger prize – but do they help? Let's just imagine how this might feel for an adult.

REFLECTIVE PRACTICE

Have You Been Good?

Your manager informs the team that a new incentive programme is going to be introduced. Rewards will be available for a whole host of activities and actions, and can be collected throughout the year. The person who collects the most rewards is then eligible for a grand prize at the end of the year. You are also told that rewards will be removed for misdemeanours.

Rewards will be available for, amongst other things:

- helping a colleague

- being on time, at work every day, with no sick days

- only having a toilet break during 'official' break times

- completing all projects on time

- eating only healthy foods

- keeping your work space clean and tidy

- being polite, kind and thoughtful

- having no performance management issues

- not making mistakes

- undertaking additional learning or Continuous Professional Development programmes.

Now consider what could happen, or how you might feel if:

- you suddenly fall ill

- you have a disability or condition requiring medical intervention

- you develop a urinary tract infection

- you have young children, or elderly relatives to care for

- your bus is late, or your car breaks down

- a parent makes a complaint about you, which is later unfounded and a misunderstanding

- you have other influences in your life, such as those discussed in Chapter 2.

I am sure you can see where this is going. There are many reasons why perhaps, no matter how hard you tried, you would not be able to achieve the 'final prize'. Sometimes situations are out of our control, other factors can influence our ability to perhaps take on additional learning, or illness stops us from behaving as we normally would. Imagine you are one day away from the 'final prize', when your bus is late or your car breaks down – how do you think you would feel? How many people would feel that all the effort had been wasted? Or, for the idea of rewards for behaviour, does that imply that we cannot 'behave' without a reward? Or indeed, that we cannot achieve something without a reward? And that is one of the main arguments against rewards, stickers, smiley faces and other incentives.

Gneezy *et al.* (2011, p.192), offer some explanations of how children [the agent] might see incentives or rewards:

offering incentives for improved academic performance in schools may signal that achieving a specific goal is difficult, that the task is not attractive, or that the agent is not well-suited for it (and thus needs the additional incentive of a reward). Alternatively, offering incentives could signal that the principal does not trust the agent's intrinsic motivation. This signal will be 'bad news' for the agent and can lower the intrinsic motivation of the agent to undertake the task.

I would urge anyone interested in this topic to read around the subject of 'intrinsic motivation', in other words the motivation to do something which is inbuilt. It is well researched, and widely acknowledged that children (indeed adults, and perhaps other animals too) learn and develop best when they are intrinsically motivated. A child excited to count out their latest collection of leaves from the outdoors, compared to a child asked to sit and count shapes on a worksheet, would be a good example. The child with the leaf collection is, for example, far more likely to be intrinsically motivated to count, stay involved for longer periods, explore other avenues, take risks with their experiences and understanding and challenge themselves, as they are motivated by their own interest. The question here perhaps is, should the child be offered a reward for counting? Or...more importantly, should we simply be encouraging children to be excited about counting, and therefore *want* to count?

An interesting place to start reading could be 'The Effect of Rewards and Motivation on Student Achievement', a Master thesis by Baranek (1996), who discusses how the environment plays a role too. Baranek covers a range of research and theory including Ryan and Grolnick (1986), who found that children who feel in control of their environment are not only internally motivated to work, but also experience positive feelings of self-worth. Additionally, Baranek considers Amabile and Gitomer (1984) and Kohn (1993) and the importance of choices and decision making in supporting deeper involvement in the learning process. *Motivation: A Literature Review (Research Report)* by Lai (2011) covers a similarly wide range of theory, research and empirical (or observed) evidence:

> The use of rewards may either encourage or diminish motivation, depending on the type of rewards and the context in which they are given. Teachers should attempt to give students more autonomy or control over their own learning by allowing them to make choices and use collaborative or cooperative learning approaches. (Lai 2011, p.2)

If we refer back to the previous reflective practice exercise ('Have You Been Good?'), perhaps the question needs to be should the actions and activities on the bullet point list happen because we want them to happen, not because we might get a prize in a year's time? And, if we turn the bullet list points into child-related activities, wouldn't we want children to be kind, toilet-trained, help tidy up, engage with mealtimes and learn and develop and so on because they want to – not because they think they might get a prize? What messages do you think that only doing things for a prize gives to children, parents and the wider community, as well as society as a whole? Are those really the messages we want to portray?

> Teaching children that they can earn praise, points, stars, smiley faces, beads, sweets, or money and treats for 'good behaviour', or lose any or all of them, be put in to time-out, or lose a favourite possession or activity can appear preferable to being hit or shouted at. However, I'm not sure it's even helpful to try and hold one up against the other as they all cause a range of anxiety, loss of power, fear, stress and distress to children. (Evans 2017)

Many reward systems for children are built around the idea of collecting several smaller incentives to transfer into a larger reward. In the reflective practice exercise, I used the example of collecting rewards over a year. For children, the average length of time is over a week, or perhaps a month. Imagine the very young child, desperately trying to please, who then on the last afternoon has a minor misdemeanour and all chances of the bigger prize are obliterated. As adults, I am sure this would cause many adults to perhaps become angry at 'losing out'; is it then any wonder that we then see a change in the child's behaviours? A week is a long, long time for a young child, and I would suggest it might be useful to reconsider the earlier sections on brain development and also on behaviours in association with this section.

In terms of nurturing PSED, we know the importance of a hug, a smile and authentic, immediate, age-appropriate, genuine praise. Interestingly, science is finding this is true of other mammals too. Cook *et al.* (2016), found that when given the choice, most dogs opted for a pat and praise from their owner, instead of edible treats, as a reward:

> Most of the dogs alternated between food and owner, but the dogs with the strongest neural response to praise chose to go to their owners 80 to 90 percent of the time. It shows the importance of social reward and praise to dogs. It may be analogous to how we humans feel when someone praises us. (MRCVS online 2016)

As with much of the discussion in this book, there are always two sides to every debate. As always, my aim is purely to ask you for further reflection and to consider future practice. The final word goes to Gneezy *et al.* (2011), who, in their serious, academic, peer-reviewed journal article, offer the following interesting, if slightly cheeky, perspective on rewards and incentives. This quote just might help with thinking about rewards in a slightly different way:

> Depending on their nature, incentives can shift a situation from a social to a monetary frame. Consider a thought experiment: You meet an attractive person, and in due time you tell that person, 'I like you very much and would like to have sex with you.' Alternatively, consider the same situation, but now you say, 'I like you very much and would like to have sex with you, *and*, to sweeten the deal, I'm also willing to pay you $20!' Only a certain kind of economist would expect your partner to be happier in the second scenario. However, offering $20 worth of (unconditional) flowers might indeed make the desired partner happier. (Gneezy *et al.* 2011, p.201)

Great Expectations?

OK, so no, not the brilliant Charles Dickens novel about Pip, the wonderful Miss Havisham and the other characters Dickens so skilfully brings to life... But, the expectations we have regarding young children. In effect, much of this chapter is about the expectations we, as adults, have about young children – and whether or not they are appropriate. The word 'expectations' is defined as:

> A strong belief that something will happen or be the case...or...

> A belief that someone will or should achieve something. (www.oxford dictionaries.com)

The issue with expectations, generally, is that we potentially all have different ones. My expectations of a great night out, for example, could be very different from yours. We will have different expectations of what constitutes a tidy house, an enjoyable meal, or a positive relationship, and so on. This is due to influences such as our upbringing, other issues in our lives and previous experiences, both as adults and as children. In addition, what we have read, seen, experienced, heard about or considered, and so on, will all add to the mix. Articles, research, blogs, social media, family, friends, colleagues, opinions and counter-opinions all add to our belief and anticipation of what could, should or might happen. Therefore, when we look at what we expect from someone else, our expectations of the other person (either child or adult) will be influenced by our previous experiences, understanding and knowledge.

In other words, our expectations of a tidy house may change if we have pressures elsewhere, our expectations of a concert or movie may rise or fall depending on reviews we see and read, and our expectations of children can be warped by our views of the world. For instance, we, as adults interested in early childhood, will expect that children will start to walk around the 12 months of age mark... But...not all children will. Or, if we use two-year-olds as an example, we might expect two-year-olds to be slightly messy, emotionally charged and determined to do things in their own way. But...and this is a big but... What if the two-year-olds you have previous experience of struggle with trying new things without being told what to do? Or, what if the latest viral internet post shows a pristine, smiling and calm toddler, who never seems to display the highly accentuated emotions that two-year-olds are so famous for?

How does this then affect our view of our world, and the expectations we place on the children in our lives? Moreover, we also need to consider the type of expectations we place on young children, in other words, are our expectations:

- too high

- too low

- or just about right (appropriate)?

In early childhood, we talk about having 'high, but appropriate expectations', in other words, expectations that support growth and development, and support children to flourish. In reality this means expectations that are not so high that they cause children to feel failures, however unintentionally... Or...not so low, that they do not encourage a child to stretch themselves and try to master new things. It is a fine balancing act.

Consider the following scenarios.

If we consider two-year-olds again, did any of the two-year-olds you have previous experience of:

- have Special Educational Needs or Disabilities, or

- have chaotic home lives, or

- spend time in care, or

- have serious illnesses, or

- were born very prematurely, or

- reach some milestones early?

And...any others you could add.

Then consider:

- Do all of these two-year-olds have the same level of development?

Probably not, and for a whole host of reasons that you could easily identify... However... Do we still place the same expectations on *all* two-year-olds?...and I think, we probably do...unintentionally perhaps... but the expectations are there all the same. My concern then is that we start to have inappropriate expectations of all children. Some young children will be advanced, or 'gifted and talented'; others will need more support and perhaps even targeted intervention. The issue for us interested in early childhood, is to consider are our expectations appropriate, do they recognise the individual child, do they allow for outside influences (such as those we discussed in Chapter 2), do they allow for our own preconceptions, and so on? Let's consider this a little more.

REFLECTIVE PRACTICE

Appropriate Expectations

What can the following children do?

- a baby of six months old
    - » Why do you think that?
- a toddler of 18 months old
    - » Why do you think that?
- a three-year-old
    - » Why do you think that?
- a four-and-a-half-year-old
    - » Why do you think that?

Where do your expectations of children come from?

- What knowledge do you have of children at the above age?
    - » Where has that come from?
- What have you seen children do (observed)?
- What else has influenced your thinking?
    - » previous experiences
    - » media and social media
    - » research, theory and other information
- How can knowing this support future practice?

Knowing where our expectations come from can be hugely beneficial, as this allows us to consider if what we are expecting young children to be able to do, or achieve, is appropriate. If, for example, we consider some of the topics we have considered in this chapter, it might be a useful exercise to reconsider each area in line with the discussion here. As always, if we put this into an adult perspective, how would we feel if other people placed inappropriate expectations on us? Imagine being told to climb a mountain, swim 10,000 metres, talk for two hours at a conference, cook a meal for 200 guests or fix a broken laptop... How would the expectation that we can all do all of these things make you feel? How do you think this would affect your PSED, and how might this be presented in your behaviours?

Everything Else?

This chapter could be huge. I am sure, like me, that there are many things that happen in early childhood that you are not sure are particularly helpful or useful to very young children. Or perhaps you question why they even happen in the first place. There are a whole host of other discussions we could have had, other situations that might have been explored. But, ultimately, the chapter must stop somewhere. So, in line with all the discussions, here are a few additional thoughts that you might want to consider in terms of your own practice:

Is it appropriate, helpful and/or useful to:

- force children to hug or kiss people goodbye
- force children to say sorry
- smell or sniff babies' bottoms, or peer down their clothes to see if they need changing
- call a soiled nappy 'dirty'
- not help children to wipe food from their faces, or runny noses, for example
- approach babies and children from behind them, when they do not know you are there, so you can lift them up to be changed, or to wipe a child's nose, for example
- use time out and other similar 'behaviour' techniques
- tell children to stop crying/be a big boy/girl
- put all children in a darkened room, or be given a mat and 'encouraged' to sleep after lunch

- keep tired children awake
- force all children to participate in 'circle time' and other similar activities
- not comfort a child, because other things need doing
- leave babies and young children to cry themselves to sleep
- not support children to understand someone they love has died.

And for each of the bullet points, ask yourself the following questions:

- What messages does this send to children?
- Does this nurture PSED and encourage understanding of behaviours?
- And if not, why not?

Imagine if these, or similar so-called 'practices', happened to adults:

- You are told you must hug or kiss someone as they are leaving, as it would be rude not to.
- You are told to immediately say sorry to a friend/partner just after a row.
- Someone looks down the back of your trousers, or sniffs you, and tells you to go to the toilet.
- You are called 'dirty' for having normal, bodily functions.
- You have dribbled food on your face, or have a runny nose, and you are poorly, or disabled or elderly and no-one bothers to help you clean yourself up.
- Someone picks you up suddenly and without warning, or pushes a cloth into your face from behind you.
- You are told you must go sit on the 'special' chair in the corner for a length of time equal to your age in years and think about what you have done, as you did not do all the things on your to-do list before 5pm.
- You are told to stop crying when you are upset.
- You are told that you cannot meet your friend for a catch up and a coffee as it is time to have a sleep.
- You are told that you cannot go to sleep when you are tired.

- You and your colleagues are forced to sit in a circle and be honest about your feelings on the day's work.

- You are not comforted when you are upset, as other things need doing.

- You are told you must not wake up through the night, or during a nap time, even if you are thirsty, cold, hot, have a nightmare, need the toilet, or just need a cuddle.

- Someone you love has died, and that person is never mentioned again in your hearing.

I am sure there are others you could add to this chapter, and indeed to this list. Just consider how would you feel in similar situations. Writing these makes me feel sad and uncomfortable, so imagine how it feels for very young children? I often put situations into an 'adult perspective', on my training programmes, and when I am reflecting on something I have read, heard about or seen. I often think, 'how would I feel if that was me...?' If that was me being shouted at for asking a question, or being told to stop being silly, when actually I am too hot and I am fed up. Or being picked up from behind when I am not expecting it. Or being excluded, when actually what I need is reassurance. Or being told to go to sleep and stop causing a fuss because headlines demand that 'children should be able to sleep through the night by x number of weeks/months/years old...', or being 'patted' on my back to send me to sleep even though I am not tired.

I stop, and just imagine myself in that position... Usually, I feel very, very uncomfortable. The process leaves me feeling sad, unsure and questioning what is going on. And, I am a grownup, and I am not even in that situation, I am merely an observer. Situations that make us feel uncomfortable, unsure or sad are likely to have a negative impact on our wellbeing. My question would be, that no matter how well-meaning, if something feels uncomfortable, inappropriate or just plain odd as an adult, then is it appropriate for children? Furthermore, if it feels odd and uncomfortable, does it nurture what we know about brain development and PSED, does it support behaviours, are we truly listening to children and does it support wellbeing? And we'll explore this more in the next chapter.

Chapter 4

PROMOTING CHILDREN'S WELLBEING

Wellbeing feels like it has become a bit of a 'buzz' word in the last few years, but we need to take it seriously. In very simplistic terms, it is just 'being happy, or well, or feeling good' in all areas. It can also feel a little like it is simply the 'in thing' at the moment or the 'latest trend'. It seems that every blog, article and magazine is trying to tell us how we can achieve 'wellbeing'. As we will explore, there is actually a wealth of science and research relating to human wellbeing. In my book *Performance Management in Early Years Settings* (2017, p.184), I considered wellbeing from an adult perspective.

The World Health Organization (WHO) define health as 'a state of complete physical, mental, and social wellbeing and not merely the absence of disease or infirmity'. In 2014, the WHO expanded this to define mental health as:

> a state of well-being in which every individual realises his or her own potential, can cope with the normal stresses of life, can work productively and fruitfully, and is able to make a contribution to her or his community. (WHO 2016)

It is interesting to note, the expansion of the definition is regarding mental health, and how publicly there is beginning to be wider acknowledgement and understanding of mental health issues. Additionally, it is now, thankfully, becoming much more acceptable to openly discuss such concerns. This correlates with the openness regarding the early years agreed principles of the importance of personal, social and emotional development (PSED) in its widest meaning. I acknowledge that we might not feel comfortable using the term 'mental health' especially in regard to very young children, and we probably prefer the term PSED, but if we consider the WHO definition,

I don't think there is actually a huge difference. Additionally, I am sure you can see how all of this links into PSED, behaviours and, therefore, wellbeing in general. Although the language might perhaps need changing ever so slightly, this definition could so easily be applied to children, and dovetails with our own knowledge of what is important for early childhood. Similarly, I looked at information from the mental health charity MIND, who offer the following:

> Mental wellbeing describes your **mental state** – how you are feeling and how well you can cope with day-to-day life.
>
> Our mental wellbeing is **dynamic**. It can change from moment to moment, day to day, month to month or year to year. (Warin 2013, p.4)

Again, although technically an adult-focused definition, we can see the relevance to young children. In real terms, this is what the area of PSED concentrates on. Of course, other areas will influence, but it is PSED that has wellbeing at its core. If we reconsider *Development Matters* (Early Education 2012, p.5):

Personal, Social and Emotional Development:

Making relationships

Self-confidence and self-awareness

Managing feelings and behaviour

It is fairly easy to see how wellbeing starts in the very earliest of years and how the WHO and MIND definitions align so well with PSED and the values, ethos and beliefs, that we, in early childhood, hold in such high regard. If we reconsider Chapter 1 for a moment, it is also easy to see how our understanding of neuroscience has influenced our understanding of how young children grow, develop and flourish, and where wellbeing fits in too. The importance of a reptilian brain that feels safe, the mammalian brain enabled to develop feelings, emotions, self-confidence and so on, and the neocortex able to think, reason, learn and thrive. Consider all of this together and it is easy to see how wellbeing and early childhood are inextricably linked…and, it would seem, not just for the children:

> The well-being of teachers and learners in themselves depends upon mutual affection, playful experimentation and the joy of consent in the making of meaning. Ancient knowledge and new ways of art and industry are passed on, as 'common sense' (Donaldson, 1992) created with love of company and with care for fear of opposition and exclusion. (Trevarthen and Panksepp 2016, p.31)

In other words, agreeing to play and test out theories and ideas, for example, with someone you like, and who likes you, helps children make sense of their world. Additionally, this supports a way of developing knowledge and new ideas, without worrying about disapproval and exclusion. Moreover, if we consider the other influences in children's lives discussed earlier, as well as the effects of hormones such as cortisol and dopamine and so on, we can see how this all starts to come together to influence wellbeing.

Oxytocin

It is worth mentioning the hormone oxytocin here. Often labelled the 'love hormone' (see Magon and Kalra 2011) it is actually so much more. It is easy to see how oxytocin has become associated with love, in that it is released in mothers as they give birth, encourages maternal behaviours and indeed synthetic oxytocin is given to induce or hasten labour. In fact, oxytocin was named in 1906, by Sir Henry Dale from the Greek words meaning 'swift birth'. Additionally, both men and women release oxytocin during sex…and oxytocin plays an important role in areas such as affection, touch, relationships, bonding, attachments, trust and connections. Furthermore, laughter, walking in the fresh air with friends, helping someone, or doing other things you enjoy, all encourage releases of oxytocin. Cuddles, with other humans or indeed pets, work too.

Significantly, oxytocin counteracts cortisol… In particular, this information is hugely important for those of us interested in early childhood. If, as we discussed earlier, we can identify when children are stressed, anxious, upset and so on, and therefore producing higher levels of cortisol…then knowing how to raise oxytocin levels can be incredibly useful.

Interestingly, very low levels of oxytocin have been linked with depression and autistic spectrum disorders (ASD). Some very early findings are showing exciting and ground-breaking signs of the possible use of oxytocin in alleviating cravings associated with addiction withdrawal, and also potentially helping people with ASD with emotional understanding. As with much of the latest brain-related research, this is very new, and there is still much to be learnt, and agreed:

> But…say researchers, oxytocin could use a rebranding. 'It doesn't induce love; it doesn't induce massive amounts of trust,' Guastella says. 'The problem we've got ourselves into is that we're trying to look for a simple answer: either oxytocin does or does not work in a patient population, or it does or does not enhance a certain social process.' But the science of life is rarely as simple as that. 'Oxytocin is known to affect circuits in different ways, and it's not going

to affect everyone in the same way,' Guastella says. 'The sorts of biology we're studying here are incredibly complex.' (Shen 2015)

Does It Hurt?

It is easy to see how hormones, play, friendships, and so on, all become interlinked with wellbeing. And, I believe, how easy it is to see how all of this starts from a very, very young age. Tiny babies watch adult faces intently for reactions: positive reactions create boosts of oxytocin in both adult and baby brains... It does not take a huge leap to see the opposite, and what could happen... I am sure we can all think of times when we have not had the positive response we had hoped for, and the feelings that we experienced. It is not very pleasant. So, imagine how that must feel for very young children? Knowing that there is a scientific and biological reason for those feelings can be helpful... And...understanding how to help with feelings that are difficult is invaluable.

Whilst researching Chapter 1, I came across a study by Goksan *et al.* (2015), entitled 'fMRI reveals neural activity overlap between adult and infant pain'. The study used new technology (functional Magnetic Resonance Imaging, fMRI) to look at how infants feel pain:

> Doctors long believed that infants do not feel pain the way that older children and adults do. Instead, they believed that the infants' responses to discomfort were reflexes. Based on these beliefs, it was a routine practice to perform surgery on infants without suitable pain relief up until the late 1980s. Even now, infants may receive less than ideal pain relief. For example, a review found that although new-borns in intensive care units undergo 11 painful procedures per day on average, more than half of the babies received no pain medications. (Goksan *et al.* 2015, p.2)

They go on to say, how even in these supposedly 'enlightened times', this practice is often still the case:

> For example, it is remarkable that current UK NHS guidelines for ankyloglossia (tongue tie) surgery state that 'in small babies, being cuddled and fed are more important than painkillers'. (NHS Choices 2015)

I found this research fascinating...scary...but fascinating. I looked into the NHS Guidelines, and it does indeed say 'being cuddled and fed are more important than painkillers'. Or, at least it did. By the end of February 2017, I was checking all the references for the final manuscript, and in the intervening few weeks from writing the above piece, the 'being cuddled and fed are more important than painkillers' has been removed from the

NHS Choices website; however, there is still the recommendation that no painkillers are needed. The focus of the guidelines, was, and still seems to be, primarily aimed at solving the problems faced by the mother if breast-feeding. It also says things such as 'quick and almost painless' and 'sharp, sterile scissors are used to snip the tongue-tie'. I am not, nor do I claim to be a medical expert, but to my early childhood, PSED, wellbeing-focused mind, any 'operation' without medication of some description, even with the all-important cuddle, seems a little barbaric. I have to say that I suspect if someone cut the skin on the inside of my mouth with a pair of sharp scissors I think I'd know about it (and I think I'd want a cuddle…).

> Infants experience pain in similar ways to adults, though they may not experience all the emotions that adults have when they are in pain. It is, therefore, important to give infants suitable pain relief during potentially painful procedures. (Goksan *et al.* 2015, p.2)

However, although interesting, this is a slight digression to explain the research; it was other findings of the study by Goksan *et al.* about how the brain works that I found particularly relevant to early childhood. The team set out to consider if, and how, new-born infants experience pain, and their results were very interesting in relation to our work in the early childhood world. Using fMRI technology, the team looked at changes in blood oxygen level dependent (BOLD) activities in the brain, and these were recorded. Goksan *et al.* found that the areas of the brain that lit up in relation to pain stimuli were similar in adults and infants, but there were two major differences, the areas in the brain called the amygdala and the orbitofrontal cortex. In very simplistic terms, the amygdala is part of the emotion network and the orbitofrontal cortex is associated with decision making.

> It is likely that the infants are too immature and inexperienced to evaluate and contextualise the…stimulus into a coordinated decision and response… Similarly, in adults the amygdala is thought to attach emotional significance…and to play a role in fear and anxiety (Simons *et al.*, 2014), which may reflect affective qualities that the new-born infant does not yet ascribe to the stimulus. (Goksan *et al.* 2015, p.4)

In other words, new-born babies do not have the emotional understanding to evaluate the pain, or make a decision as to their emotional reaction to the pain. Or, to put it another way, children have to *learn* about pain and emotions, and the *associated decisions* – and it is us, as adults, that help them to do that. I know we probably all knew that anyway, or at least suspected it, but here I had found a scientific study that was not looking at

PSED, but by accident almost, had provided the evidence for what many in early childhood had long suspected: it is how *we*, as adults, react that causes children to learn and develop their emotional understanding of fear, anxiety and so on, and the associated decision-making skills. So, what implications does this have for those of us interested in early childhood?

Consider how we, as adults, see very young children take risks, test their abilities, try new things, test their bodies, overcome challenges, fall down, get back up, persevere and try, and try again…and never give up. We attend to numerous cut knees, bruised heads, bloody elbows, scrapes, grazes and bumps… And still, children get back up and try again…

But then suddenly they stop…

They become uncertain, fearful, anxious, worried and so on…

They stop trying again and again…

They stop trying new things, and start to use words like 'dangerous', 'scared' or 'too hard'.

…Because someone, somewhere has 'helped' the child to learn an emotional reaction to the pain (or even potential pain, that might not actually occur) and make a decision about it, and make a decision about the activity that caused the pain (no matter how minor or short-lived the pain is, or may be)… Or even, perhaps, to avoid any potential pain, just in case it might happen… Because someone, somewhere has stopped the child from testing their body and abilities… Because someone, somewhere has 'helped' the child decide that they are not capable of overcoming challenges and therefore it is not worth trying… Or perhaps, because someone, somewhere, had a ridiculously over-the-top reaction to something the child did, or did not do…

In other words, someone, somewhere has 'helped' the child to stop using their natural abilities to understand risk and challenge… I am *not* saying that children should be exposed to extreme danger, severe pain or emotional trauma and so on, but I am sure that you can think of children, and perhaps even some adults, who seem to have extreme reactions to the slightest pain, or emotional reactions that seem a tad over the top in relation to the pain? Perhaps the adults, when they were children, did not have the opportunities to develop their own understanding of pain, emotional response and reaction? And the children? Well, it would not be too big a leap to consider that children's reactions have been developed due to adults' responses, interventions or directions…

In terms of wellbeing, what we do know is that doing things such as whizzing down a slide, overcoming challenges and celebrating being brave enough to do things such as walk across a wobbly bridge, all help us to feel good. And, that all of these things require us to have an understanding of risk, be able to take on challenges, test our abilities, problem solve and so on. We also know that the links to risk and challenge and resilience and self-regulation are vitally important, and we will come back to these a little later. We also know that wellbeing is linked to mental health (in adults as well as children), and we know that all of these 'areas' are intertwined! Perhaps, then, what we need to consider is the role of the adult in this, and if we what do actually does help or, however unintentionally, actually hinders, obstructs or deters.

Risk and Challenge and Wellbeing

In my book, *Performance Management in Early Years Settings* (2017, p.155), I looked at risk and challenge from an adult perspective. The following is a variation.

In ECCE, Health and Safety is often blamed for not allowing children to do certain things. However, much of Health and Safety is misrepresented, and indeed the Healthy and Safety Executive (HSE) often speaks out in relation to 'myths', such as children being allowed to take risks. For example, Judith Hackitt, the Chair of the HSE, in an interview entitled 'The Myths of 'Elf n Safety', said:

> A challenge of the next decade will be a generation of 'cotton-wool kids' who have not been exposed to risk in childhood and will grow up to be risk-naive adults – and therefore vulnerable... I worry how they will behave once they are in the workplace. It will increasingly become an issue in the next few years. They need to be able to live ordinary lives. They should be able to play, fall over and hurt themselves. (*The Independent* 2015)

Neither I or, Ms Hackitt, or the HSE, or indeed anyone who advocates risk and challenge in early childhood are saying that children should not be safe. However, research from a range of disciplines is recognising, more and more, the importance of being able to manage risk and challenge as an essential part of growing up the links to other areas of development, and how this links to feeling secure, and to our wellbeing in general. Further evidence is being presented which shows how falling over, getting hurt, being able to get back up, and overcoming challenges and so on, all help to develop abilities such as resilience and self-regulation – which as well as being vital to PSED and understanding behaviours, are also essential elements of wellbeing. In early childhood, we know that much of this happens through play. Play England (2017), on their website, offer the following benefits, which will come as no surprise to many in early childhood:

Research shows that play has many benefits for children, families and the wider community, as well as improving health and quality of life. Recent research suggests that children's access to good play provision can:

- increase their self-awareness, self-esteem, and self-respect

- improve and maintain their physical and mental health

- give them the opportunity to mix with other children

- allow them to increase their confidence through developing new skills

- promote their imagination, independence and creativity

- offer opportunities for children of all abilities and backgrounds to play together

- provide opportunities for developing social skills and learning

- build resilience through risk taking and challenge, problem solving, and dealing with new and novel situations

- provide opportunities to learn about their environment and the wider community.

(www.playengland.org)

Additionally, it is easy to see how each of the bullet points links to PSED, brain development and behaviours (and increase oxytocin and/or dopamine levels). If we go back to Chapter 2 and the discussions around mammals, then maybe that is useful here too? Humans are mammals, and therefore perhaps we need to consider how children develop, as mammals, too? There are many examples of baby animals 'playing' in order to learn about the world they live in. I am sure we can all recall lion cubs, baby elephants and lambs, for example, innocently appearing to be simply playing and gambolling about, when in fact they are learning the life skills they need to survive. Similarly, if we go back to the baby Spider Monkey, her daddy did not scream at her to 'get down', or tell her to 'stop climbing' or warn her that she 'is going to fall' or 'hurt herself'. No, Daddy Spider Monkey stepped in and supported his little one to find her own way – yes, she needed his help, but she also needed to find out for herself. I am guessing the baby Spider Monkey probably did not go too far up the tree for a little while, but I am pretty sure neither she or her daddy decided she should never do it again either! In other words, she needed to manage her own risks, overcome her own challenges and learn from her own mistakes, and therefore build up her own confidence, resilience and self-regulation. Perhaps even by doing so, our baby Spider Monkey also gave her wellbeing a boost too!

> Children are active participants in their own development. Reflecting the intrinsic human drive to explore and master one's environment. (Shonkoff and Phillips 2000, p.27)

OK, so I am *not* saying we should have small children having near-death experiences from the tops of very tall trees, but they do need to master the environment they are to live in. Otherwise, we are in danger of, as Judith Hackitt describes, having a 'generation of "cotton-wool kids" who have not been exposed to risk in childhood and will grow up to be risk-naive adults – and therefore vulnerable'. This is a very strong statement from the Chair of the HSE, in other words children who have not experienced risk are vulnerable. So how does not experiencing risk cause vulnerability, and what has that got to do with wellbeing and nurturing PSED and behaviours?

REFLECTIVE PRACTICE

Risk, Challenge and Vulnerability

Consider your day so far (sorry if you are reading this at bedtime). What risks and challenges have you overcome or avoided?

Initially, this feels a simple question – unless you have had a near-miss with a bus, it can feel like a pretty uneventful day – but now consider these questions:

- Did you use electricity, water, gas or other potentially hazardous materials?

- Did you use a range of substances, potions and lotions correctly and safely?

- Did you cross the road, safely, perhaps many times?

- Did you manoeuvre your body through an indoor environment without any major trips, falls or accidents?

- Did you manoeuvre your body through an outdoor environment without any major trips, falls or accidents?

- Did you negotiate a bridge, a staircase or other high obstacle?

- Did you eat and drink without choking or poisoning yourself?

- Did you use anything extremely hot or extremely cold without inflicting damage on yourself or others?

- Did you use implements, equipment and resources appropriately?

- Did you walk, climb, run, swim or engage in other physical activity requiring you to move your body?

- Did you pick something up, hold something or use something that required you to move your arms?

Do I need to go on? Without wanting to sound like some wild-haired banshee in a cartoon GIF, 'life *is* a challenge'. From the moment we are born, and probably even from before that, everything we do has the potential to be a risk or a challenge. However, this section also mentions 'vulnerability', so let's consider those questions again.

Imagine you have not had the experience of how to:

- use electricity, water, gas or other potentially hazardous materials

- use a range of substances, potions and lotions correctly and safely

- cross the road, safely

- manoeuvre your body through an indoor environment without any major trips, falls or accidents

- manoeuvre your body through an outdoor environment without any major trips, falls or accidents

- negotiate a bridge, a staircase or other high obstacle

- eat and drink without choking, or poisoning yourself

- use anything extremely hot, or extremely cold without inflicting damage on yourself or others?

- use implements, equipment and resources appropriately

- walk, climb, run, swim or engage in other physical activity requiring you to move your body

- pick something up, hold something or use something that requires you to move your arms.

I think it is pretty clear where the vulnerability comes in. Imagine not being able to do these things, simply eating or walking in the street could be a life-threatening activity. Yet, children have to learn how to do these things. Are we going to stop children eating solid foods or only let them live indoors? Of course not, that would be ridiculous, so maybe we need to consider some of the other things we, as adults, stop children from doing too? I am sure you can see how all of this then starts to link together, and influence children's PSED, wellbeing and behaviours.

Imagine seeing others do some of the things on the bullet point list. Now consider the following:

- Imagine that you can do lots of the things on the bullet point list, or at least, you want to try to do them...and some well-meaning person stops you.

- How would you feel *personally, socially* and *emotionally*?

- How do you think your *wellbeing* would be affected?

- How might this be presented through your *behaviours*?

I'm sure you can see the importance of supporting children to understand risk and challenge, and therefore avoid some of the vulnerabilities that Judith Hackitt is, rightly, so concerned about. Perhaps, one of the easiest ways we advocate risk and challenge in early childhood is through outdoor play. Across the world, and certainly within the UK playwork sector, the principles of playing and learning within the natural elements of earth, air, fire and water (in other words outdoor play) are highly regarded. Additionally, risk, and understanding how to manage risk, are central to playwork practice. I'm also sure you will be able to think of many examples of children playing, developing understanding of risk and overcoming challenges through being outdoors and see how this links to supporting their wellbeing. If you refer back to the MIND definition at the beginning of this chapter, I am sure you can see the correlation: climbing, running, jumping, digging in soil (or sand), playing in long grass, looking at flowers, being in the wind, the sun, the rain and the snow and playing in, and with water, for example, all support wellbeing. (Incidentally, as a slight detour, it might also be interesting, for your own reflections to explore the work, in Germany, of Kain Karawahn, and Günter and Gryta Julga who support young children in developing an understanding of fire. Imagine not knowing how to light your cooker, a barbecue or a candle safely, for example, and you can perhaps begin to see where this area of practice comes from?)

Perhaps, then, it is worth considering how being outdoors is one of the easiest ways for children to understand risk and challenge, and develop wellbeing? I am *not* saying supporting wellbeing can only happen outside, or that young children should be left to roam freely. Nor am I saying that risk and challenge can only happen in the outdoor environment. We all know that toddlers, for example, need to learn about chewing food and hot radiators, or older children may need help to understand how sharp knives and tools should be handled appropriately. What I am saying is that we need to support children to negotiate the world we live in, not take everything out of this world. Let's consider some normal, everyday occurrences in a child's life.

REFLECTIVE PRACTICE

Safe or Sorry?

Consider the following 'normal' events in any ECCE setting:

- A child staples their own finger.
- A child falls off the climbing frame.
- A child throws snowballs in the outdoor area.
- A child cuts another child's hair with the scissors.
- A child falls playing in the puddles in the rain.
- A parent brings in balloons for a child's birthday.

Now consider the following questions for each bullet point:

- How do the children react?
  - » Why do you think that is?
- How do the adults react?
  - » Why do you think that is?
- How is children's PSED nurtured?
  - » Why do you think that is?
- What behaviours are adults likely to exhibit?
  - » Why do you think that is?
- What behaviours are children likely to exhibit?
  - » Why do you think that is?

In effect, what often happens with these and similar 'incidents' is that the 'offending' item is removed from the children, or the children are removed from the 'offending' item. Health and Safety is often the reason given. On its website, the HSE has a health and safety 'Myth Buster' panel, which is a great read over a coffee (especially for those of us who have small children in our lives). The Myth Buster panel looks into requests from members of the public, and either offers the reasons why something is true, or 'busts the myth'. You can check out the above points if you do not believe me, but contrary to popular belief, none of the 'offending items' on the list have been 'banned' by 'health and safety', and yet, at some point Health and Safety has been blamed for the banning of all of the points on the list.

What happens in reality is that 'adults' hide behind, or are confused by, health and safety, rather than, perhaps, supporting children to understand more appropriate ways to use 'offending items', such as scissors. All too often removing the 'offending item', or removing the children, seems an easier option. But…what about being able to negotiate the world and what about the wellbeing bit? What about experiencing the exhilaration of being able to splash in puddles, or the satisfaction of scissors that help you make a model and cut through paper, string and card, or testing yourself to see how far you can throw a snowball? All of these things, and more, help children to understand their world, their own bodies, minds, emotions, abilities and so on, and help children to stretch themselves and develop in ways that only real-life experiences can. (After all, you cannot truly understand snow unless you feel it!) In other words, all of these have a direct influence on children's PSED, wellbeing and behaviours.

The alternative is taking all of these things away (or taking the children away). I am sure you have all experienced the annoyance, quickly followed by sheer exasperation and frustration, when using stupid, senseless, plastic scissors that do not cut anything. If we put this into a child's perspective, what does this tell them? In all probability, the messages children then receive is that all scissors are blunt and do not cut anything – which of course is simply not true! Here then perhaps lies the longer-term danger: what happens later, when the child does pick up scissors that are sharp, and simply does not know how to handle them appropriately, and then playfully 'pretends' to cut a friend's hand? Or, how does the child feel when continuously frustrated with equipment that will not cut…and then, what behaviours are we likely to see?

In terms of wellbeing, the link between taking risks and overcoming challenges is well researched. In 2012, a High-Level Statement was issued from the Play Safety Forum and Health and Safety Executive which stated:

Play is great for children's wellbeing and development. When planning and providing play opportunities, the goal is not to eliminate risk, but to weigh up the risks and benefits. No child will learn about risk if they are wrapped in cotton wool. (Ball, Gill and Spiegel 2012, p.107)

Additionally, Ofsted are also clear on their viewpoint:

The provider ensures that staff have a good understanding of how to manage, and minimise, risks for children without limiting opportunities for their development. (Ofsted 2015b, p.35)

There are also additional, specific concerns that you may need to consider: children with disabilities or additional need, the responsibility of adults to support children to stretch themselves, and fears that children who do not have opportunity for risk and challenge may seek it elsewhere:

All children both need and want to take risks in order to explore limits, venture into new experiences and develop their capacities, from a very young age and from their earliest play experiences. Children would never learn to walk, climb stairs or ride a bicycle unless they were strongly motivated to respond to challenges involving a risk of injury. Disabled children have an equal if not greater need for opportunities to take risks, since they may be denied the freedom of choice enjoyed by their non-disabled peers.

It is the job of all those responsible for children at play to assess and manage the level of risk, so that children are given the chance to stretch themselves, test and develop their abilities without exposing them to unacceptable risks.

This is part of a wider adult social responsibility to children. If we do not provide controlled opportunities for children to encounter and manage risk then they may be denied the chance to learn these skills. They may also be more likely to choose to play in uncontrolled environments where the risks are greater. (Ball, Gill and Spiegel 2012, p.111)

Added to this innate, built-in need to take risks and challenge ourselves, are the influences of various vitamins, minerals, hormones and so on. There is much research, for example, regarding the role of dopamine. As we discussed in Chapter 3, dopamine is released as a result of a pleasurable experience, but it also seems to have a more sinister side:

Dopamine supports us to take action toward goals, desires and needs. Procrastination, self-doubt and lack of enthusiasm are linked with low levels of dopamine (*as are some addictions*). Celebrating small goals and successes as well as big ones, helps to release dopamine, as does gentle exercise. (Adapted from Nguyen 2014)

Similarly, research by Schultz (2007, p.262) found that:

> Impulsivity, gambling, attention deficit hyperactivity disorder (ADHD), and restless leg syndrome are based on altered dopamine function or dopamine receptor polymorphism [occurring in different forms] (Perez-de-Castro *et al.* 1997, Stiasny *et al.* 2000, Sagvolden *et al.* 2005).

It is widely accepted that physical activity raises dopamine levels, as do the feelings of accomplishment associated with the 'I did it' moment when we achieve something we set out to do. I think it is fairly easy to see the link here between supporting children with risk and challenge in order to alleviate the potential difficulties associated with low dopamine levels. Of course, there is still much to learn, and as always, there will be two sides to every debate, and there continues to be new information being discovered about the role of hormones. Indeed, three UK-based scientists won the €1m 2017 award 'The Brain Prize' (the biggest prize in the field of neuroscience), for their three decades of work looking at the effects of dopamine. One area of knowledge that does seem to be gaining momentum is the role of dopamine in both Parkinson's and Alzheimer's diseases, and we'll come back to this in Chapter 6.

In terms of early childhood, perhaps what we need to consider is how we ensure young children are able to achieve challenges, learn through trial and error, and experience more of those dopamine-releasing, 'I did it' moments. If we consider very young babies, they do not give up. I have never heard of a young baby who decides that learning to crawl or walk is too much like hard work, and just stops trying. Some babies achieve these milestones very early, and walking at nine months is now not uncommon; others take longer, and maybe do not become upright until around 18 months of age. This is considered well within 'normal parameters', there is no need for alarm, and unless there appear to be other concerns around developmental or physical delay, would not be investigated further. The children would continue to try, until they overcome the challenge, and experience the 'I did it' moment.

In evolutionary terms, human babies would have probably been carried for much of their earliest years of life, only being placed on to the ground when it was absolutely safe to do so. If we look at animal programmes such as *Planet Earth* (BBC 2012), *Planet Earth II* (BBC 2016a) and *Spy in the Wild* (BBC 2016b), as well as other wildlife documentaries, we see that most animals are at their most vulnerable from the moment of birth until they are able to walk, or at least move independently, which of course, for some animals is incredibly soon:

Active at birth, or precocial, describes species that are physically mobile and able from the moment of birth or hatching. Wildebeest calves, and many other grazing animals, need to be up and running from the word go, to avoid becoming dinner for nearby predators. Newborn dolphins have to be able to swim immediately. Precocial birds, like ducks and chickens, can often feed themselves as soon as mum shows them what is edible. Offspring that are helpless at birth – humans and mice, for example – are the opposite, altricial. (www.bbc.co.uk/nature/adaptations/Precocial)

In terms of risk, challenge and vulnerability, new-borns who do not overcome these early challenges, who do not begin to develop an awareness and understanding of risk, are likely to continue to be vulnerable. (Think back to Chapter 1, and the deer who does not get up and learn to walk quickly, and indeed run, when spotted by the lion.) For humans, whilst we may not have to worry about lions, we do have other risks and challenges to overcome in daily life, and to not build up an understanding and awareness could leave us very vulnerable indeed. It then begins to make sense that children who do not overcome other challenges, and develop understanding of managing risk, become more susceptible to later vulnerabilities. It is also worth bearing in mind that this is also the case for developing awareness around emotional risk and challenge too. Learning how to trust, negotiate, deal with conflicts and disagreements, and being able to overcome disappointments are some examples. Thankfully, most of us have other people in our lives who help with the daily trials and tribulations that life throws our way. And, as we discussed earlier regarding oxytocin, science is now showing that having love, relationships and connections in our lives helps immensely.

Love, Relationships and Connections

In terms of nurturing PSED and understanding brain development and behaviours, the foundations are laid within love, relationships and connections. To my mind, and I know many, many others, one of the greatest advocates for developing understanding of human connection is Dr Suzanne Zeedyk. Suzanne explains the science of connection in ways that cause reflection, deeper understanding and the desire to change lives. I was delighted when Suzanne agreed to write the foreword for this book. Suzanne's foreword, on the importance of relationships in terms of neuroscience, puts the central messages of connection into context brilliantly.

Another valuable resource for practitioners around the area of love, relationships and connections, is the work of Dr Jools Page, on the role of 'professional love' in the ECCE sector. The Professional Love in Early Years Settings website (Page 2015b) offers the following:

The *Professional Love in Early Years Settings (PLEYS)* research project was set up to examine how those who work in early years settings can safely express the *affectionate and caring behaviours* which their role demands of them. The outcome was a set of Professional Development Materials which comprise the *Attachment Toolkit.* (http://pleysproject.wordpress.com/contact-us)

The website, and toolkit, is a wealth of evidence, information, case studies and opportunities for reflection on practice, and I would strongly encourage you to discover more. I do not want to simply repeat Dr Page's work here, but the following quote might be useful:

> 'Professional Love' provides practitioners with the language to appropriately describe the close, loving, intimate and affectionate bond which, over time, is inevitably developed with the children in their care in the context of reciprocity (meaning with mutual agreement) and shared understanding. (Page 2015b, p.15)

All of this grounded research and evidence-based understanding further adds to our knowledge of the importance of nurturing PSED in very young children. Brain development, emotional development, resilience, self-regulation, and so on, all depend on a secure and sound base of love, relationships and connections. Let's consider this from a slightly different viewpoint.

REFLECTIVE PRACTICE

All in a Day (1)?

One day, you get up for work and the following happens:

- At home, no-one talks to you as they are too busy.
- The journey to work is stressful, everyone is rushing, no-one smiles and everyone is harassed.
- You are the first to arrive, so nothing is ready.
- You are just getting organised and feeling settled, when you are pulled away for a break.
- After break, you have a disagreement with a colleague, but there is not time to sort it out as it is nearly lunchtime.
- At lunchtime, the staff room is chaotic and busy, it is too hot in the room and you realise you do not actually fancy the lunch you have brought today.

- After lunch, everyone is busy, but you could really do with some fresh air.

- You get on with what you should be doing, and then are asked to work elsewhere, but you do not know anyone in that section.

- Everyone else has left for the day, most of the building is in darkness and locked up, you are desperately trying to finish off some last-minute jobs before your lift home arrives, but the caretaker is jangling keys, and pointing at the clock in irritation.

Now consider the following questions, for each of the bullet points:

- What do you think would be happening to your reptilian brain?

- What do you think would be happening to your mammalian brain?

- Do you think your neocortex will have problems engaging or concentrating, for example?

  » Why do you think that?

- How do you think you would be feeling personally, socially and emotionally?

- Would you feel loved, safe and secure?

- What about relationships and connections?

- What if you haven't the resilience and self-regulation to handle the situation appropriately?

- What if you have additional influences in your life, such as those discussed in Chapter 2?

Again, I am sure you can see the analogies here, and how each bullet point is potentially representative of a section of a child's day. If we consider the beginning and ends of the day, for example, there is growing understanding that these times of the day need to be taken more seriously in ECCE. Ofsted (2005, p.4) in their document 'Early Doors: Experiences for Children in Day Care During the First Hour of the Day', found that:

> Good nurseries plan to have sufficient staff at the start of the day to cope with partings from parents. They plan activities to engage interest from first opening, setting these out at the end of the previous day so that the nursery is bright and cheerful, and there is plenty for children to do when they arrive.

However, they go on to paint a rather bleak picture of some children's experiences:

> Although most nurseries offer a balanced day for children, activities at the start of the day are not good enough in over half of the nurseries visited. Children were present for over an hour and in some cases up to two hours before the 'normal' nursery day started. (Ofsted 2005, p.6)

In terms of the bullet point list 'All in a Day (1)?', we covered meal and snack times elsewhere in some depth, but what about some of the other points? Let's just consider one more. What about transitions, for example?

> …define transitions as any kind of change that may alter the routines… This does not just mean moving from room to room or between settings. The change can be something as simple as the introduction of a new member of staff, a staff member leaving, an unexpected visitor to the group, or someone different bringing the child to, or collecting them from, the setting. (Allingham 2015, p.5)

In terms of nurturing PSED and behaviours, are all these points considered as transitions? How are young children supported during these times? What do we as adults do that helps (or indeed hinders)? How does considering these types of questions support your understanding of children's behaviours? Dr Suzanne Zeedyk regularly talks of the importance of drop-off and pick-up times; for example, this is from Dr Zeedyk's website, and the article on Childcare Practice:

> We can pay attention to drop-off routines at the beginning of the day and pick-up routines at the end of the day. These are the two most important moments of the day, for a child in childcare. These are the moments that involve reunion and parting. You are saying goodbye to Mummy or Daddy or Granny, and hello to your key person. Then, later on, you get to say hello to Mummy or Daddy or whoever picks you up, but you have to say goodbye to the people you spent the day with. Such transitions are emotionally tricky and often involve a fair amount of anxiety for children. (Zeedyk 2017)

Additionally, in an interview for Kathy Brodie's Early Years Web Summit (March 2017), Dr Zeedyk talks of the end of the day, for example, and how we, as practitioners, often meet the parent at the door to share information on the child's day. Meanwhile, the child and parent have to wait for their re-connection moment. What Dr Zeedyk suggests is that we support the re-connection of parents and their child first, and then offer the necessary information. This is such a simple, yet highly sensible way of working, and one that is completely free to implement. Working in this way would need no further resources, but could influence perceptions about relationships, for example. What all of the bullet points in the 'All in a Day (1)?' reflective practice exercise have in common are the influences each has on our PSED, wellbeing and/or behaviours. For young children, the importance of relationships, connections and PSED, as well as feeling safe, secure, loved (professional or otherwise), and so on are vital…and this includes the importance of touch…

The Importance of Touch

There is much debate, nationally and internationally, regarding cuddles and hugs in early childhood. We mentioned this briefly in earlier sections (see 'What about Daddies' and also the note on 'Self-Soothe and Self-Settle'). Moreover, parents and early childhood practitioners are bombarded with information from both sides of the debate of whether to cuddle or not. Does picking up a crying baby 'spoil' them? Does cuddling boys make them 'soft'? Or, the flip side – the importance of work such as that of Dr Page on PLEYS (Professional Love in Early Years Settings). Additionally, if we go back to Dr Zeedyk's website, and the article on Childcare Practice:

> We can be sure there are plenty of cuddles on tap throughout the day. In the modern world, we have become scared of touch. We are on guard against allegations of 'inappropriate touch'. Many childcare settings now have policies that encourage staff to limit the amount of cuddles they offer to children. Sometimes those policies are supported by the belief it will encourage independence in children. But that's not what the science of connection tells us. It shows without question that children need lots of touch – especially when they are upset or anxious. The reassuring arms of someone they trust produces a burst of the hormone oxytocin, and that's what helps children to start to feel calmer. It is not too strong to say that childcare settings who are reluctant to give cuddles are harming children emotionally – even though that is probably the last thing they intended to do. (Zeedyk, 2017)

In researching this book, I came across the work of Professor McGlone, who had been quoted in an article in the *Times Educational Supplement* (TES, 17 February 2017). The headline, by Blume (2017) said:

> Refusing to touch pupils is a form of child abuse, psychologists say.

Well, of course, with a headline like this, I was immediately interested. I read the article, and found that Professor Francis McGlone is a Professor in Neuroscience at the School of Natural Sciences and Psychology at Liverpool John Moores University, and he was quoted as saying:

'Touch isn't just good – it's absolutely essential,' he said. 'Denying it is like denying a child oxygen, I get very exercised [angry] about the demonization of touch. It is cruel, in my mind. It's another form of abuse. The scientific evidence is incontrovertible. I'm not just talking pyschononsense; I'm talking about proper, evidenced, neuroscience.'

Wow! Was I excited… Here we had a real, authentic, 'proper' neuroscientist saying we need to touch, cuddle and hug children. Professor McGlone is a highly regarded academic and researcher, and has written numerous publications. His work concentrates on touch, temperature, pain, itch and pleasure. Professor McGlone's research is mainly in the area of a class of peripheral nerves called c-fibres:

C-fibres [are] widely recognised as coding for pain and itch when the skin of the body is damaged but another type of c-fibre has recently been found innervating the skin that does not signal negative skin based events (pain/itch) but the positive and rewarding sensations we experience when being gently touched. These c-fibres are called c-tactile afferents – CTs for short. CTs play a vital role in all manner of social interactions, from the nurture of a mother to her baby out to the reassuring touch to an elderly relative in a care home. (Professor F. McGlone, personal communication, 30 March 2017)

In conversation with Professor McGlone, he talked of how his research looks at the 'feeling aspect of touch' as opposed to 'the sensing aspects of touch', and how the evidence is uncontroversial: similar fibres respond specifically to the same feeling of a touch in many social animal species. For example, rat mothers who lick their pups, or mothers who gently stroke their babies are stimulating the same areas of the brain. We also discussed the TES article, mentioned earlier, and Professor McGlone added that 'withholding touch denies the child of reassurance and the ability to develop future trust of adults'. Professor McGlone also directed me to the following two articles which have been incredibly useful:

'Affective touch is a potential way in to understanding the development of the normal social brain,' says Francis McGlone, a neuroscientist at Liverpool John Moores University in England and a leader in the field. 'It's giving the brain knowledge of me and you, and the emotional quality of gentle, nurturing touch is a very important feeling that underpins a lot of social interaction.' (Denworth 2015, p.32)

Similarly, it also appears that touch plays a role in other areas of life too:

Fist bumps and bum slaps, high fives and back pats – most sports teams can't keep their hands off each other. Watch a group of players on a winning streak and you'll see a lot of touching. Keep a tally and it might even give you a way to pick the champions. The teams at the top of the rankings at the end of the US National Basketball Association season, for example, engage in more hands-on interaction from the start than those who ended up at the bottom, according to work by a group at the University of California, Berkeley. (Geddes 2015)

This makes absolute sense when put this way; we all see teams (even male ones) celebrating in this way, and it is considered perfectly normal. Additionally, the fact that those teams that engaged in more physical touch, backslaps and high fives, etc. performed better fits with our understanding in early childhood. Furthermore, this also fits with our understanding of hormones such as oxytocin. Yet, as we discussed earlier in the section on daddies, somehow we seem to be giving different messages about touch to the men in our world. Professor McGlone's work in this field tells us the exact opposite, and to requote the TES article '…the demonization of touch. It is cruel, in my mind. It's another form of abuse' (Blume 2017).

Professor McGlone and I also discussed the terrible cases of the babies and young children in the Romanian orphanages, which horrified the world in the early 1990s. Whilst much of the research around the Romanian children is often cited as part of the 'neuromyths' problem (see Chapter 1), as it is used incorrectly, there is still much we can learn. Indeed, an open access article by Barke *et al.* in *The Lancet*, looking at some of the Romanian orphanage children who are now aged between 22 and 25 years, was published just days before a telephone conversation with Professor McGlone:

> Notwithstanding the resilience shown by some adoptees and the adult remission of cognitive impairment, extended early deprivation was associated with long-term deleterious [harmful] effects on wellbeing that seem insusceptible to years of nurturance and support in adoptive families. (Barke *et al.* 2017, p.1)

In other words, for some of the children from the Romanian orphanages of the 1990s, despite being adopted into nurturing and supportive UK families, the long-term effects were still present in later life, particularly for those who had spent longer than six months in institutionalised care. As Professor McGlone went on to explain, in relation to his academically sound and proven research, part of the issue was the fact that, although perhaps unintentional, these babies and very young children experienced extreme neglect, in that they were left isolated, in cots, with no physical human contact.

The research by Professor McGlone (and the team he works with) is truly fascinating, grounded in academic enquiry, highly relevant, and should influence our approach to nurturing PSED in very young children, and our understanding of brain development and behaviours: I would urge you to look into this more.

> This kind of touch – variously called social, emotional or affective touch – also seems to be activated more by warm temperatures, meaning a touch from cold hands is less rewarding. 'They [CT-Fibres] are exquisitely tuned to exactly the type of affiliative touching that you see between parents and baby...' says McGlone. (Blume 2017)

Or, indeed, what perhaps we should be expecting to also see between *practitioners* and babies/young children? Interestingly, the word 'affiliative' also means 'connection', or 'attach' – so here we are back in territory we know well, with the work of the likes of Bowlby (1951), Ainsworth *et al.* (1978) and, of course, the continuing work of Dr Jools Page and Dr Suzanne Zeedyk!

For future practice, you might want to reconsider the other points in the 'All in a Day (1)?' bullet list, and consider the links between the adult role, love, relationships, connections and the importance of touch and so on, and how these influence children's PSED and behaviours. I am sure that it is easy to see how all of this starts to link together and influence young children's wellbeing, and how emotions and reactions will be revealed in a whole range of behaviours. In turn, this all feeds into the ability to cope with, and respond accordingly to, life's challenges, and this is termed resilience and self-regulation.

Resilience and Self-Regulation

Love, relationships, connections, PSED, brains that feel safe, our wellbeing, managing risk and challenge, and so on, are all the foundations of how we build resilience and self-regulation. In turn the effects of these, or indeed lack of, are then presented through our behaviours.

> Self-regulation – (of a system, organization, or activities)
> Controlled by the people involved in them, rather than by outside organizations or rules

> Resilience – the quality of being resilient
> a. the ability to bounce or spring back into shape, position, etc.
> b. the ability to recover strength, spirits, good humour, etc. quickly; buoyancy

> Behaviour – manner of behaving or conducting oneself. (Collins Dictionary)

Therefore, in simple terms, we are hoping to support children to be able to:

- control their reactions and learn from experiences and challenges (self-regulate)
- 'bounce back' or 'recover quickly' or overcome challenges (resilience, sometimes referred to as 'bouncebackability')
- conduct themselves appropriately (have suitable behaviours).

In other words, learn to cope with what life throws at them. Newman (2004) describes resilient children as children who resist adversity, manage to cope with uncertainty and are able to recover successfully from trauma. (And bear in mind the discussions in Chapter 3, regarding how trauma can be different things to different people.) Of course, as with much of this work, the research is ongoing, and there is much still to learn. If we go back to the longitudinal ERA (English and Romanian Adoptee) study (Rutter *et al.* 2007 and Barke *et al.* 2017), Tomlin reported:

> One in five people from this severely deprived group did not experience any mental health problems into young adulthood. This remarkable finding should inspire future research into the resilience of this population, which may help us to develop better interventions for others. The next steps of the research will involve an in-depth genetic analysis of the most exposed adoptees who did not develop mental health problems, to distinguish whether genetic and epigenetic differences contribute to resilience. (Tomlin 2017)

In terms of wellbeing, it is widely agreed that adults who are resilient and able to self-regulate have higher levels of wellbeing, and, in turn, are less likely to be in danger of mental health issues or engage in impulsive, high-risk behaviours, such as alcohol or drug misuse, sexual promiscuity, gambling, involvement in 'gang' culture/peer pressure, or self-harm, for example. Similarly, it is widely agreed that the building blocks for self-regulation and resilience are laid in early childhood.

There is much research regarding this area of practice, and I do not want to simply repeat it here, but we cannot consider how we nurture PSED and behaviours without some exploration in this area. For example, the research by Shonkoff and Phillips (2000) and Eisenberg *et al.* (1998) is interesting, wide ranging and easily relatable to practice, and I would encourage you to have a read. Topics covered include the developing brain, resilience, reactions to anger, nature vs nurture, empathy and sympathy, the language of emotions and the role of gender, for example. Also, as mentioned earlier, there is a general agreement that exposure to risk in play supports resilience. Barnardo's (2004) offer a summary of the work of Newman (2004):

> Some of the processes that are thought to play a part in *promoting resilience* include *managed exposure to risk.* (Newman 2004)

In relation to the adult role, Eisenberg *et al.* (1998) as well as Valiente *et al.* (2007) found that responding appropriately to children's emotions helped to teach effective strategies for self-regulation. Additionally, Sheese *et al.* (2008) found evidence of self-regulation in very young infants who were appropriately supported. It is therefore easy to see the links between a range of research and the importance of early childhood, and importantly the role of adults in early childhood. Eisenberg *et al.* (1998) also quote Kopp (1989, p.248) who noted that:

> caregivers' responses during distress not only provide external support for emotion regulation, but also allow infants to make an association between the caregiver and relief from distress.

So, here we are back at the very beginning, and attachment, and the importance of not just what we do, but *how* we do it! In other words, babies and children expect adults to respond to their stress and distress, and they expect relief. Moreover, all of this happens from a very, very young age. For instance, Lamb and Malkin (1986) found that babies from as young as just four weeks old would soothe, before being picked up, simply by the sight or sound of a caregiver.

Additionally, the research demonstrates that children who are consistently *not* supported when experiencing so-called negative emotions, or are sanctioned for expressing negative emotions, grow into adults who suppress their feelings or express them inappropriately. (See, for example, Buck 1984; Gottman, Katz and Hooven 1996; and Gross and Levenson 1997). I am sure this comes as no surprise to many of us interested in early childhood; additionally I am sure many of us can think of adults we know who are in this position.

In terms of the way we, as adults, attempt to regulate children's emotions, Spinrad *et al.* (2004, p.45) developed a way of coding seven strategies:

- *Distraction* was rated when the mother attempted to focus the child's attention away from the distressing or exciting situation (e.g. *'Look at the picture on the wall!'*).

- *Direct request* referred to the mother making a direct request for the child to regulate his or her affect (e.g. *'Come on now, stop crying'*).

- *Soothing and acceptance* was scored when the mother attempted to soothe the child (e.g. *'It's OK, you're all right'*).

- *Granting wish* was defined as the mother meeting the child's needs or requests (e.g. *'All right, you can have the toy'*).

- *Questioning emotion* was coded when the mother asked the child why he or she was upset or excited (e.g. *'Why are you crying?'*).

- *Explanation* was scored when the mother attempted to explain the emotion or the situation (e.g. *'We'll be done in a bit'*).

- *Bribery* referred to the mother offering the child something in return for the child regulating his or her emotions (e.g. *'If you stop crying now, we can go to McDonald's when we're done'*).

REFLECTIVE PRACTICE

Adult Regulation of Children's Emotions

Consider your own experiences and practice. Can you think of a time when you have used each of the seven strategies, as described by Spinrad *et al.* (2004)?

- Distraction:
  - » Did it work?
  - » How did the child/ren react?
  - » Why do you think that it is?
- Direct request:
  - » Did it work?
  - » How did the child/ren react?
  - » Why do you think that it is?
- Soothing and acceptance:
  - » Did it work?
  - » How did the child/ren react?
  - » Why do you think that it is?
- Granting wish:
  - » Did it work?
  - » How did the child/ren react?
  - » Why do you think that it is?

- Questioning emotion:
  - » Did it work?
  - » How did the child/ren react?
  - » Why do you think that it is?
- Explanation:
  - » Did it work?
  - » How did the child/ren react?
  - » Why do you think that it is?
- Bribery:
  - » Did it work?
  - » How did the child/ren react?
  - » Why do you think that it is?

I am sure you will be able to see fairly quickly which strategies are more likely to work and why, and importantly, the ongoing consequences of a particular strategy. Additionally, you should also be able to see which strategies nurture children's PSED, help children's brains to feel safe and therefore in turn support the whole range of behaviours. It might also be an interesting activity to go back through this list and consider times as an adult, when other people have used similar strategies with you. Just change the question 'how did the child/ren react', to 'how did you feel?' I am certain that this reflection would also give you further insight into the lives of small children. Additional to this exercise, you might also want to reconsider the reflective exercise in Chapter 2 around 'Behaviour Management or Self-Regulation'.

Whilst I acknowledge that much of this research is primarily based around work with parents (mainly mothers), children often spend a great deal of time in ECCE settings too. Therefore, I think it is fairly easy to see how much of the research is equally as important and easily transferable into our work with young children; after all, we play a large part in children's' 'surrounding culture'.

Whether children come to view their emotions as threatening, something to be controlled, and something to enjoy and that can enhance relationships, or as a deterrent to rational thinking emerges from the way their families and the surrounding culture deal with emotion, and children's fit on this dimension within their family and culture. (Eisenberg *et al.* 1998, p.24)

We know from everything else we have discussed this far, how well we are in control of emotions, other factors in our lives and how we are supported (or not, as the case may be), directly influence our ability to learn, develop and thrive, whether we are little people or big people. Additionally, we also know that some people (whether little or big) cope with these situations and circumstances better than others. Therefore, I was intrigued when Professors Chis Pascal and Tony Bertram (2016), from the Centre for Research in Early Childhood (CREC), released the findings from their High Achieving, White Working Class Boys (HAWWC Boys) project.

As you may know, white, working class boys, in England, tend to be amongst the lowest academic achievers in the country. Using the EYFS Profile data, the HAWWC Boys project identified a group of approximately 40 boys, who, at the end of the reception year of school, were achieving academically, despite some very difficult, traumatic and chaotic home lives. But, and this is hugely important, not only were this group of boys achieving well, they were achieving in the top percentage in the country, and outstripping some of their more affluent peers.

The HAWCC Boys project team had extraordinary access to the information surrounding these children, in that they were able to consult with the children and their families, their current teachers and the early years practitioners that had worked with the children before they started school. The HAWCC Boys project's findings are truly remarkable. In every section of the report, there are links to the topics and themes we have discussed throughout this book. However, to take just one example, the section on 'Child Temperament and Capacities' looks at suggested action points which could help other children elsewhere. In terms of resilience and wellbeing, the HAWWC project offers:

> Supporting and sustaining strong, secure and trusting attachments of young boys to key adults and peers, both within and outside of their home, is critical to healthy development, resilience and wellbeing.

> Building in regular and sustained periods of outdoor and physical activity will enhance the young boy's learning, motivation and wellbeing. (Pascal and Bertram 2016, p.16)

In other words, here we are back at the importance of at least one supportive adult, what Pascal and Bertram refer to as the 'significant other', who becomes a 'companion and not an instructor'. As Professor Pascal pointed out:

This is a key point – these boys were not 'pushed' or 'instructed' they had someone to share their daily activities and passions with who enjoyed their company. (Professor C. Pascal, personal communication, 29 March 2017)

It is also interesting to note, that we again see that word 'outdoor' which creeps up time and time again. Another key finding was the ability of the parents involved to support their children, even in the most difficult of circumstances, and this also has implications for our role as early childhood practitioners. In other words, how do we develop our support systems for parents? As Professor Pascal went on to say:

Another key point is the quality of 'parenting' and that the extraordinary thing is that the significant other was an excellent parent in the most challenging circumstances i.e. they had 'parenting resilience' and often the early childhood practitioner was a vital part in that.

This is a hugely, hugely influential project, and I would strongly urge you to explore the CREC and HAWWC Boys project website, documents, podcasts and interviews. The fact that a section of the, usually, least academically successful group in the country have built up the resilience and self-regulation to overcome even the most difficult of circumstances is extraordinarily remarkable – and the rest of us need to know why! Every single practitioner, leader, manager and parent – indeed anyone interested in early childhood – needs to read, explore and understand this research – to not do so would be to drastically underestimate the potential of, and potentially fail, the children that usually fall into this group, as well as the other children this research could help us to support.

I believe the HAWWC Boys study will become one of those seminal studies discussed for a long, long time into the future. In the final chapter of this book we will explore the lifelong influences of some of the things we know and understand in early childhood. I suspect that the HAWWC Boys study will prove long term, that the positive effects of the childhood of these children will be felt throughout their lives, and it will be interesting to watch further research from the HAWWC Boys project and CREC unfold.

The foundations for resilience and self-regulation are formed in very early childhood; this we have known for some time. The long-term impacts of this are still being discovered. Each discovery adds to our knowledge, supports us to be curious and encourages us to reflect on practice. Wellbeing, as I mentioned at the beginning of the chapter, should not be seen as just a 'buzz word'. Our knowledge, understanding and practice regarding wellbeing, and therefore happiness, resilience, mental health and so on, is vital, not just for supporting children, but adults too. As humans, we need to consider the long-term impacts and implications of this growing area, and how we further support the wellbeing of the children and adults around us, and we will explore this further in the next section. Schore (2016, p.xli) explicitly talks of this in his research exploring the importance of early childhood:

> Mental health, especially the field of infant mental health, is now poised to actively move towards the goal of not only treating but also potentially preventing psychiatric illness and personality disorders. The new information that science is providing on attachment, trauma, emotions and right brain development is directly relevant to the creation of more effective early intervention and prevention models.

What Helps: Five Ways to Wellbeing

The section discussed here is a variation of the one in my book, *Performance Management in Early Years Settings* (2017, p.194). I previously considered the report, *Five Ways to Wellbeing* (Aked *et al.* 2008), by the New Economics Foundation (NEF), from an adult perspective; the discussion *here* considers the research from the perspective of young children.

NEF gathered evidence from a range of up-to-date and sophisticated research and data to consider what supports and promotes wellbeing. It came up with a list of just five very simple things that we can do every day to improve wellbeing (or happiness):

The Five Ways to Wellbeing is a set of evidence-based actions which promote people's wellbeing:

- Connect.
- Be active.
- Take notice.
- Keep learning.
- Give.

These activities are simple things individuals can do in their everyday lives. The Five Ways to Wellbeing were developed by NEF from evidence gathered in the UK government's Foresight Project on Mental Capital and Wellbeing (New Economics Foundation and Foresight (Government Office for Science) 2008). I am sure that these Five Ways to Wellbeing will come as no surprise to those interested in early childhood, as it is what we do every day. We support children and families to connect with us and with each other. I am sure being active, taking notice and keeping learning need no further explanation. We also encourage children to 'give', which NEF describe as including smiling, doing something nice for a friend, being involved in the local community or creating connections with the people around you.

REFLECTIVE PRACTICE

Developing and Supporting Wellbeing in Young Children

Consider the 'Five Ways to Wellbeing' (Aked *et al.* 2008); how can we use the five ways to develop and support wellbeing in young children? You might also want to look at the following websites for more information:

www.fivewaystowellbeing.org and

www.neweconomics.org/publications/entry/five-ways-to-well-being-the-evidence

	We do this by:	We need to do more of this by:
Connect		
Be active		
Take notice		
Keep learning		
Give		

(Note: you might want to create and complete additional grids for each age group of children, or perhaps parents or colleagues?)

I am sure you will be able to come up with many, many examples. In ECCE, we know the benefits of the 'five ways', and how these types of actions help to build self-esteem, confidence, resilience, self-regulation and the 'characteristics of effective learning' (Early Education 2012, p.5), and so on. Additionally, we know how all of these create a strong foundation for children to learn, develop, flourish and thrive. Furthermore, this shows how the abilities needed to do these, and similar, things are developed in early childhood, so here we have yet more reasons to celebrate and develop the work we do with very young children.

REFLECTIVE PRACTICE

All in a Day (2)?

As we have discussed many times, all of this is inextricably linked. In relation to wellbeing, and bearing in mind some of the topics discussed this far, consider the following questions, which are based on some of the issues considered in the reflective practice exercise 'All in a Day (1)?':

- How do welcomes and arrivals support all children?
  - » What works well?
  - » What needs developing?
- How do the routines of the day support children?
  - » What works well?
  - » What needs developing?
- How are all children supported with disagreements and conflict?
  - » What works well?
  - » What needs developing?
- How do snack and mealtimes support all children?
  - » What works well?
  - » What needs developing?
- How is the outdoor area/access to outdoors used to support all children?
  - » What works well?
  - » What needs developing?
- How do transitions support all children?
  - » What works well?
  - » What needs developing?
- How does the end of the day support all children?
  - » What works well?
  - » What needs developing?
- How do all of the above support children's wellbeing?
- What else might you need to consider?

Whichever language we use, it all comes back to how we interact with each other, whether children or adults. Our relationships, connections and interactions directly influence our PSED and our behaviours, and our expanding knowledge of neuroscience seems to only demonstrate this further. I seem to find that with much of the research, theory, observations and conversations I engage with, the messages are always similar, and this is evident in the area of wellbeing.

We cannot contemplate wellbeing in early childhood without considering the work of Professor Ferre Laevers. Professor Laevers' work is easily available elsewhere, so I do not intend to go into too much detail here. Professor Laevers is highly respected in the early childhood field for his work on wellbeing and involvement. Working with the Research Centre for Experiential Education at Leuven University, Professor Laevers developed the 'Well-being and Involvement in Care: A Process-oriented Self-evaluation Instrument for Care Settings (SICS)'. The instrument is well respected, based on observations of children and used worldwide as a way of supporting children's wellbeing, and I would urge you to look into this further if it is something you have not come across before. Professor Laevers offers wellbeing as:

> 'Like a fish in water' – that is how you can describe children who feel alright. They express their positive feelings in various ways. (Laevers *et al.* 2005, p.7)

I have been lucky enough to hear Professor Laevers speak several times, and it is always a delight. His understanding of young children and the way he describes his work is an absolute inspiration to listen to. Definitely something you should do if you ever have the opportunity. When talking about 'wellbeing', Professor Laevers often discusses 'like a fish in water' or 'being OK in your skin'. I am sure we can all think of children, who sadly, and for whatever reasons, do not seem 'OK in their skin'. Similarly, I am sure we can all recall times when we, as adults, feel like 'a fish out of water', or just 'not OK in our skin'. So, here again, we can clearly see how these abilities to feel OK, have resilience, be able to talk to others and ask for help, bounce back, and so on, are lifelong, and we will explore this more in Chapter 6.

For now, I'd just like to concentrate a little on the wider topic of mental health, and in particular the importance of supporting boys. Historically, discussing mental health was considered taboo, whether for children or adults, and the statistics regarding suicides in young men in the UK are staggering (see Chapter 6). Thankfully, there is a growing public awareness about the importance of wellbeing, including mental health, and in particular with men. For example, the charity 'State of Mind', established after the tragic suicide of former international rugby league player Terry Newton in 2010, is bringing mental health awareness to the fans, players, people and world of sports:

> Speaking to Dr Phil Cooper, a mental health nurse consultant with the NHS and a co-founder of State Of Mind, he explained how the initiative came to be.
>
> 'Terry taking his own life in 2010 was a catalyst. I work in the NHS, and I remember reading several articles at the time suggesting that the NHS and the sport should be working together. Alongside his former teammates such as Brian Carney and Terry O'Connor, we initially started with ideas to do a conference, or offer free education sessions to players for the Rugby Football League.'
>
> Before long, though, they made the decision to expand their horizons to include fans of the sport, rather than just the players.
>
> 'Lots of blokes don't come to mental health services, so being a big rugby league fan, it was an obvious choice, really. The interesting thing about the game is that anyone that's ever played it will tell you that you're taught not to show any weakness on the pitch so your opponents can't exploit it, and that mentality can have negative knock-on effects away from the field. The RFL [Rugby Football League] and Rugby League Cares have been fantastic to us. For me as a mental health professional, I've been to many sporting occasions and rugby league games over my lifetime, but there are very few where I'd have something like State Of Mind thrust in front of me.' (Bains 2017)

I think it is very easy to see how this links to early childhood… How often do we give these same messages (such as weakness) to our little boys…and then complain that, when they grow up, they become men who do not 'open up', or talk about their emotions? Surely, we should be encouraging all the males in our world to talk about and recognise feelings and emotions? (You might also want to look at the work of Mantality Magazine or Andy's Man Club, which started the hashtag #itsoktotalk that you may have seen. See bibliography for more information.)

Additionally, the royal family are also adding their support to raising awareness and understanding, around mental health issues. The charity 'Heads Together' is working with a range of national charities and is spearheaded by the Duke and Duchess of Cambridge and Prince Harry:

> Through our work with young people, emergency response, homeless charities, and with veterans, we have seen time and time again that unresolved mental health problems lie at the heart of some of our greatest social challenges.

Too often, people feel afraid to admit that they are struggling with their mental health. This fear of prejudice and judgement stops people from getting help and can destroy families and end lives. Heads Together wants to help people feel much more comfortable with their everyday mental wellbeing and have the practical tools to support their friends and family. (Heads Together website, 2017)

These, and other similar messages, are not about being an ECCE practitioner, an adult or a young child, they are about being human – and ones we need to take on board in ECCE. Perhaps there is even more to it? The abilities to love (and indeed hate), have relationships, overcome challenges and be resilient, for example, are traits once held in high regard to be only accessible to humans; however, the wildlife documentaries and animal research I refer to so often are challenging that view. So perhaps it isn't 'just' about being human after all? Perhaps, in future years, science will reveal more secrets as to how all the life on this planet interacts, the things we can learn from other species, the ways in which our environments are so finely in tune and how the way in which we nurture our young influences their wellbeing and lifelong development. Only time will tell:

In the area of development, research in the past 20 years or so has generated profound insights into the human mind and had revealed that the cognitive and social cognitive capacities of very young children are much more sophisticated than was once believed… (Gazzaniga and Mangun 2014, p.xiv)

They go on to say:

One flourishing area in cognitive neuroscience revolves around trying to understand…the social brain… For humans, many of the most challenging adaptive problems result from the necessity of interacting with other humans…selecting mates, cooperating in hunting and gathering, forming alliances, competing over scarce resources, and even warring with neighboring groups… There is remarkable convergence…that highlights the important role of the amygdala across animal species. (Gazzaniga and Mangun 2014, p.xv)

I am sure you can think of many, many instances where this happens, albeit on a small scale, within groups of children, and indeed animals. For the young of this planet, many of the most challenging situations they face involve social interactions of some sort. I am not taking about extreme traumas here, just the day-to-day challenges of life! Relationships, cooperating, sharing or competing over resources, and developing understanding around conflict, are daily occurrences for all young animals, and indeed in early childhood.

And, importantly, I am sure you can see how these lessons, learnt in early childhood, help us to understand our world, throughout our lives. The more we research, the more we understand, the more we talk to each other, then our knowledge is also expanding. Information comes from an ever wider range of areas, with information and evidence also coming from areas not usually associated with early childhood:

> History is what you choose to believe. To my father archaeology was the study of antiquities, pottery and flint implements... Forty years ago animals had little to do with archaeology, except in artistic representations, and the relationships between humans and animals, if thought about all, were classed as anthropology or biology... To me, archaeology is the history of humans in their environment, and their progressive domination of a world that appears to be rapidly diminishing in size as we travel higher and faster around it... I see that the master predator is indeed an animal with unique consciousness and capabilities, but an animal all the same. (Clutton-Brock 2015, p.1)

So, is this about being interested in early childhood, about being human, or perhaps about much, much more than we fully understand – at least at the moment anyway? Who knows? What I do know is that we need to keep listening. Listening to science, listening to a range of research areas, listening to each other, and to the young children who will, in turn, create their own histories. And we'll explore this more in the next chapter.

Chapter 5

THE IMPORTANCE OF LISTENING

It is well recognised that children 'speak' to us, or communicate, in many ways, through not only words, but also actions, deeds, behaviours and so on. Interestingly, as you probably know, babies can hear (listen) before they are born, but it is also generally believed that our hearing is the last sense to fail, as we die. But of course, 'listening' is not only about the sense of 'hearing'. In this chapter, we will re-examine the many ways we listen to very young children, but also – what we *do* with what we *hear*. So, yes, this chapter is entitled 'the importance of listening', but I am not going to go through lots of theory about *how* we should listen, or consider active listening techniques and so on; there are lots of other places where you can find that information if you are interested. I am going to look at this from a slightly different angle. Let me tell you a little story.

Whilst writing this book, I was talking to my husband about starting this particular chapter, and talking through my thoughts for what should (and should not) be included. We talked about how listening is more than what we do with our ears. We also talked about a small child who had been staying with us recently, and how this little person, with very little language, had made it perfectly clear that tiredness was beginning to set in, and how our ears were perhaps the least important or useful 'tool' at that moment. I am sure those of you interested in early childhood are beginning to build up a mental picture of what happens to small children when they are tired, what we as adults experience, and how we 'listen' to the messages that we are receiving. As Covey's website offers:

> Communication is the most important skill in life. You spend years learning how to read and write, and years learning how to speak. But what about listening?

So this then is my starting point, listening is not about ears (necessarily). Also, those of you who have read my *Performance Management in Early Years Settings* (2017) book will know that my husband has Asperger's Syndrome. It is well documented that Asperger's Syndrome has, as an indicator, difficulties with reading body language, and other non-verbal clues:

> Comprehension of other people's expressions and gestures is poor and the person with Asperger Syndrome may misinterpret or ignore such non-verbal signs. (Wing 1981, p.116)

Moreover, we are constantly told that 'listening' is also about non-verbal communication. In terms of communication about feelings and attitudes, it is generally accepted that 7 per cent is made up of the words we use, 38 per cent is the tone of voice and 'musicality' and 55 per cent is non-verbal (Mehrabian 1981). Hmm…so, here's my dilemma: communication (which obviously includes listening) is said to be *more* about non-verbal than verbal communication, and yet generally, people with Asperger's Syndrome struggle with non-verbal signs and signals, particularly in relation to feelings and attitudes. However, my husband could clearly identify the ways in which one small person had plainly indicated his feelings and attitudes, in other words, the onset of tiredness…

Move this to a different scenario, let's say in a restaurant, a child from an adjacent table starts laying down on the floor, touching potentially dangerous things, falling over and so on. My husband could not state with any definitive assurance that the child was indeed tired…and I do not think we, as early childhood 'experts', could either. So, if we go back to our little guest, how did my husband recognise the onset of tiredness? There was virtually no language, so therefore no tone of voice either, so the 'clues' to tiredness had to be non-verbal, and yet, in theory at least, my husband should not be able to interpret such signs. So perhaps, the idea of listening and body language, facial expressions and other non-verbal clues, is still only part of the story. Let's explore this a little further.

REFLECTIVE PRACTICE

Listening to Messages?

Imagine the following:

- A baby holding tightly to a comforter.
- A toddler falling over ten times in as many minutes.
- A toddler hurting another child.
- A child in a pushchair in the supermarket trying to touch everything as they pass.
- A child laying on their tummy, face down, on the grass in the park.
- A child laying down to play with toy cars.

Now consider the following questions:

- What non-verbal clues is the child presenting?
- Is the child tired?
- How do you know?

It's the bottom question that I think answers the middle question. In short, we don't. And herein lies the answer to my dilemma. I think that unless we have some *knowledge* of the child, knowledge of child development and/or *context* to the situation, we cannot be absolutely certain as to what their non-verbal cues actually mean. Without some knowledge or context, for example, we might struggle to decide if in fact the children in the bullet points are tired or not. Oh, I know we could probably have a good guess – but we might not be correct. I believe that the reason my husband could identify that our little guest was indeed tired was due to the *context* of the situation, and the *additional knowledge* my husband already understood about *this* child. In other words, my husband's ability to identify the behaviours is based on the *context* and previous *knowledge* of this *particular child*. For example, my husband knew the time of day, what usually happens at that time, the behaviours that this child *usually* presents (when not tired, for example) and could also identify behaviours that are not normally present (such as falling over and touching potentially dangerous objects, such as the TV).

This is exactly what happens with parents. I acknowledge that parents would not necessarily say they are using their knowledge of the context and of child development – but they are, they are using their knowledge of the development of their child. Isn't that child development? This then is my point: listening is so much more than verbal and non-verbal communication, and especially in early childhood where children are still learning about vocabulary, non-verbal communication and indeed how to control their bodies. The work of Dr Suzanne Zeedyk, and others, has added to the generally now accepted view that even from infancy babies can interpret and respond to non-verbal signals from close adults, but it still takes a little time for children to develop and fine-tune these skills within themselves and in their interactions with others. And, let's be honest, even as adults we can misinterpret these signs, so it's little wonder that children are confused sometimes.

Additionally, we need to remember that, just as we discussed in Chapter 2, there are a whole host of other influences going on. Understanding the complexity of this plays a huge part in understanding and, therefore, listening to children, and how they are experiencing their world. All adults, whether parents, relatives, practitioners or otherwise, use some form of 'method' to look at, consider and plan what their next steps should be, in order to support young children. Which is exactly what my husband had done with our tired little house guest. With no training or knowledge of the early childhood world, my husband had successfully (and easily) carried out an observation, made an assessment and knew what to plan in order to assist. In other words, my husband had carried out an OAP. He had:

- observed a change in behaviours (falling over regularly, laying down to play, touching things that are not normally touched, such as the TV, etc.) and

- assessed what the situation entailed (it is around the normal bed time, and it has been a very busy day) and

- planned the necessary action (perhaps an early bedtime is needed).

OAP

Observation, Assessment and Planning is often the most bemoaned topic on any training programme I deliver. I regularly hear comments about too much paperwork, takes away from spending time with the children, feels like I am sitting doing nothing, parents are not interested and so on. However, my belief is that we cannot truly *listen* to children *without* OAP. As Clough and Nutbrown (2010, p.154) consider:

Factors for success depend upon...the ability of the adults...involved to listen, really listen, to the children's voices.

I acknowledge that this quote is from a text book to help students undertake research projects; however, I think the message is still relevant. The quote is from a passage regarding inclusion, and how we as practitioners need to be fully aware of *all* the messages, that *all* children are sending. Additionally, as this particular quote is regarding children with disabilities, that offers us an opportunity to consider what we mean by the term 'voices'. I acknowledge that some children with Special Educational Needs and Disabilities (SEND) will have a voice in the traditional understanding of the word; however, some will not.

'Listening as a Way of Life' leaflets were originally published by the National Children's Bureau (NCB) as part of the government funded projects, 'Listening as a Way of Life' and the 'Young Children's Voices Network'. The leaflets are easily available, very accessible and contain a wealth of information, and I would urge to you to explore them. The updated leaflet 'Listening to Young Disabled Children' offers that listening is, amongst other things:

- an active process of receiving (hearing and observing), interpreting and responding to communication – it includes all the senses and emotions and is not limited to the spoken word

- an ongoing part of tuning in to all young children as individuals in their everyday lives.

Understanding listening in this way is key to providing an environment in which all young children, including babies, feel confident, safe and powerful, ensuring they have the time and space to express themselves in whatever form suits them. (Dickins and Williams 2017, p.3)

So here we have more clues to what we mean by 'listening', which are relevant to all children. Clues such as receiving, hearing, observing, 'not limited to the spoken word', tuning in, 'all young children, including babies', 'express themselves in whatever form suits them'. So, in other words, the importance of listening to everything other than just what young children say. Furthermore, especially when we consider very young children (under twos) and children with English as an additional language, we may want to think about other ways to interpret and share what children express to ensure that their 'voices' are heard and inform decision making. The philosophy of Reggio Emilia is world famous for their approach to the one hundred languages of children, and of using what they describe as 'the third ear':

> We may listen, but what do we hear? ...it is essential for teachers to listen with the third ear. (Forman and Fyfe 1998, p.249)

However, the 'third ear', or abilities such as sensitivity, intuition and awareness, are not always present in all people. Some people seem to have copious amounts of sensitivity, intuition and so on, whereas others appear to have none. These abilities are almost ethereal, intangible and imperceptible, not something you can exactly 'put your finger on'. Indeed, would it be possible to 'teach' these 'skills', or decide in an interview if a potential early childhood practitioner indeed had these 'qualities'? That is perhaps a debate for you and your colleagues. But, if we go back to my example of our small guest and my husband, it is widely accepted that people with Asperger's Syndrome generally struggle with these 'third ear' and similar 'qualities', and yet, my husband could still support our small guest. So, perhaps there is still yet more to explore?

In her book, *Observation, Assessment and Planning in the Early Years: Bringing It all Together* (2013), Kathy Brodie offers an exceptionally useful and accessible guide to some of the most well-respected early childhood theorists. As well as the work of Reggio Emilia as discussed earlier, Brodie considers:

> Friedrich Froebel...believed the role of the adult was to observe the children and understood that the support needed by children in their early years is different to support required later on... He was very child centred...he was well known for listening to children. (p.4)

> Margaret McMillian...close observations...benefits of outdoor activity, freely taken by children...would not have been able to make such a strong case for outdoor play without her detailed observations. (p.5)

> Maria Montessori...observed children in asylums and noticed how their development depended on adults and environment that the children were in (Mooney 2000) ...observed how the children's development was significantly improved when given appropriate objects to play with. (p.5)

> Lev Vygotsky...believed that the observation of children was more important than test scores... (p.6)

> Susan Isaacs is considered a modern day pioneer of naturalistic observations. These are observations of children while they play, with no interactions or hindrance...the practitioner, observes, supports and scaffolds the learning. (p.6)

Margaret Carr is best known for her development of learning stories… observations should be about what children can do, not what they can't do. (p.7)

Additionally, Brodie (2013) cites the work of Chris Athey as '…a master class in observations of all descriptions' (p.8). What all of these expert, highly regarded, well-understood child development theorists have in common is their absolute belief in the power of observation. Additionally, as we discussed in the previous chapter, the work of Professor Ferre Laevers is also based on observation…and all the key theorists hold the belief that observations help adults to build knowledge of children. I am not going to go into details regarding how to undertake OAP, as there is plenty of information elsewhere, such as Kathy Brodie's book. In addition, you might want to consider some of the research around 'pedagogical documentation':

> Pedagogical documentation is the process of learning to understand what it is that children might be thinking. It is a visible process of thinking and reflection on children's learning. It may take the form of photographs or film combined with notes of what children say and do. (Keyte-Hartland 2017)

I think it is easy to see why observations are seen as the bedrock of early childhood practice. In addition, observations then help adults to work out what to do next, in order to support children to grow, develop, flourish and thrive…in other words, how we use our knowledge and reflections, to support our observations, assessments and planning.

This is exactly what I believe my husband did with our very tired little visitor. My husband used his observations of this small person, built up over a period of time, to inform his knowledge of what needed to happen next to support the child. My husband would not call this knowledge 'child development' but in some ways, it was exactly that. My husband could see that falling over, laying down to play and touching potentially dangerous things were all things that this child does not normally do. And this is where I think the importance of OAP and listening comes in. My husband 'listened' to the child. The spoken word, facial expressions and body language (in the most generally understood way) were virtually non-existent, but my husband still listened, and he knew what to do with what he 'heard'. (And, just in case you are interested, our very tired little guest did indeed go to bed not long after…and slept from almost seven o'clock until almost six o'clock the next morning, with barely a murmur.)

The Importance of OAP in Listening

OK, so let's explore this a little further. *Development Matters* (Early Education 2012, p.3) talks of the importance of how OAP can 'help practitioners to support children's learning and development, by closely matching what they provide to a child's current needs'. I recognise that *Development Matters* is primarily aimed at professionals, and I also acknowledge that some of the arguments against OAP are that parents are not interested. However, if we consider the document 'What to Expect When', the very first page offers:

> One way of using this document could be to use it as a reference – see what you notice your child can do [observe and assess]. Use it as a prompt to explore and try new things together [assess and plan]. (4Children 2015, p.2)

As you may know words in [square brackets] are included by the writer to explain a technical word, or to help a quote make more sense to the reader. So yes, I have added the words observe, assess and plan to the quote. However, I am sure you can see my point. The 'What to Expect When' document was produced by 4Childen, and is aimed at, and was supported by parents. Whilst some of the terminology may be slightly different, overall, it is written in the same language as the Early Years Foundation Stage (EYFS). It covers the same seven areas of Learning and Development (L&D), and within each section are the same aspects as used in *Development Matters* (Early Education, 2012). Additionally, the age brackets are the same overlapping ones we would use in ECCE, also from *Development Matters*.

Whenever I have shown 'What to Expect When' to adults, practitioners or parents, it is always very, very well received. If we refer back to Chapter 2, 'Influences on PSED, Part 2: Adults: Parents and Practitioners', I reiterate here:

> I have never met a parent who is not interested in their child. I have worked with literally thousands of parents: I have met stressed parents, ill parents, worried parents, anxious parents, over-worked parents, vulnerable parents, misinformed parents, etc. but never a non-interested parent.

In addition, as also stated in Chapter 2, if we believe parents *are* interested in their own children… And, that part of our role, as professionals, is to support parents and share our knowledge… And, that 63 per cent of parents would prefer support for their child from someone that *knows* their child (Zero to Three 2016, p.21)… And, that we need to consider why some parents may not engage with ECCE settings…then I do not see how we can do any of this without OAP. Let's consider this from a slightly different perspective.

REFLECTIVE PRACTICE

Life without OAP?

Imagine the following happens to you:

- You go to the doctors with a headache. The doctor tells you that you are carrying some dreadful, terminal illness.

- You take your car to the garage as a brake light is broken. The mechanic tells you the engine on your car is failing and will cost thousands of pounds to repair.

- You call into the estate agents to see about selling your house. The estate agent tells you that your house is only worth a few hundred pounds.

- You show your partner/parents/housemates the lovely, new scented candle you have bought. They tell you that you cannot burn candles as the house will burn down.

- You ring a plumber to tell them your kitchen tap is leaking. They tell you that your water will have to be disconnected until further notice.

I am sure you can see where this is going. First, let me clarify, this is not intended as a slur on any profession, these are purely analogies that I feel most people will be able to relate to regarding the aim of OAP. Can you imagine any of the above happening, without Observation, Assessment and Planning? We, as adults, would be in uproar! Furthermore, I doubt we would feel listened to. Therefore, I believe, it goes hand in hand that OAP is one way we truly listen to very young children. Furthermore, I think these analogies show the importance of OAP and listening in terms of nurturing personal, social and emotional development (PSED) and understanding brain development and behaviours. I think it is fairly easy to see how, as adults, we would be affected, and what behaviours we then might present, when feeling not listened to and without some 'method' of OAP in place.

So, if we go back to the beginning of this chapter it seems we have some answers. It would appear that listening to very young children is complex. Listening is about more than just ears, and also, not just about the spoken word. It also seems that listening is supported by building knowledge and understanding and includes verbal and non-verbal communication covering what Loris Malaguzzi, the pedagogical leader of the Reggio Emilia early years philosophy, describes as 'The One Hundred Languages of Children':

The possibilities for the 'languages' are endless – dancing, dreaming, playing, questioning, singing, reasoning, imagining, listening, laughing, crying, loving, hating, painting, sculpting, exploring, experimenting. (Nursery World, 21 March 2007)

In terms of *how* to carry out observations, assessments and planning, then I would strongly recommend Kathy Brodie's book (2013) for further reading. In relation to the comment regarding OAP and 'too much paperwork', that is often said to me on training programmes, so let's just consider how life without OAP could affect your work.

REFLECTIVE PRACTICE: CASE STUDY

Vroom, Vroom, Ne-Ne, Ne-Ne (Part 1)

Imagine the following scenario, and you as the key person.

Zamir is 22 months old, and loves playing with cars. One day, you observe Zamir playing with some small cars on the table; you go over and say hello. Zamir has ten small die-cast vehicles. Of these, one is a fairly life-like car transporter, in that the cab turns at a right angle to the back, just like a real articulated vehicle. It also has a tailgate which can be used to drive smaller vehicles onto the transporter, as well as be lifted into an upright position, to hold the smaller vehicles in place. Of the other vehicles, two are fire engine-related, two are tractors and one is a helicopter. On the table Zamir also has an open book, which due to how it has been opened is forming a ramp.

At the side of the book, Zamir has placed all the vehicles in one long line; additionally, all the vehicles are facing the same way. As you sit down next to him, Zamir looks up and you smile. Zamir looks back at his cars, and takes the car transporter from the end of the line. 'Vroom, vroom' he says, as he pushes the transporter passed the line of the vehicles. As he gets to the end of the line, Zamir tries to 'turn' the vehicle, but the end of the transporter moves too quickly, and hangs over the end of the table. Zamir looks puzzled, picks up the transporter and places it at the other side of the line of cars. 'Vroom, vroom' he says again, and pushes the transporter up the 'ramp' of the book. This goes on for several minutes; every time Zamir reaches the end of the line, and the transporter has to make a turn, the end of the vehicle hangs over the end of the table. He tries turning another couple of the smaller vehicles, which turn easily in the small space at the end of the long line of other vehicles, and do not hang over the end of the table. Zamir continues to look confused, and is becoming slightly agitated.

Now consider the following questions:

- Is this level and type of play generally, representative, of this age group?

  » Why do you think that?

- Do schemas need to be taken into consideration?

  » Why do you think that?

- How can you help Zamir with his learning and development?

  » Why do you think that?

- What might happen if you do not help Zamir with his learning and development?

  » Why do you think that?

- Why might Zamir's parents be interested in this type of play?

  » Why do you think that?

- What else might you need to consider?

I am absolutely certain that this needs very little explanation – we would not know all of these things without OAP. This is a case study, and I acknowledge that without knowing Zamir, it is perhaps a little harder to inform practice, but we have other knowledge we can call on. Previous observations of other children, along with our knowledge of child development, will inform the answers to these questions. In terms of listening, Brodie (2013, p.86) talks of 'listening to children's interests', and that is exactly what is happening in this case study – we can 'listen to Zamir's interests'. I am sure we can all see that Zamir needs help to understand how the car transporter cab can be turned at a right angle so it does not hang over the end of the table and continue to confuse and frustrate him. Additionally, if we are considering brain development, PSED and behaviours, as Zamir becomes more frustrated and agitated, his body will start to produce more cortisol, making the situation more stressful. I am certain we could predict, with some degree of accuracy, what will begin to happen quite rapidly, without an adult stepping in to support. The trick here, I suspect, is knowing when to step in.

REFLECTIVE PRACTICE: CASE STUDY

Vroom, Vroom, Ne-Ne, Ne-Ne (Part 2)

The next time Zamir reaches a corner, you quietly lean over, and turn the cab of the car transporter to a right angle and show Zamir how doing this stops the transporter from hanging over the edge of the table, and able therefore to turn in the small space. Zamir pushes the transporter back up the ramp. 'Vroom, vroom' he says. When the transporter reaches the next corner, Zamir looks at you. 'You try,' you say, and smile and nod encouragingly, and Zamir turns the transporter at a right angle. The transporter turns, and does not hang over the edge of the table. 'Vroom, vroom' shrieks Zamir loudly and continues pushing the transporter up and down each side of the line of other cars; at each corner, Zamir turns the transporter at a right angle.

After several minutes, Zamir picks up the two fire engine vehicles, looks at you, and says 'Ne-ne, Ne-ne' (imitating the fire engine siren noise). 'Yes, they are fire engines, ne-ne, ne-ne,' you reply, smiling. Zamir places the two fire engines on the back of the car transporter, and pushes them to the end of the line of cars. When he reaches the end, he again turns the car transporter at a right angle, but in doing so accidently dislodges both fire engines, which fall off the transporter and on to the table. 'Oh, oh…crash,' says Zamir, and places his hands on his face, his fingers spread widely across his cheeks, and makes a big O shape with his mouth in 'mock-horror'. 'Oh, oh, the fire engines crashed,' you reply. Zamir picks the fire engines up and carefully places them back on the car transporter, making sure they are both facing the same way. As Zamir pushes the transporter up the 'ramp', as the tailgate is not in the 'up' or 'locked' position, both fire engines roll off the back (just as real cars would if they were not secured). Zamir watches them roll back down the 'ramp' and across the table. 'Ooh,' he says and looks at you. 'Ooh, did they roll off?' you reply. Zamir tries again, several times, but each time he reaches the 'ramp' of the book, both fire engines roll off and roll away across the table. By this point, Zamir has been playing with the cars for a total of 20 minutes.

Now consider the following questions:

- In the last 20 minutes, what do you think has happened:

  » To Zamir's reptilian brain?

  – Why do you think that?

  » To Zamir's mammalian brain?

  – Why do you think that?

» To Zamir's neocortex?

- Why do you think that?

» To Zamir's wellbeing?

- Why do you think that?

- What do you think could happen next?

» Why do you think that?

- Is this level and type of play generally representative of this age group?

» Why do you think that?

- What do you think is the adult's role in this?

» Why do you think that?

- What do you think the adult should do next?

» Why do you think that?

- How can the adult continue to support Zamir's development?

» Why do you think that?

- What else might you need to consider?

Usually, in my case studies, as it says in all 'good' books, the characters are 'not based on any person living or dead', but this one is different, because this one is a true story. I was lucky enough to witness this amazing, 22-month-old child playing with the little cars...and so I know what happens next, but I'm not sharing just yet... (I'll leave that for the endnote, if you are interested?)

There is lots going on in this case study, so let's consider things in a bit more detail. In the bullet points from the beginning of the chapter, we could not answer the questions regarding if the children were tired or not because we do not have enough detail of the individual children. However, in this case study, there is much more detail for us to consider. For example, can you answer the following questions:

- What is Zamir interested in?

- How do you know?

- Can Zamir relate his toys to, and explore, the 'real world'?
  - How do you know?
- Does Zamir understand that some things are not supposed to happen?
  - How do you know?
- Does Zamir understand facial expressions and non-verbal communication?
  - How do you know?
- Can Zamir sustain an interest for a length of time?
  - How do you know?

Additionally, if we consider *Development Matters* (Early Education 2012):

- How do you feel Zamir is developing in terms of the areas of Learning and Development?
  - The Prime Areas (PSED, Physical and Communication and Language.)
  - The Specific Areas (Literacy, Mathematics, Understanding of the World, Expressive Arts and Design.)
- How do you feel Zamir is developing in terms of the Characteristics of Effective Learning?

Finally, could you offer some suggestions for developing Zamir's interest in terms of:

- the Prime Areas
- the Specific Areas
- exploring other areas of play/environments within the setting (such as)
  - books
  - water and sand
  - mark making
  - art/creative area
  - outdoors?

I am absolutely certain that the majority of practitioners in the early childhood sector will be able to answer many, if not all of these questions. In other words, will be able to carry out some method of OAP, and come to some decisions about Zamir's learning and development. Importantly in terms of this chapter, we are able to 'listen' to Zamir and support his PSED and indeed behaviours...with very little language, non-verbal communication, or any other signs of what we would traditionally describe as communication.

And, just to finish, some final thoughts on the importance of OAP in terms not just of listening, but also in terms of brain development and nurturing PSED and behaviours. Imagine Zamir's parents approached you. Could you answer the following questions, if you were asked them?

- Does Zamir has speech and language problems?

- Does Zamir has any Special Educational Needs or Disabilities?

- Is he is entitled to additional funding?

- What progress Zamir has made?

- What information is there to share with the Health Visitor for the Integrated Check?

- Is Zamir is settled and making friends?

- What other things Zamir is interested in? (Or indeed what Zamir avoids?)

- Is Zamir ready to transition into another room?

- What is Zamir finding difficult? Or alternatively, is Zamir advanced for his age/stage of development, and possibly a gifted or talented child?

I'm sure you can see the direction we are going here, and I am sure you could add many more questions. Questions that we would struggle to answer without OAP. All this is before we even start to look at the more difficult circumstances that some children sadly find themselves in, such as child abuse, domestic abuse in the home, or a parent in prison, for example. I am not saying that these more difficult circumstances will always show in our observations, but that chances are that our observations will show changes over time, no matter how small. OAP shows progression, or indeed lack of; it shows changes that might otherwise go un-noticed. OAP shows where children are struggling with certain areas of development, and where children might be exceeding. OAP gives us valuable evidence that we may not otherwise notice, or remember over time… Imagine, for example, in a year's time, we are asked to provide information for a social worker, or for a court case, or to another colleague about the child's progress, or asked if, and when, a child's behaviours changed. Or if a parent needs reassurance, or the child transitions to another setting. Or a parent of a child with disabilities needs support to see the things their child can do, as well as the things they cannot do. Without previous observations to compare to, how can we possibly share this kind of information?

There are many, many questions we could not answer without building up a picture. Over time, through OAP, we begin to build a holistic, rounded, picture of each unique child. And this is why the observations have to be collected and stored in some way. Therefore, there will always have to be some 'record', whether on paper, or electronic, or indeed any futuristic way we develop. We cannot possibly expect to store all this knowledge about each child in our heads, whether for 13, four or even one very young child. By having the 'paperwork' that is so often lamented, we have the ability to answer the last set of bullet list questions, and more beside. I am not saying observations should be reams and reams of paperwork, and neither are the DfE:

2.1. Assessment plays an important part in helping parents, carers and practitioners to recognise children's progress, understand their needs, and to plan activities and support. Ongoing assessment (also known as formative assessment) is an integral part of the learning and development process. It involves practitioners observing children to understand their level of achievement, interests and learning styles, and to then shape learning experiences for each child reflecting those observations. In their interactions with children, practitioners should respond to their own day-to-day observations about children's progress and observations that parents and carers share.

2.2. Assessment should not entail prolonged breaks from interaction with children, nor require excessive paperwork. Paperwork should be limited to that which is absolutely necessary to promote children's successful learning and development. Parents and/or carers should be kept up-to-date with their child's progress and development. Practitioners should address any learning and development needs in partnership with parents and/or carers, and any relevant professionals. (DfE 2017, p.13)

I believe, that in terms of nurturing PSED, and understanding brain development and behaviours, we need to listen to children, and perhaps the most effective way to do this, especially for our youngest children, is through effective use of Observation, Assessment and Planning, and the key person approach. As we have explored throughout this chapter, listening is far more complex than most people would initially consider. Additionally, in order to listen to very young children, we have to take on board all of the 'one hundred languages' children use, and the ways that very young children creatively communicate with us. Of course, as children grow and develop, so their vocabulary, facial expressions and non-verbal communication skills will grow and develop too. Our abilities, as adults, to talk, listen, question, support, scaffold, encourage, plan, model, discuss, involve, prepare, interact and so on, all support this growth and development. Furthermore, if we take notice of one of the central messages from this book – we notice and support what children are communicating through their behaviours. We use our knowledge, skills and understanding of child development. We work in partnership with parents and other professionals. We use our knowledge and understanding of research, theory and best practice. We consult, we support, we share. In other words, we are professional people, doing a professional, and very important job. And, we need to Observe, Assess and Plan (OAP) to support us in doing all of these things… And…therefore, isn't all of this the actual role of an ECCE practitioner, and therefore the role of a key person?

The Role of the Key Person in Listening

I am not going to go into a huge amount of detail here, as there are a range of excellent resources readily available to support thinking, understanding and developing practice regarding the role of the key person. In terms of *OAP, it is* **not** *'sitting doing nothing'* – it is a fundamental, vital and core aspect of supporting young children. In essence, what we have discussed here is the core role of a professional early years practitioner and/or the key person. Indeed, nurturing PSED and understanding brain development and behaviours, is perhaps *the core of the role of the key person*, and in some ways, that could so easily have been the title of this book. Providing empathetic, respectful, warm, caring relationships, routines and intimate care practices that meet individual young children's needs, being aware of other influences and developing wellbeing are what truly happens when we listen to children – and what truly happens in a genuine and authentic child–key person relationship. Along with knowing children well, sharing information with, and supporting parents, safeguarding (in the widest sense of the word), creating and evolving plans to support learning and development and supporting children in their play, is, I believe, what the key person role is for.

> 1.10. Each child must be assigned a key person (also a safeguarding and welfare requirement – see paragraph 3.27). Providers must inform parents and/or carers of the name of the key person, and explain their role, when a child starts attending a setting. The key person must help ensure that every child's learning and care is tailored to meet their individual needs. The key person must seek to engage and support parents and/or carers in guiding their child's development at home. They should also help families engage with more specialist support if appropriate. (DfE 2017, p.10)

I would just like to finish this section with the words of three very highly regarded and well-respected experts in this area. Elfer, Goldschmied and Selleck (2012) consider the key person, and offer the following:

> The key person approach is a way of working in early years settings in which the whole focus and organisation is aimed at enabling and supporting close attachments between individual children and practitioners. The key person approach is an involvement…commitment between a member of staff and a family. (p.23)

They go on to say:

> The Key Persons approach is intense, hard work and a big commitment… makes very real physical, intellectual and emotional demands upon the Key Person…develop a sense of really mattering to a child and to their family… likely to have a powerful impact on the child's wellbeing, his mental health, and his life chances to think and learn.
>
> The term 'key worker' and 'Key Person' are often used interchangeably… We would like to draw a clear distinction between the two terms… 'Key Person'…refers to a professional relationship that has direct emotional significance…someone who is 'key' to the child. (p.24)

The Dangers of Not Listening?

We have discussed in some detail the importance of listening, and briefly considered what might happen when you are not listened to in the 'Life without OAP?' reflective practice exercise. Let's just consider this in a little more detail.

REFLECTIVE PRACTICE

I Can't Hear You...

How do you feel when you have, and have not felt listened to? Think carefully – and don't just put 'body language' – try and work out what actually happened/did not happen or what was actually said/not said.

Think of a time when you have felt really listened to.

- What did the person do (or not do) that made you feel listened to?

- What did the person say (or not say) that made you feel listened to?

- How did you feel?

- How did you react?

Now, think of a time when you have not been listened to.

- What did the person do (or not do) that made you feel not listened to?

- What did the person say (or not say) that made you feel not listened to?

- How did you feel?

- How did you react?

This is a very simple, yet powerful activity, and I use it regularly on various training programmes to highlight the importance of listening, not just to young children, but also each other. The likelihood is that both of these sets of questions will have elicited some very strong emotional reactions in you. In the feedback session on this activity on training programmes, for the first half of the exercise, there are usually words such as eye contact, smile, touch, nod, acknowledgement, happy, affirmation, praise, cared for, supported, and so on... As I am sure you can imagine, the words for the second half of the activity are very, very different. Words such as turned away, not looking, carried on with what they were doing, deflated, stopped talking, stopped trying, sad, lonely, frightened, angry, worried, worthless, and so on, are common. I am sure you have come up with equally emotive words.

Now imagine these or similar things happening to very young children. And...this is why this section is called 'the dangers of not listening'. I acknowledge that we never intentionally do not listen to children. Equally, I wonder, how often in the busyness of a normal day, are children left, however unintentionally, feeling scared, worried or angry and so on, because someone did not listen? Bearing in mind everything we have discussed in this book, imagine these very young brains, trying to understand some of those very difficult emotions you considered in the previous reflective practice exercise... In terms of understanding neuroscience and nurturing PSED and behaviours, I don't think we need to say much more... Additionally, I think it is fairly easy to see how the practice and the theory we have discussed so far easily translates into lifelong practice.

Chapter 6

THEORY INTO LIFELONG PRACTICE

Throughout this book, we have explored the world from a child's eye view – and often asked the question 'how would we react if this happened to us as adults?' In this chapter, I want to take that further, and ask, what could happen if we don't take on board some of the messages? How does some of the theory we have considered translate into lifelong practice? Are there crossovers between age groups and disciplines? Can the early childhood practices we have discussed help in other areas of life? How can theories and research support us as we go through life? How do we know which ones to trust?

Throughout the book, I have acknowledged that there are ongoing debates on some of the issues we have discussed, such as neuroscience and *how* important early childhood is, whether animals 'feel' emotions and the issues around men and early childhood, for example. Additionally, I have encouraged you to reflect on debates, theory and practice and how this could, should or might impact on children and/or the adults who support them, and I hope you will continue to do so.

I have also said words to the effect of 'do not believe everything you read'. As I write this, the media is in a frenzy over 'fake news', social media responds in a millisecond, 'information' is cascaded, presented, digested, regurgitated and shared. Information may have been misunderstood, misinterpreted and even perhaps purposely altered. Some information will be useful, some will be unhelpful and some possibly down-right dangerous (in my opinion). I say on my training programmes all the time, 'information' is only as good as what you do with it later. Whether it is information from training, exploring or reading, articles, research and theory, or any other form of Continuous Professional Development (CPD), the 'information' you gather is only useful *if* you then consider, question, dissect, challenge, discuss and, as Dr Suzanne Zeedyk often says, 'are curious'. Being 'curious' is perhaps helpful terminology; it feels as if we have permission to do things such as ask questions, doubt and explore further.

Let's consider one example, and how what seems like one thing can mean something completely different. Throughout the world, media headlines, the sharing of information, different interpretations of language, and so on, sometimes land us in a bit of a pickle. Let's explore a piece of research that was published very recently, and caused a bit of a stir on social media.

Being Curious about Fadeout?

Academics Bailey, Duncan and Odgers published an article in the *Washington Post* (17 February 2017), considering their research. The headline read: 'Preschool can provide a boost, but the gains can fade surprisingly fast'. The article was shared many times on social media, and probably discussed around the world. However, let's look at this further, let's be 'curious'...

For a start 'preschool' means different things to different people (whether American, British or otherwise), so my first curious question would be: what exactly are we discussing here? Does 'preschool' mean the same thing to you as it does to me, or to parents, for example? The headline also includes the word 'can' – so does that mean that sometimes the benefits fade (known as 'fadeout'), but that sometimes there is no fadeout?

The article then goes on to say:

> Unfortunately, our investments in many early-childhood programs may be based on an inflated sense of their promise... We reviewed data from 67 high-quality interventions...most of which targeted economically disadvantaged children...effects faded startlingly fast: falling by half within a year and by half again two years later...

OK, so maybe the next 'curious' thing is 'early-childhood programs'? What does this mean to the reader, the writer, to parents, or to the public, for example? And, importantly, what does this mean to *their* understanding of what we in early childhood do? Moving on, what about 'quality interventions', and, 'targeted economically disadvantaged children'? These terms would indicate, in the UK at least, that these are more 'structured intervention' programmes perhaps? However, how many people would make that differentiation? And finally, in the same paragraph, the article goes on to say:

Head Start – perhaps the best-known early-childhood program – was no exception.

OK, so the term 'Head Start' is widely known across the world, and generally highly regarded, but what is Head Start? And here is a perfect example of what I mean by being curious and questioning everything. But also, as I have discussed elsewhere, how research can take us down paths we had not previously considered... So, time for a bit of a side-track, a different route to explore, off we go to the Head Start USA website:

> Head Start programs promote school readiness of children ages birth to five from low-income families by supporting their development in a comprehensive way...offer a variety of service models...programs are based in centers and schools. ... [or] in child care centers and family child care homes. Some programs offer home-based services...weekly visits to children in their own home and work with the parent as the child's primary teacher.
>
> Over fifty years ago...was created to serve pregnant women, infants, and toddlers...recently, many Early Head Start programs have been funded to partner directly with existing infant and toddler child care programs, resulting in higher quality services to all children enrolled in the child care program. (Office of Head Start website)

Or perhaps the National Head Start Association (NHSA) which talks of the four major components to Head Start, as education, health services, parental involvement (such as classes and workshops on child development) and social services.

Are we still talking about that same word 'preschool'? Do we still have that same understanding of what we thought we understood at the beginning of this section? For instance, so far in this section alone, in around 400 words, I, or the documents I have referenced, have used the terms:

- preschool
- early childhood programmes (or programs)
- interventions (and structured interventions)
- Head Start
- school readiness
- centres, schools, childcare centres and family childcare homes
- home-based services

- infant and toddler childcare programmes

- childcare programmes

- education

- health

- classes and workshops on child development

- social services

- outreach.

OK, so can you see what is happening here? Fourteen different terms for 'early childhood' or 'early years' from a headline using the term *'preschool'*. And how many more could we add? What was originally termed 'preschool', and a term we thought we recognised and understood, now looks like something completely different. But, and it is a huge *but*, how many people will have taken the time to be curious enough to explore the headline 'Preschool can provide a boost, but the gains can fade surprisingly fast'.

Or, perhaps was this headline simply read, discussed, regurgitated and so on and then shared around the world? Accompanied perhaps with an angry response, hands thrown up in horror and a general feeling of frustration as to the lack of understanding around the importance of early childhood. Or, more dangerously perhaps, how many people will have seen the headline and decided that 'early childhood' is a waste of time, effort and money?

Yes, we may be angry that headlines are misinterpreted, misconstrued and inaccurate sometimes, but we need to encourage people to be more curious about what they see, hear and read. Articles such as these will have been seen by hundreds, possibly thousands or even hundreds of thousands of people: people who are not in 'our world', who perhaps make decisions about funding, or perhaps people who are parents, grandparents, aunties and uncles, or people who believe children start learning at five, people who for whatever reason do not have the curiosity about young children the way we do. People who will see the term 'preschool' and do not understand the vastness of the term, because they do not inhabit our early childhood world. People who take at face-value the headlines they see, because they have no reason to be curious about it. However, that is half the issue here; yes, the terminology is so vast that this adds to the confusion regarding the true importance of early childhood (or whatever we want to call it), but there is also more to it.

Public Perception of Preschool?

I have used the term 'preschool' for this section partly because that is the term in the article discussed previously, but also partly because I like the alliteration of the letter P. However, whatever we call it, in terms of theory into lifelong practice, we in early childhood, who advocate so passionately for our world, need to consider how sometimes we actually add to the public perception of early childhood importance (or indeed the lack of importance). Are we, by sharing these types of misguided headlines, simply adding to the lack of understanding? Do the 'others' who do not live in our world, or perhaps make funding decisions about our world, read these and similar stories and simply decide that our work is not to be valued? How do we challenge this? Are we curious enough to explore, delve, question, consider, reflect and so on, and to then do we share the information we uncover as widely as we possibly can?

I had not intended to cover this kind of debate in this book, but a Twitter exchange one evening with Suzanne Zeedyk and other passionate, early childhood advocates, made me feel this had to be included somewhere. Suzanne had re-posted a Tweet from Arthur Rolnick, who I quoted in Chapter 3. I replied to the Tweet, Suzanne replied back and included a new article, from the Heckman Equation. Curious as ever, I looked into it:

> A new study, Persistence and Fadeout in the Impacts of Child and Adolescent Interventions, was featured in a Washington Post analysis on February 17, 2017, making the claim that the cognitive gains of early childhood education programs fadeout over time. It ignores an overwhelming body of recent evidence that shows to the contrary: so-called fadeout doesn't exist. (Heckman 2017)

But, in order to understand the discussion from the Heckman Equation statement, I had to go back and read the *Washington Post* article first, and then explore all of the above. The Heckman Equation website, the full statement from which the above quote is taken, and the accompanying links, go on to supply a huge wealth of research and evidence as to the importance of what they term 'early childhood education programs', and I would urge you to have a look and consider some of this research in terms of future practice.

Hopefully, it is now beginning to make sense as to why I decided to include this here, in this chapter, after all I could have included it anywhere, or simply ignored it. Or, I could have taken the article headline at face value, and started to doubt my own values and the early childhood field I so passionately champion. Thankfully, I am 'curious', and the more I looked (researched), the more I read (articles, theory, documents or simply information), the more it informed my future practice... And that is what I am urging you to do in terms of your lifelong practice. And, as I said at the beginning of this chapter 'do not believe everything you read'.

So, yes, I felt that putting this section here fits incredibly well with the title: theory into lifelong practice. Much of the 'information' we read, hear and see, is potentially 'theory'. Theory simply means things such as a thought, a model, a concept or an idea. Therefore, *anything* has the potential to influence lifelong practice, whether it is about early childhood or not. It is what we do with that information that counts.

However, if we do not challenge, question, dissect, reflect, discuss, stay curious and so on, then we are simply allowing those with the loudest voices to be heard. In other words, we need to ensure we consider what we see, hear and read carefully, and make informed decisions regarding future or lifelong practice...and this could mean challenging others, expressing a different viewpoint or offering another angle, for example. In our book, *Leadership for Quality* (L4Q), Andrea (Lancaster) and I called Chapter 5, 'The Leader as a Champion'. In the chapter descriptions, we talked of how:

> The Leader as a Champion...act with integrity and lead by example, standing up for what they believe is right. (Garvey and Lancaster 2010, p.16)

OK, so you might not look at yourself as a 'leader' in terms of your role or job title, but you are leading in the sense Andrea and I advocate. In relation to lifelong theory into practice, part of our role is to champion early childhood. In other words, act with integrity and stand up for what we believe is right. Isn't that exactly what we are hoping the children we so passionately care for will do? Do we not support children to challenge and explore, ask questions and be curious? Does then that mean that we are leading by example? I think it does. That does not mean we have to shout the loudest, be the most prolific on social media, or read everything and anything, but it does mean we need to be curious, take what we read, see and hear, consider it carefully, ask questions and if appropriate, use it in practice. Let's now consider some of the other 'theory' we have discussed, and how this could influence not just early childhood practice, but other areas too.

Back to the Beginning?

In the introduction, I started with the link between animal behaviours and early childhood development. Especially in relation to my two cats, Merry and Pippin, and whilst acknowledging the cries of 'anthropomorphism', offered that my two cats seem to purr when content. However, purring can also have a different message, that perhaps we as humans need to understand too. Bolt (2014) offers that it is not just cats that purr: rodents, bears, bats and primates, for example, are other mammals with purring abilities, and that as widely accepted, purring is often associated with making connections or responsive behaviours (including cuddles and play!). Bolt, goes on to explain:

> However, purring also occurs... [for example] ...domestic cat purrs when giving birth and when severely wounded, and in these situations of extreme pain and stress, purring is thought to function as an appeasement signal, advertising helplessness towards a nearby individual [Leyhausen, 1979; Beaver, 1992], or as an 'autocommunicatory signal' which allows the animal to self-soothe [Peters, 2002, p. 264]. (Bolt 2014, p.202)

I am sure all of us that have cats in our lives will recognise the healing and soothing power of a cat curled up on your knee purring. But, I also wonder how many of us would associated purring with pain or stress too? Or as a signal to others nearby, for support or help perhaps? Or, how it can also be a self-soothing mechanism? So here we are back at Dr Suzanne Zeedyk's work, and the messages around connection, cuddles and the ability to 'grow an internal teddy bear' in order to self-soothe/self-regulate. How many of us, whether human or animals, would feel abandoned to Suzanne's metaphorical 'sabre-toothed tigers' if our cries for support were ignored? Or perhaps, like the purr, if our cries were misinterpreted or not listened to appropriately? So perhaps again here, science is providing more insight and information that we can use for lifelong practice.

Lifelong Impact?

In Chapter 2, we looked at the many influences and factors that impact on early childhood. It is easy to see how many of the influences we discussed could still cause distress many years later, when children become adults, or indeed if these influences happened to us *as* adults. For instance, we looked at the importance of the role of both the physical and emotional environment and the impact these have on children. In terms of *this* chapter, we can further explore how these influences often have a lifelong impact. In an article by Davis (2015), we are offered the work of Gabor Maté:

> Gabor Maté observes an extremely high rate of childhood trauma in the [adult] addicts he works with and trauma is the extreme opposite of growing up in a consistently safe and loving environment.

Similarly, many people have built on the work of the ACE Study (1998, Felitti *et al.*), to consider the categories of 'Adverse Childhood Experiences (ACE); these were:

- emotional abuse
- emotional neglect
- physical abuse
- physical neglect
- sexual abuse
- witnessed domestic abuse
- living with substance abusers
- living with mental illness/suicidal adults
- family member in prison
- loss of a parent (divorce, separation or death).

Felitti and his colleagues studied the results of thousands of people, and found that:

Persons [adults] who had experienced four or more categories of childhood exposure [ACE categories], compared to those who had experienced none, had

- '4- to 12-fold increased health risks for alcoholism, drug abuse, depression, and suicide attempt'
- '2- to 4-fold increase in smoking, poor self-rated health, [more than] 50 sexual intercourse partners, and sexually transmitted disease'
- '1.4- to 1.6-fold increase in physical inactivity and severe obesity.'

(Felitti et al. 1998, p.245)

So here we have more messages regarding what research is telling us, and the potential to explore the theory around the lifelong impacts early childhood experiences can have. Likewise, it is easy to see how some of the areas we have discussed within this book, and how our roles in supporting early childhood, can have a lasting influence. Additionally, it is also clear how the discussions and theory in Chapter 4 around promoting wellbeing, and the links to risk, resilience and self-regulation are likely to have lifelong influences:

Longitudinal research on resilience suggests that, in addition to enhancing positive outcomes… *matching challenge and skill* in daily life may *protect against negative outcomes.* (Schmidt 1999)

In other words, being presented with challenges that match our skills increases positive outcomes, and develops resilience. Here again perhaps a chance to consider how theory can influence lifelong practice? Perhaps even how we consider how we support (and indeed, appropriately challenge) an ever-increasing, ageing population? Or, how having challenge that matches skills in early childhood can help protect against later negative outcomes? Or, how having challenge that matches skills in early years, helps build resilience, which can then support lifelong approaches? Additionally, we also looked at information regarding resilience and self-regulation in Chapter 4, and there is a wealth of other research regarding the link between resilience, self-regulation and emotions, and not just in early childhood.

We learnt that after September 11 nearly everyone felt sad, angry and somewhat afraid. And more than 70 percent were depressed. Yet the people who were originally identified as being resilient in the early part of 2001 felt positive emotions strongly as well. They were also half as likely to be depressed. Our statistical analyses showed that their tendency to feel more positive emotions buffered the resilient people against depression.

Gratitude was the most common positive emotion people felt after the September 11th attacks. Feeling grateful was associated both with learning many good things from the crisis and with increased levels of optimism. Resilient people made statements such as, 'I learned that most people in the world are inherently good' (Fredrickson 2003, p.333).

So, once again, we find that the practices we advocate in early childhood ring true across the age groups, and across even the most difficult of times. The ability to name, understand and control emotions (self-regulate), 'bounce-back' (be resilient) and show thanks, gratitude and appreciation to others, are all practices that we so desperately strive to support children with. Barker (2015) quotes Korb (2015, p.194):

> Everything is interconnected. Gratitude improves sleep. Sleep reduces pain. Reduced pain improves your mood. Improved mood reduces anxiety, which improves focus and planning. Focus and planning help with decision making. Decision making further reduces anxiety and improves enjoyment. Enjoyment gives you more to be grateful for... Enjoyment also makes it more likely you'll exercise and be social, which, in turn, will make you happier.

Hygge

It is often quoted that Denmark has the happiest people in the world, and, for example, research by Veenhoven found that Danish happiness, or wellbeing, levels have remained consistently high over the last four decades

(Wiking 2014, p.12). This bears out in various, academically sound studies. People from organisations across the world, such as the OECD (Organisation for Economic Co-operation and Development) and the United Nations (UN), amongst others, regularly publish research that backs this up. Media articles follow quickly afterwards, often quoting Denmark's own assertions that they have some of the worst weather, the shortest hours of daylight during the winter, the shortest hours of darkness during the summer and the highest taxes.

In other words, factors that would usually be associated with low levels of wellbeing do not appear to be issues. It seems that despite rain, drizzle, snow and cold weather, short winter days with very little sunlight, lack of darkness (for sleeping, for example) in the summer, and some of the highest taxes in the world – living in Denmark is associated with very high, and consistent, levels of wellbeing. And, it seems that everyone is interested in the Danish way of life, and if it is possible for citizens from other countries to learn lessons in order to replicate similar levels of happiness and wellbeing.

In 2016, 'hygge' was ranked by several sources as one of the 'words of the year' and hygge has now become synonymous with wellbeing and happiness. Originally a Norwegian word, meaning something like 'wellbeing', it appeared in Denmark around the 18th century and has become recognised as at the core of Danish culture:

> Hooga? Hhyooguh? Heurgh? It is not important how you choose to pronounce or even spell 'hygge'. To paraphrase one of the greatest philosophers of our time – Winnie-the-Pooh – when asked how to spell a certain emotion, 'You don't spell it, you feel it.' (Wiking 2016, p.4)

If you haven't heard of hygge (suggestions on pronunciation also include hue-gah, to rhyme with 'cougar'), it is the Danish 'way of life', and is so engrained in the culture of Denmark, that it notoriously difficult to explain in other languages. The Oxford Dictionaries offer:

> A quality of cosiness and comfortable conviviality that engenders a feeling of contentment or well-being (regarded as a defining characteristic of the Danish culture). (www.oxforddictionaries.com)

Similarly, the Visit Denmark website attempts a definition:

> Hard to explain and even harder to pronounce, the Danish word hygge (sounds a bit like 'hooga') roughly translates to coziness, but that definition doesn't quite cover it.
>
> Hygge is as Danish as pork roast and cold beer and it goes far in illuminating the Danish soul. In essence, hygge means creating a nice, warm atmosphere and enjoying the good things in life with good people around

you. The warm glow of candlelight is hygge. Friends and family – that's hygge too. And let's not forget the eating and drinking – preferably sitting around the table for hours on end discussing the big and small things in life. (www.visitdenmark.co.uk)

Meik Wiking is CEO of The Happiness Research Institute, a Research Associate for Denmark at the World Database of Happiness...and a researcher, who studies happiness and wellbeing. Using his knowledge of a wealth of research, as well as personal experience, Wiking wrote *The Little Book of Hygge* and offers the 'Hygge Manifesto' (2016, p.46):

1. Atmosphere: turn down the lights.

2. Presence: be here now. Turn off the phone.

3. Pleasure: coffee, chocolate, cookies, cakes, candy. Gimme! Gimme! Gimme!

4. Equality: 'we' over 'me'. Share the tasks and the airtime.

5. Gratitude: take it in. This might be as good as it gets.

6. Harmony: it's not a competition. We already like you. There is no need to brag about your achievements.

7. Comfort: get comfy. Take a break. It's all about relaxation.

8. Truce: no drama. Let's discuss politics another day.

9. Togetherness: build relationships and narratives. 'Do you remember the time we...?'

10. Shelter: this is your tribe. This is a place of peace and security.

I am certain you can see how much of this would easily translate into early childhood practice. OK, so we might not want children eating lots and lots of chocolate, cakes and cookies, but we considered elsewhere ways for children to find pleasure and socialisation experiences with food and mealtimes, and I am sure you can think of other ways that this could easily be encouraged. There are several hygge books and articles available, and I have included more information in the bibliography. As always, there are those who welcome this approach and those who are sceptical; however, the science behind the wellbeing of the population of Denmark is very real:

The Happiness Research Institute is an independent think tank.

Our mission is to inform decision makers of the causes and effects of human happiness, make subjective well-being part of the public policy debate, and improve the quality of life for citizens across the world. (www.happinessresearchinstitute.com)

Based in Copenhagen in Denmark, The Happiness Research Institute covers a range of interdisciplinary research areas, and is a wealth of information, and I would encourage you to explore the website. Annual reports and other publications include *The Happy Danes* (why are Danish people often said to be the happiest in the world, 2014), World Happiness Report and Job Satisfaction Index (both published annually), all of which develop, explore and interpret research and data to consider wellbeing… And, all of which hold easily transferrable lessons into our work and lifelong practice. After all, if the Danes are considered the happiest people in the world, and we are interested in wellbeing and happiness, then an organisation that looks at research and theory in these areas, and is actually based in Denmark, seems to me like a good place to start.

Finally, we know happiness is catching, and surely developing understanding around this has to be a good thing? Fredrickson and Joiner (2002, p.174) found that 'positive emotions – through their effects on broadened thinking – predict future increases in positive emotions'. In other words, positivity breeds positivity, which we in early childhood know helps with overall growth and development. Doesn't this then again offer us in early childhood yet more reasons to continue to carefully consider research from a range of areas and ask ourselves: how does this impact on our very youngest children and our early childhood world? In terms of lifelong practice, however, the young children we are caring for now will first have to cope with becoming teenagers.

Teenage Dirtbag?

For those of you not into rock music, 'Teenage Dirtbag' is the title of a song released in 2000, by the US rock band Wheatus. It was the band's most famous song to date, and has been covered by such diverse artists as Girls Aloud and The Ukulele Orchestra of Great Britain. The song is a typical story of unrequited teenage love, and one of my favourites to sing along to in the car… But, the reason I choose the title for this section is the word 'dirtbag', and how teenagers (just like the two-year-olds discussed in Chapter 2) often get a very raw deal. In terms of theory into lifelong practice, perhaps we need to consider that young people maybe need some nurturing of their personal, social and emotional development (PSED), and greater compassion and understanding of their brain development and behaviours too.

REFLECTIVE PRACTICE: CASE STUDY

One Rule?

Consider the following statements:

- Hats and Hoodies Banned by Shopping Centre: After various complaints from members of the public regarding groups of women, a local shopping complex has implemented a ban on wearing hats and hoodies. Any woman entering the complex with a hat or hoody will be asked to either remove the hat/hoody or leave.

- Residents approach local council to remove playground after groups of women congregate there at night.

- People afraid to use public transport due to local women.

- New research shows why women are lazy, and refuse to do chores.

- Women told to stop using 'stroppy' behaviour.

- Women are often smelly, uncommunicative and rude.

- Neighbours warn that they have to cross the road if they see a group of women coming.

OK, do I really need to go on? ... I am sure you can see where this is going. All of the above are my versions of headlines that are regularly used regarding not women, but young people. Can you imagine if these types of things were said about women, or men, or anyone else for that matter? Yet, it is deemed acceptable to say things such as this about our young people. Except they are not called young people or even teenagers, are they? More often they are referred to as layabout-hoody-wearing-tattoo-covered-long-haired-drug-addicted-knife-wielding-yobs!

Hmm…do you know any teenagers? Do you have teenagers in your life that you love and care about? Are they young people who, generally, are caring, considerate and helpful, but 'get it wrong' sometimes? Are they layabout-hoody-wearing-tattoo-covered-long-haired-drug-addicted-knife-wielding-yobs? Just as we discussed with our terrific toddlers in Chapter 2, we are labelling our young people. Perhaps unintentionally, perhaps even without thinking, but we are labelling them and in doing so we are allowing others to do the same.

OK, so yes, there are some young people who hit the headlines for all the wrong reasons, but then there are some adults that do too. We do not then go around saying 'all adults are murderers/rapists/thieves...' In any parts of society, across any culture, across any age group there will be some who will show behaviours that are not acceptable to the rest of that society or group. However, that does not give us carte-blanche to demonise the rest. I am becoming increasingly concerned about this. The statistics regarding the PSED of our young people, as shown on the YoungMinds website are staggering:

- One in Four (26%) young people in the UK experience suicidal thoughts

- ChildLine (UK) has revealed that it held 34,517 counselling sessions in 2013/14 with children who talked about suicide – a 116% increase since 2010/11

- Among teenagers, rates of depression and anxiety have increased by 70% in the past 25 years, particularly since the mid 1980's

- Suicide is the most common cause of death for boys aged between 5–19 years, and the second most common for girls of this age

- The number of children and young people who have presented to A&E with a psychiatric condition have more than doubled since 2009. (8358 in 10/11; 17,278 in 13/14)

- 55% of children who have been bullied later developed depression as adults

- 45% of children and young people under the age of 18 detained under s.136 [of the Mental Health Act 1983] were taken to police custody in 2012/13.

(YoungMinds 2017)

And these are just some of the mental health statistics on the YoungMinds website. The majority of this book could be so easily re-written or re-read with teenagers/young people in mind. It is how we reflect on the theory and inform future practice that counts. There is not room in this book to go into too much depth here, but this subject worries me; after all today's little children will, all too soon, be tomorrow's teenagers. Perhaps I'll just remind you that under UK law, children are classed as children until they are 18. I'm going to finish this section with the wise words of Dr Suzanne Zeedyk (2016):

To feel safe, children need to know the adults around them will not desert them when they are struggling emotionally, with traumas big or small.

Neuroscience and Later Life?

Back in Chapter 1, we looked at what multidisciplinary science is telling us about brain development and how these messages can support early childhood development. We considered how areas such as hormones, PSED and behaviours are all intertwined, and how this can support understanding of early childhood. However, there are other implications too. We explored this a little further in Chapter 4, and particularly the direct link to hormones, and mentioned briefly, for example, dopamine in relation to both Parkinson's and Alzheimer's Diseases. So, in terms of theory into lifelong practice, what can these messages tell us? The Parkinson's UK website offers the following in relation to dopamine:

The loss of dopamine in Parkinson's

- The nerve cells that die and lead to the development of Parkinson's are responsible for producing a chemical known as dopamine.

- Dopamine allows messages to be sent to the parts of the brain that co-ordinate movement.

- With the loss of dopamine-producing nerve cells, these parts of the brain are unable to work normally, causing the symptoms of Parkinson's to appear.

- The level of dopamine then continues to fall slowly over many years, causing symptoms to further develop and new symptoms to appear.

Additionally, there is a wealth of academic research in this area:

Recent experimental work revealed that the dopaminergic system may well be involved in the occurrence of cognitive decline, often being predictive of rapidly progressive forms of AD [Alzheimer's Disease]. (Martorana and Koch 2014, p.1)

In other words, declines in dopamine levels seem to indicate rapid deterioration of some abilities and the onset of some forms of Parkinson's and Alzheimer's Diseases. Therefore, science is helping us to understand the importance of dopamine throughout life. This is hugely important for us in early childhood, in terms of supporting children with those 'I did it' moments (which release dopamine), as well as supporting children to manage risk and challenge, and therefore avoid so-called risky behaviours in order to achieve 'dopamine-hits' for want of a better term. Moreover, it also seems that science is showing us the importance of dopamine in later life too. So here we have science showing us the importance of hormones, and how they link to abilities and behaviours, and potentially have a lifelong impact. As in many areas of science, we have to acknowledge that we do not fully understand the importance of these links yet. The work in this field of research is ongoing, and the researchers themselves recognise that further work is needed:

> Future clinical trials are needed to verify the potential therapeutic effectiveness of dopaminergic drugs in AD patients. (Martorana and Koch 2014, p.4)

Similarly, Dr Zeedyk (2014c) discusses frequently the link between research in early and later life:

> Research with dementia patients is teaching us the same thing that research with infants has taught us: human beings are innately communicative. Human brains are biologically programmed to search for meaning in other people's behaviour. Dementia 'patients' have not lost that biological programming. Whatever other deterioration their brain is undergoing, it continues to search for responses from the people around them.

Too Young or Too Old?

All too often it is our youngest or oldest people who, sadly, receive the least amount of attention, funding and support. The media is full of headlines regarding insufficient staffing, funding and quality of care for both our youngest and oldest, and therefore most vulnerable, citizens. In terms of theory into lifelong practice, I have been convinced for some time that much of the work we advocate as excellent practice in early childhood could be easily transferable to elderly care. Not for one minute am I saying that all early years practices are appropriate for older people, or indeed that older people should be treated like babies, but I do believe there is a crossover. Our core values and ethos of mutual respect, empathy, kindness, understanding, compassion, integration and so on, are universally about being human. The underpinning, solid, grounded and highly regarded foundation of 'unique child [person]', 'positive relationships' and 'enabling environments' (Early Education 2012) are so easily transferrable.

In Chapter 3, for example, we considered the many things that we do that are well-meaning, but do not always have the outcomes we intended. I am also sure can you think of older family members, or have seen, read or heard information regarding elderly care practices, with similar difficulties. Just as the early childhood practices we discussed are never intended to cause distress and alarm, so I am sure it is the case for practices in elderly care. Moreover, I suspect that there are many areas within this book that could be shared not just with elderly care, but across the health, education and other caring professions. Likewise, I believe, my references to how our views are changing regarding animal behaviours are also helpful to wider theory into lifelong practice.

REFLECTIVE PRACTICE

Lifelong Practice?

Imagine you find yourself caring for a young baby, a young animal, an elderly relative, an elderly pet, a sick baby, a sick animal or a sick relative. Would the questions we need to consider work across all these potentially vulnerable areas:

- Do they need help personally?
- Do they need help socially?
- Do they need help emotionally?
- Do they need support with intimate care (washing, feeding, bodily functions, etc.)?
- Do they need treating with respect, empathy, compassion, kindness, understanding and so on?
- Do we need to consider them as unique individuals?
- Do we need to consider their relationships?
- Do we need to consider their environments?
- Do we need to consider their reptilian, mammalian and neocortex brains?
- Do we need to consider their behaviours?

I am sure you can see where this is going. I strongly believe that the qualities, attitudes, ethos and values, and so on, we hold in such high regard in early childhood are so easily transferable. For example, in Chapter 2, we looked at the role of the adult; however, in an ever-increasing ageing population, this is becoming increasingly important in our later years too. Additionally, science is changing our perception of animals, so our roles needs further consideration here too. As I said in Chapter 3, I often ask myself how I would feel if that was me, or indeed someone (or something) I cared about. How we carry out each of these bullet points is what counts, and only history will tell us whether we got it right; after all, in terms of theory into lifelong practice, the children we care for now are the carers of the future.

In Chapter 4, we explored the research of Professor McGlone and his team on the importance of touch. Interestingly, during our discussions, Professor McGlone, as well as discussing the importance of touch, also mentioned that research has shown that 'loneliness is the second biggest killer, only to smoking'. Here, again, are practices across early childhood that could so easily be transferred into lifelong practice. For instance, we advocate making healthy choices, friendships, relationships, empathy and helping each other. I am sure you will have all seen the headlines around the issues of loneliness in elderly people, and also how every winter we are encouraged to check on elderly relatives and neighbours. I would encourage you to watch the TEDx video with Helena Backlund Wasling that is in the bibliography, but be aware you might want to make sure you have a box of tissues handy! Additionally, the 'Campaign to End Loneliness' website is full of helpful information. In terms of the dangers of loneliness, they offer the following:

> Loneliness is a bigger problem than simply an emotional experience. Research shows that loneliness and social isolation are harmful to our health: lacking social connections is a comparable risk factor for early death as smoking 15 cigarettes a day, and is worse for us than well-known risk factors such as obesity and physical inactivity. Loneliness increases the likelihood of mortality by 26%. (Campaign to End Loneliness, 2017)

This is why Professor McGlone had also mentioned the studies around the babies in Romanian orphanages, which we considered in Chapter 4. In a Huffington Post article, author Maia Szalavitz (2010) begins by describing this in animals. Szalavitz considers what used to be termed 'runt syndrome' and how the runt of the litter (the smallest and therefore weakest) is often not licked or nurtured in the same way as the other bigger, stronger babies, who have more chance of survival. Szalavitz the goes on to explore how lack of physical contact affects human babies, and offers:

> But how could simply being in an orphanage kill a baby? Basically, they die from lack of love. When an infant falls below the threshold of physical affection needed to stimulate the production of growth hormone and the immune system, his body starts shutting down.
>
> In humans, the immune system seems to be profoundly affected, making these children especially vulnerable to all types of disease – probably because not being nurtured is extremely stressful and high levels of stress hormones can turn off the immune system...

In fact, 'failure to thrive' in human infants has been shown to result from lack of individualized, nurturing, physically affectionate parental care, whether in an orphanage or due to extreme parental neglect. Babies' brains expect that they will experience nearly constant physical touch, rocking and cuddling: without it, they just don't grow. And without receiving kind empathetic care, they are less likely to behave that way towards others as they get older. (Szalavitz 2010)

Perhaps then here, there are links to be explored regarding the effects of isolation as we age too? Additionally, as we discussed in Chapter 4, the impacts of the experiences of some of the Romanian children are still present many years later. So, again here, we have more evidence of the importance of early childhood experiences on lifelong practice. We also know that the ability to show empathy with others is part of being sociable, which of course counteracts loneliness. Goleman states:

Empathy, another ability that builds on emotional self-awareness, is the fundamental 'people skill'... Chapter 7 will investigate...the social cost of being emotionally-tone deaf, and the reasons empathy kindles altruism. People who are empathetic are more attuned to the subtle social signals that indicate what others need or want. (Goleman 1996, p.43)

Yet more evidence perhaps of the importance of early childhood experiences: babies and children not supported during the 'sensitive period' are less likely to be empathetic to others as they get older, therefore more likely to be socially isolated and excluded, and therefore more likely to be lonely, with the associated higher mortality risks.

Additional to the loneliness elements, Professor McGlone also discussed how the ERA study (English and Romanian Adoptee research) by Barke *et al.* 2017 found a higher percentage of children on the autistic spectrum. In terms of lifelong practice, perhaps there is yet more to understand about the links between research, the importance of touch (especially in babies and very young children) and the development of empathy or the incidence of neurological disorders, for example, and perhaps other lifelong impacts?

Of course, there is always going to be some debate about research and theory, and some of this is very new, and still developing scientific research. Genetics, hormones and other influences and factors such as those we discussed in Chapter 2, will also play a part. However, my question would be, are we as adults, as practitioners, as parents, grandparents and loved ones, as a society – prepared to take the risk? Should we worry too much about the debate? Shouldn't we be actually saying, for example, 'touch and cuddles are important', we know *some* of the reasons why, and then the children can say in the future, 'history has shown us more'?

Staying Curious?

Throughout this book, I have quoted and referred to a whole range of literature, and there is much, much more in the bibliography. I would urge you to use the bibliography; it isn't there to just meet the legal requirements of naming the people, documents and information I have referred to. It is there to help you continue to explore theory as you develop your lifelong practice. I find bibliographies fascinating, and would not have read many of the documents I have without having a look through someone else's bibliography. For example, I would urge you to read Daniel Goleman's *Emotional Intelligence* (1996). It truly is a fascinating read, not least as mentioned in the previous quote, for Chapter 7, which considers 'life without empathy', and looks at the minds of abusers and psychopaths. Not entirely what we would normally read in regard to early childhood, but a definite insight into why developing empathy is so fundamental to humanity.

I used the word 'humanity' here on purpose. It is interesting to note that the word 'altruism', as used in the previous Goleman quote, means unselfishness, or selflessness, but it also means humanity. In terms of not just this book, but much of my life, work and writing, humanity is a word I like, as well as aspire to live and work by, and I feel it fits very nicely here in a chapter about the lessons we can learn and use for lifelong practice...and as Suzanne discusses in the foreword, much of the discussions throughout this book are about being human.

Lifelong Practice

I am going to finish this chapter with some key information that I believe we should be taking with us into lifelong practice.

On 14 April 2016, the World Bank Group and UNICEF made an announcement:

> The two organizations announced the establishment of a new alliance that aims to make ECD [Early Childhood Development] a global policy, programming and public spending priority, to give all young children access to quality services that improve their health, nutrition, learning ability and emotional well-being.
>
> Advances in neuroscience and recent economic studies show that early childhood experiences have a profound impact on brain development and on subsequent learning, health, and adult earnings.
>
> 'What we are learning about all the elements that affect the development of children's brains – whether their bodies are well nourished, whether their minds are stimulated, whether they are protected from violence – is already changing the way we think about early childhood development. Now it

must change the way we act,' said UNICEF Executive Director Anthony Lake.

Through the new alliance, the World Bank Group and UNICEF are inviting governments, development partners, civil society, foundations and the private sector to make early childhood development a global and national development priority. The objective is to support country-led efforts to invest in nutrition, early stimulation and learning, and protection, and to engage with communities to drive demand for these high-quality ECD services for every child.

On 8 November 2016, Ben Schiller wrote an article entitled 'Meet the Billionaire Philanthropist Placing Big Bets on Early Childhood Development'.

When J.B. Pritzker invests his family's philanthropic dollars, he thinks about it in the same way as his other investments. After all, he's a business guy – one of the Midwest's biggest tech venture capitalists – and he prefers to think of himself as such. 'I hate the term philanthropist,' he says.

And to Pritzker, there's no area with as much potential upside – socially speaking – as early childhood. In setting up pre-K [pre-Kindergarten] schools, supporting home visit programs, and looking to technology to aid and support early childhood, there's a possibility of big gains, multiplied through people's lives. Pritzker, the 512th richest man in the world, clearly finds the area awe-inspiring for its possibility.

'When you're someone who cares about making a difference in the world and you have resources to do that, you have literally hundreds of choices you could make about how to do that,' he says. 'Why was early childhood so attractive? Because, literally, the return on invested dollars in [the] first five years is more than almost every other philanthropic endeavor.' (Schiller 2016)

And finally, also in 2016, the Center on the Developing Child at Harvard University published *From Best Practices to Breakthrough Impacts: A Science-Based Approach to Building a More Promising Future for Young Children and Families*. This, from page 41 (emphasis added), is the final thought:

The challenges facing cancer researchers and space explorers are no greater than ours – and those challenges have not deterred the progress that has been made by mobilizing scientific knowledge, 'real-world' wisdom, 'can-do' problem-solving, and a dogged refusal to accept failure as an option.

...*How* can we come together across multiple sectors and work collaboratively with families and communities to learn from both failure and success? The possibility for substantial progress in our ability to dramatically improve the life prospects of all young children is real. *The time to aim higher is now.*

Endnote

Reflecting on Personal, Social and Emotional Development

As anyone has read my other books will know, I love the endnote, because I love the opportunity to reflect on the writing and the learning journey a particular book has taken me on. This one was no exception... And, here we are, almost at the very end. I have loved the journey, and discovered many new things along the way. Every time I thought I had finished a chapter, I would come across a new piece of research, or be taken down a new and interesting path, and I just felt implored to explore that too. The discoveries being made around neuroscience (and the associated disciplines), personal, social and emotional development (PSED) and behaviours are solidifying previous knowledge, but they are also ever-evolving and ongoing, which in some ways makes it all the more interesting. And, of course, means we can continue to research, and continue to inform future practice. It creates some interesting debates too. What you read in one book will perhaps be denounced vehemently in another. But, I suppose that is the way of the world. We do not always agree with each other, we debate, we discover new information and then may (or may not) change our minds, I suppose it all adds to an interesting mix. In addition, in terms of early childhood, it is not just 'our world' we have to take notice of, and this ongoing complex mix of information comes from a range of research areas and from a range of disciplines:

> The body of research that the committee reviewed is extensive, multidisciplinary, and more complex than current discourse would lead one to believe. It covers the period from before birth until the first day of kindergarten [USA, age 5]. It includes effort to understand how early experience affects all aspects of development – from the neural circuitry

of the maturing brain, to the expanding networks of a child's social relationships, to both the enduring and the changing cultural values of the society in which parents raise children. (Shonkoff and Phillips 2000, p.3)

As we often say, the world of early childhood is never boring! I welcome this exciting, complex, extensive and multidisciplinary world that is ever changing, and offers ever more interesting things to consider. As a passionate, enthusiastic and 'curious' early childhood 'champion', and now, even more so, as a writer, it is hugely motivating. And whilst I will always love reading, researching and finding out more...I still find calling myself 'a writer' a little strange... In 2010, Andrea Lancaster and I were delighted with the publication of our book, *Leadership for Quality in Early Years and Playwork: Supporting Your Teams to Achieve Better Outcomes for Children and Families* (affectionately known as L4Q). In terms of writing books, I genuinely thought that would be it for me. They say everyone has 'one book in them', and I thought that L4Q would be my 'one' (and if I'm honest, my only one!). When Jessica Kingsley Publishers (JKP) took over the publishing of L4Q, I did not expect the turn of events that followed.

In April 2016, I received an incredibly polite email from the Senior Commissioning Editor, Andrew James, asking if I would be interested in writing something new. I spoke to Andrea (Lancaster), but commitments to her own studies meant that if I was going to do this, it would be on my own. I had thought about a PSED book for a while, so tentatively emailed Andrew back and suggested we have a phone conversation, not honestly expecting much to happen.

The day of the phone call arrived, and I had some thoughts in my head of what a book about PSED in early childhood might include. However, I was fairly certain that after the phone call, JKP (and indeed Andrew) would realise I was not really a 'clever writer' and nothing would come of the ideas, and it would not go any further. (By the way, this is known as 'imposter syndrome' and maybe I'll get around to exploring that in another book one day.) To my immense surprise, the exact opposite happened. By the end of the phone call, and with Andrew's gentle encouragement, help and expertise, I had agreed to write two books! I came off the phone in a bit of a daze: had a well-established, well-known and highly regarded publisher just agreed to work with me to develop two 75,000-ish words books? Had I really just agreed to write something in the region of 150,000 words on two seemingly different subjects in less than a year?

Yes, pretty much – that is exactly what happened. The more Andrew and I talked, the more it began apparent that there were two books floating around in my head, one that became this book (*Nurturing Personal, Social and*

Emotional Development in Early Childhood: A Practical Guide to Understanding Brain Development and Young Children's Behaviour) and one around *Performance Management in Early Years Settings*, also published in 2017. The hard part was going to be deciding which bits of my 30-ish years' interest in all of this went into which book. What I realised fairly quickly was that they both had the same central theme.

What both books have in common is the vital need to understand brain development in our interactions with other humans. In the *Performance Management* book, I looked at this from an adult perspective. This PSED book considers the world through the eyes of a young child, and asks many, many times 'how would you feel if this happened to you?' I use this question a lot, personally, on training programmes, and indeed throughout this book. At differing points in this book, I have felt sad, angry, frustrated, excited, confident, worried and even, at times, tearful – and if I feel like that I can only begin to imagine what it must feel like for young children. I truly have been on the full roller-coaster of personal, social and emotional experiences... As Suzanne said in the foreword, it has been a bit of a bumpy ride.

I know there are some sections, such as the one on Christmas, which are perhaps going to be controversial, but I hope they come across in the way they are intended. My hope is that this book encourages further discussion, thought and reflection. I hope it supports you to ask those 'what if' and 'why not' types of questions in your own head, with your colleagues, and indeed with anyone interested in early childhood. I hope, as Suzanne suggests in the foreword, that you are courageous, and explore and discover new things. I am not saying that either you, or I, have to agree with, or disagree with, the other researchers, writers, bloggers and so on that I have mentioned throughout this book, simply that this is some of the information I came across in my research. I hope that you will, as I did, research some of the topics and draw your own conclusions, and maybe even find some new things that you had not considered, or known about before. So, for example, the research I undertook around the topic of Christmas brought a new document that I had not discovered before. As such a huge fan of Christmas, this surprised me... And I was intrigued...

In 1897, the editor of The Sun (a prominent New York newspaper at the time), declared, in response to a letter from a little girl, that 'Yes Virginia there is a Santa Claus'. (Incidentally, long before the 1947, 20th Century Fox Film Corporation, original version of *Miracle on 34th Street* proved the existence of Santa Claus.) This discovery made me smile, not only because of the mental image of a Victorian editor responding to an eight-year-old little girl, but also the fact that Virginia went on to be an 'educator', and obtain a Doctorate of Philosophy (PhD) from Fordham University. Why have I included this here? Simply because it helps to show how eclectic, assorted, diverse and wide-ranging reading topics sometimes all start to link together. So, what's the connection? The title of Virginia's dissertation is 'The Importance of Play'. Doesn't it sometimes feel like a small world? Or, maybe just that everything (just about) comes back to early childhood in the end? I also discovered that it is possible to read 'The Importance of Play' dissertation from 1930, by Virginia Douglas (née O'Hanlon). I particularly liked the following quote, which still resonates today, and comes from a book published in 1914:

> Cabot says 'Play is a little heaven.' That is what we hope to make it. (Douglas 1930, p.3)

There is only so much you can put in a book, and as a writer you have to make decisions about what is, and what is not, included. If, for example, we consider the modern world, compared to the world of children in Virginia's childhood, and the work quoted from over one hundred years ago, the digital influence we experience now is beyond what anyone could have ever imagined. This is one area I would have liked to explore a little more. Mary Aiken points out in her book *The Cyber Effect* (2016, p.16), 'The impact of technology on human behaviour begins at birth and ends at death.' Or perhaps the work of Professor Susan Edwards on integrating technology and digital play in the early years would have brought further areas for consideration? Or even perhaps, the opportunity to explore the impacts of a technology-driven childhood and if there has been a decrease in the world of imaginary friends:

> They seem to be the products of special minds, but researchers have struggled to identify any substantial differences between children who have them and children who do not.... One recurrent theme...invention of an imaginary friend should not be interpreted as a symptom of emotional or interpersonal problems. In fact, children who create imaginary companions tend to be particularly sociable individuals who enjoy the company of others and are somewhat advanced in social understanding. (Taylor 1999, p.157)

Again, there is much research regarding technology, perceived safety fears and the impact on playing freely outdoors. Consider also, the research regarding the importance of being outdoors in relation to mental health, and that would also have been an interesting area to research further. Similarly, the work of Scottish mill owner Robert Owen in the 1800s and his belief that children should not work, and should have access to education, fresh air and play, still resonates today. But, as mentioned previously, there is only so much room. So, just one quick quote, from Amii Spark and her article in Teachwire: 'Step Away from the Laminator'.

> Time in nature is what children are so greatly deprived of, so it's this we need to give them. In this way, we can be sure that every child who attends our settings benefits from at least some of the time they so desperately need to engage with the natural world, without being inundated with pre-academic pollution. (Spark 2016)

Or, at some other time, perhaps we could explore the work of Sandi Phoenix, of Phoenix Support for Educators, based in Queensland, Australia. On Kathy Brodie's Online Early Years Summit (March 2017), I listened enthralled as Sandi described developing the concept around five metaphorical 'Phoenix Cups': Fun, Power, Freedom, Love and Survival. Sandi's incredibly simple philosophy is that we each have the five cups, but importantly, we each have differing sized cups – including children. Understanding your own personal, and indeed children's individual, differing cups, is called a 'needs profile'. The Phoenix Cups approach considers what happens to all of us when our cups are full, or conversely, what happens when our cups are depleted, or indeed empty.

Sandi used herself as an example and talked of how some people need to have control (they are likely to have a bigger power cup), or how some people can still function when tired, not so well and have not eaten for a while (and are therefore likely to have a smaller survival cup). Sandi went on to explain that regardless of the size of our own metaphorical 'cups' – we all need our cups to be full – including children. Sandi described how our role as educators is to ensure children's cups are full, and to consider what we, as adults, need to do when cups need filling up. I love this so easily understandable, visually represented analogy, and would urge you to look at the Phoenix Support for Educators website, and Phoenix Cups resources in more detail. My favourite line from the interview though was Sandi's take on how to support children's behaviours:

> It is about following children's lead…they are magically wired to know what they need… If you're not sure what to do – plonk them outside… we have issues when we put children in captivity and then take away their outdoor play time…we make it worse!' (Phoenix, March 2017)

But, just because these topics are not included in this book in any great detail, that does not mean they are not important, plus, you can always research these in relation to your own CPD. Or maybe consider them as part of your RAPP? (See the appendix.) This is one of the reasons why

I have mentioned several times that the bibliography is so important. As I discussed elsewhere, I love looking at other people's bibliographies; it gives an insight into what has been read, and perhaps even some understanding into their interests as a person, and as a professional. I know certainly when I have been involved in marking academic papers, the first thing I look at is the bibliography – what have people been reading? If you explore my bibliography, you will see some diverse topics, from a range of sources, such as media articles, websites, books and academic journal articles. A truly eclectic and varied mix, which probably does reflect the diverse (and sometimes bizarre) nature of the things I read that influence my thinking.

My initial research, based on watching Merry and Pippin, was constructed on observations of the animal kingdom, and that still interests me. I often find areas that cross over, such as the topic of daddies that we looked at in Chapter 2. Advances in technology are supporting science in exploring more the role of male animals, for example, who are involved in their offspring's upbringing, such as in the Spider Monkey example, but also the Brown Kiwi who incubates the eggs and raises his chicks. Or the male Sand Grouse, who will fly up to 60 kilometres to find water, where he will sit and wet his breast feathers, before making the return journey to provide water for his partner and babies. Or indeed the tiny male Glass Frog, no bigger than a fingernail, who protects his offspring from potential predators. All of these daddies bring me back to human daddies who also go to extraordinary lengths to support, nurture and care for their children. Reading research, and watching programmes about animals, nearly always leads me back to thinking about young children. For example, in the bibliography, you will see articles such as the one from National Geographic by Handwerk (2010), which looks at how chimpanzee youngsters seem to have a preference for so-called 'girls' or 'boys' toys. Or indeed any of the other animal-related articles, documents, websites and research, such as the one mentioned earlier in the book, on why whales mourn their dead (Watson 2016).

The article regarding whales led to thoughts about how children cope with grief, and perhaps how boys, (and men?) in particular, are helped, or indeed hindered, when showing and expressing emotions. Packham (2017) talks of a mum (Sullivan) who posted an article about comforting her son when he was injured playing sports:

> Sullivan said boys are wrongly taught that sadness is weakness and talking about their fears or short-comings makes them 'less of a man'. Because of this, she said boys don't mourn properly, they struggle to grieve and they're afraid to cry. (Packham 2017)

This of course links back to the topic of mental health that we considered in the chapter on wellbeing. However, we have only briefly considered how, sadly, some children find themselves in a whole host of situations that cause them serious difficulties and result in some children being very vulnerable. Supporting children to cope with pain (physical and/or emotional), and coping with loss and death, is another topic that we might have discussed further. It is widely attributed that Benjamin Franklin said, 'the only two certainties in life are death and taxes'. Well, hopefully young children do not have to worry about taxes, but what about supporting our more vulnerable children, such as those experiencing death, loss and pain? I think that is a whole other topic that would be interesting to explore in more detail; maybe that is a whole book in itself?

Sometimes, as a writer, I am aware of a publication, a document, a piece of research or theory, for example, but then choose not to include it, and keep it for a future topic perhaps. Some things are simply not included in a book because they are already in existence elsewhere. Perhaps, for example, a particular subject has already been covered by highly regarded authors and writers, and it is easy for readers to explore those topics elsewhere, as part of their own, ongoing research and CPD. Sustained Shared Thinking (SST) is one of those areas that is not included in this book as there are in existence, other highly regarded books on this topic, and I would urge you to explore further. Interestingly, and linking back to the discussions in Chapter 3 on well-meaning, in the book *Sustained Shared Thinking in the Early Years*, Brodie (2014) offers her very first example of SST based on how one preschool put on a Christmas show based on a book they had been heavily interested in, rather than the traditional Christmas performance. In her article 'Sustained Shared Thinking: How Important is it?' Brodie (2009a) defines SST as:

> The important aspect is the 'meeting of minds' and subsequent learning that occurs on both sides.
>
> The practitioner has the opportunity to learn extensive amounts about how the child sees the world, their level of cognitive development, schemas, community and self esteem (to name but a few!).
>
> The child may learn things such as social interaction techniques, how to think creatively, cause and effect and factual information.

I agree with this definition, and for me SST is a large part of PSED, and understanding behaviours, and could support many of the things we have explored throughout this book. Adults engaging in SST can easily support behaviours, wellbeing, and learning and development, and demonstrate truly listening to children, for example. SST is one of the reasons I included such a detailed case study in Chapter 5. The scene with little Zamir, was, I believe, Sustained Shared Thinking. If we reconsider Brodie's definition, it was 'a meeting of minds and subsequent learning occurred on both sides'...

Hmmm, so, what about Zamir from Chapter 5? Do you want to see if you agree with me: is this case study a good example of SST? Do you want to know how Zamir got on? Do you want to know what happened next? Well I hope so...because this is what happened.

REFLECTIVE PRACTICE: CASE STUDY

Vroom, Vroom, Ne-Ne, Ne-Ne (Conclusion)

Over the next 25 minutes, with very minimal support from the adult who was sitting with him, Zamir:

- worked out how to lift the tailgate on the car transporter, into the 'up' or 'lock' position

- discovered how to stop the fire engines rolling off the car transporter

- found that some vehicles could 'drive' up the tailgate of the transporter

- realised that some vehicles could also 'reverse' down the tailgate of the transporter

- explored that some vehicles could reverse quickly down the tailgate, and zoom across the table if you let go, whilst the transported was still on the ramp (book)

- recognised how having three vehicles on the transporter meant that the tailgate would not close

- noticed that two cars and the helicopter would fit on the transporter, and the tailgate would still close

- pointed at the vehicles, in turn, saying 'two' or 'three' (pointing at all the vehicles/counting)

- noticed that the tractors had tiny 'hooks' on the back of them, but that the hooks did not connect to each other

- found that the 'forks' on the front of both tractors, as well as having a 'down' position, could also be lifted into an 'up' position (above the cab)

- discovered that the tractors did not connect with the 'forks' in the 'down' position

- realised that the two tractors did connect, if the 'forks' were in the 'up' position

- worked out that two tractors could be connected via the 'hook' on the back of one tractor to the front of the other tractor

- found that the tractors could 'drive' together and stay connected

- explored the helicopter 'flying' in the 'sky', saying 'vroom, vroom'.

Throughout, Zamir tested every scenario, by 'driving' the vehicles parallel to one side of the line of other vehicles (the side nearest to him), and then 'turning' at the bottom. Zamir then leant over the line of vehicles in order to 'drive' back up the other side of the line of vehicles, up the 'ramp' and back to where he started. And, when something did not work, he went 'back to the drawing board' and continued testing until it did work the way he wanted it to...and then, Zamir...

- 'explained' all of the above to his mummy and daddy when they came to collect him.

WOW! I do so hope this reads as amazingly as it actually was to witness. It was a truly magical experience. This little boy is not yet two, only spoke the words 'Vroom, vroom', 'Ne-Ne, Ne-Ne', 'Oh, oh', 'Crash', 'Two' and 'Three' a handful of times, yet concentrated intensely throughout the 45 minutes he 'played' with the vehicles. Yes, you read that correctly, 45 minutes, and not yet two years old! And then, when Mummy and Daddy arrived, spent another ten minutes showing them exactly what all the different vehicles could (and couldn't) do.

I was absolutely mesmerised the whole time. The adult supported with offering simple language, such as 'You try' or 'Wow, look what happened', or by modelling the appropriate language, such as when matching the words to the child's pointing actions and own language, the adult supported by speaking all the numbers from one to ten. The adult only stepped in to 'help' when and if Zamir began to become frustrated or, for instance, offered the cars to the adult for help. So, for example, when the vehicles kept whooshing off the transporter, Zamir, looking puzzled, offered the transporter to the adult, and was clearly 'asking' for help. The adult only offered minimum help each time, such as pointing out that the tailgate could 'lock' in an 'up' position, or the fact that the 'forks' on the tractors lifted into an 'up' position, above the cab of the tractor. The rest of the bullet points mentioned here, this tiny little person worked out all on his own!

This interaction was a cost-free, uncomplicated, simple way to build on the relationship already established between the child and the adult, develop trust and a sharing of ideas. The interaction showed the child was listened to, and supported all areas of the child's learning, development and wellbeing. In my humble opinion, this was a stunning example of Sustained Shared Thinking at its absolute, purest, uninterrupted best. Furthermore, it was a fabulous example of 'Nurturing Personal, Social and Emotional Development in Early Childhood' and showed a true 'Understanding of Brain Development and Young Children's Behaviours'.

Reflective Action Plan for Practice (RAPP)

The following Reflective Action Plan for Practice (RAPP) is for you to record your thoughts, reflections and intended actions. The aim of the RAPP is, as throughout this book, intended as a point to aid reflection. You do not have to complete it, or indeed, you may well have in place an action plan format that you would prefer to use. My only wish is that, unlike the 'wrap' at the end of a movie (see preface), I do hope that this is 'not the end' in terms of your reflection. As Andrea and I discussed in L4Q:

> Reflection should be seen as an integral part…supporting developments, understanding and the sharing of ideas…reflect on own and others' practice and share feedback appropriately… How we translate this reflection into practice is one way in which we develop our learning potential. In other words, what we do with the 'thinking' process' or the 'reflection'. (Garvey and Lancaster 2010, p.22)

Reflection is not about getting something 'right' or 'wrong', it is about considering our thoughts and deciding on a course of action, which may or may not be different based on the reflection. As a starting point, reflecting on practice may include the following:

- Something happens, or you notice something (incident or occurrence).
- You think about what happened/is happening (reflect).
- You gather people's thoughts (consult).
- You gather more information on the subject, from possibly a range of sources (research).
- You decide what to do next (plan) and/or
- You decide what you will do next time if it happens again (plan).

- You put the knowledge, understanding, etc. you have gained from the above into practice (action).

- You notice the effect (impact/s).

- You consider if it is making a difference (even if the difference is in small, incremental steps). How do you know? (review and monitor)

- You consider the end result/consequence (outcome/s).

- You consider your learning from the experience (evaluate).

- New learning becomes part of your practice (reflexion).

There are two copies of the RAPP:

- a sample version

- a blank version.

The sample version has some thoughts and questions included that you might want to consider to get you started. The bullet points ideas in the grid are not exhaustive, they are meant as a starting point. I am sure you will be able to come up with other questions and points to consider. The blank version is for you to complete, and you may wish to complete more than one action plan, if considering different areas of practice, or different age groups of children, for example.

Finally, you may want to share these reflections with others, either in terms of support for your own reflections or to support others to reflect. Therefore, it may be useful to consider links to supervision, appraisals and team meetings, for example, and how working with others can further support reflection and development.

Reflective Action Plan for Practice (RAPP): Sample Questions

Page no:	Areas to Consider:	Reflections:	Actions:
• For reference	• Area covered in the book? • Area within the setting? • Areas of learning and development? • Age group of children? • Area to research?	• Implications for you? • Implications for colleagues/team? • Implications for organisation? • Implications for children/families? • Your thoughts? • Your comments? • Your questions? • Future CPD need? • Why are you considering this area specifically?	• What are you going to do? • Changes to practice? • What help might you need? • Who are you going to speak to? • Links to support – such as supervision, etc.? • When do you see this happening? • How will you monitor your progress? • How will you review the impact?
Impact on children/families:			

Page no:	Areas to Consider:	Reflections:	Actions:
Impact on children/families:			

Blank Reflective Action Plan for Practice (RAPP)

Page no:	Areas to Consider:	Reflections:	Actions:

Impact on children/families:

Page no:	Areas to Consider:	Reflections:	Actions:

Impact on children/families:

Page no:	Areas to Consider:	Reflections:	Actions:

Impact on children/families:

Bibliography

4Children (2015) *What to Expect When*. London: 4Children

Aiken, M. (2016) *The Cyber Effect: A Pioneering Cyberpsychologist Explains how Human Behaviour Changes Online*. London: John Murray.

Ainsworth, M.D.S. and Bell, S.M. (1970) 'Attachment, exploration, and separation: illustrated by the behaviour of one-year-olds in a strange situation.' *Journal of Child Development 41*, 49–67.

Ainsworth, M.D.S., Blehar, M.C., Waters, E. and Wall, S. (1978) *Patterns of Attachment: A Psychological Study of the Strange Situation*. Hillsdale, NJ: Erlbaum.

Ainsworth, M.I.S. and Wittig, B.A. (1969) 'Attachment and the Exploratory Behaviour of One-year-olds in a Strange Situation.' In B.M. Foss (ed.) *Determinants of Infant Behaviour*. London: Methuen.

Ainsworth, M.D.S., Blehar, M.C., Waters, E. and Wall, S. (1978) *Patterns of Attachment: A Psychological Study of The Strange Situation*. Hillsdale, NJ: Erlbaum.

Aked, J., Marks, N., Cordon, C. and Thompson, S. (2008) *Five Ways to Wellbeing*. London: New Economics Foundation.

Allen, G. (2011) *Early Intervention: The Next Steps. An Independent Report to Her Majesty's Government*. London: HM Government.

Allen, S. and Daly, K. (2007) *Father's Involvement Research Alliance: The Effects of Father Involvement: An Updated Research Summary of the Evidence*. Canada: University of Guelph.

Allingham, S. (2015) *Transitions in the Early Years: A Practical Guide to Supporting Transitions between Early Years Settings and Key-Stage One*. London: Practical Pre-School Books.

All-Party Parliamentary Group (2015) *1001 Critical Days, The Importance of Conception to Age Two Period*. London: Parent Infant Partnership PIP (UK).

Amabile, T.M. and Gitomer, J. (1984) 'Children's artistic creativity: effects of choice in task materials.' *Personality and Social Psychology Bulletin 1*, 209–215.

Ball, D., Gill, T. and Spiegel, B. (2012) *Managing Risk in Play Provision: Implementation Guide*. London: National Children's Bureau.

Banks, R. and Yi, S. (2002) *Dealing with Biting Behaviors in Young Children*. Accessed February 2017 at http://ecap.crc.illinois.edu/poptopics/biting.html.

Baranek, L.K. (1996) 'The Effect of Rewards and Motivation on Student Achievement.' *Masters Theses*. 285. Accessed February 2017 at http://scholarworks.gvsu.edu/theses/285

Barke, E., Kennedy, M., Kumsta, R., Knights, N. *et al.* (2017) 'Child-to-adult neurodevelopmental and mental health trajectories after early life deprivation: the young adult follow-up of The Longitudinal English and Romanian Adoptees Study.' *The Lancet 10*, 1016/S0140-6736(17)30045-4.

Barnett, R.C., Marshall, N.L. and Pleck, J.H. (1992a) 'Adult son-parent relationships and their associations with son's psychological distress.' *Journal of Family Issues 13*, 4, 505–525.

Barnett, R.C., Marshall, N.L. and Pleck, J.H. (1992b) 'Men's multiple roles and their relationship to men's psychological distress.' *Journal of Marriage and the Family 54*, 2, 358–367.

Barrett, P., Zhang, Y., Davies, F. and Barrett, L. (2015a) *Clever Classrooms: Summary Report of the HEAD Project. (Holistic Evidence and Design)*. Salford: University of Salford.

Barrett, P., Zhang, Y., Davies, F. and Barrett, L. (2015b) 'The impact of classroom design on pupils' learning: final results of a holistic, multi-level analysis.' *Building and Environment Journal 89*, 118–133.

BBC (2012) *Planet Earth.* London: BBC.

BBC (2016a) *Planet Earth II.* London: BBC

BBC (2016b) *Spy in the Wild.* London: BBC.

Beaver, B. (1992) *Feline Behavior: A Guide for Veterinarians.* St Louis: Mosby.

Bell, S.M. and Ainsworth, M.D.S. (1972) 'Infant crying and maternal responsiveness.' *Journal of Child Development 43*, 1171–1190.

Berlinski, S. and Schady, N. (2015) *Development in the Americas: The Early Years Child Well-Being and The Role of Public Policy.* New York: Palgrave McMillan.

Biller, H.B. (1993) *Fathers and Families: Paternal Factors in Child Development.* Westport, CT: Auborn House.

Black, P. and Wiliam, D. (2001) *Inside the Black Box: Raising Standards Through Classroom Assessment.* London: King's College, School of Education.

Blount, J.M. (2005) *Fit to Teach: Same-sex Desire, Gender and School Work in the Twentieth Century.* Albany, NY: State University of New York Press.

Bolt, L.M. (2014) 'Male-specific use of the purr in the ring-tailed lemur (Lemur catta).' *Journal Folia Primatologica 84*, 4, 201–214.

Bowlby, J. (1951) 'Maternal Care and Mental Health.' *World Health Organization Monograph.* (Serial No. 2.)

Bretherton, I. (2009) 'Origins of Attachment Theory.' In S. Goldberg, R. Muir and J. Kerr (eds) *Attachment Theory: Social, Developmental and Clinical Perspectives.* New York: Routledge.

Brodie, K. (2013) *Observation, Assessment and Planning in the Early Years: Bringing It All Together.* Maidenhead: Open University Press.

Brodie, K. (2014) *Sustained Shared Thinking in the Early Years: Linking Theory to Practice.* Abingdon: Routledge.

Brogaard Clausen, S. (2015) 'Schoolification or early years democracy? A cross-curricular perspective from Denmark and England.' *Journal of Contemporary Issues in Early Childhood 16*, 4, 355–373.

Bronfenbrenner, U. (1979) *The Ecology of Human Development.* Cambridge, MA: Harvard University Press.

Bronson, M.B. (2000) *Self-Regulation in Early Childhood, Nature and Nurture.* New York: The Guildford Press.

Broström, S. (2017) 'A dynamic learning concept in early years' education: a possible way to prevent schoolification.' *International Journal of Early Years Education 25*, 1, 3–15.

Brown, T.T. and Jernigan, T.L. (2012) 'Brain development during the preschool years.' *Journal of Neuropsychology Review 22*, 4, 313–333.

Bruer, J.T. (2000) *The Myth of the First Three Years: A New Understanding of Early Brain Development and Lifelong Learning.* New York: The Free Press.

Bryce-Clegg, A. (2015) *Continuous Provision: The Skills: Enhancing Children's Knowledge Through Skill-Based Learning.* London: Featherstone.

Buck, R. (1984) *The Communication of Emotion.* New York: Guilford.

Burgess, A. (2006) *Evidence and Insights to Inform the Development of Policy and Practice The Costs and Benefits of Active Fatherhood. A Paper Prepared by Fathers Direct to inform the DfES/HM Treasury Joint Policy Review on Children and Young People.* Marlborough: Fatherhood Institute.

Cabot, R.C. (1914) *What Men Live By.* New York: Houghton Mifflin Company.

Campbell-Barr, V. and Leeson, C. (2016) *Quality and Leadership in the Early Years: Research, Theory and Practice.* London: Sage.

Cardona, V.E. (2008) *Families' Perceptions and Practices of Parent Involvement in Early Childhood.* Wyoming: University of Wyoming.

Casey, B.J., Tottenham, N., Liston, C. and Durston, S. (2005) 'Imaging the developing brain: what have we learned about cognitive development?' *TRENDS in Cognitive Sciences, 9*, 3, 104–110.

Center on the Developing Child at Harvard University (2016) *From Best Practices to Breakthrough Impacts: A Science-Based Approach to Building a More Promising Future for Young Children and Families.* Cambridge, MA: Harvard University Press.

Cherry, K. (2017) *How Many Neurons are in the Human Brain?* Accessed March 2017 at www.verywell.com/how-many-neurons-are-in-the-brain-2794889.

Children's Food Trust (2012) *Eat Better, Start Better: Voluntary Food and Drink Guidelines for Early Years Settings in England – A Practical Guide*. Sheffield: Children's Food Trust.

Christakis, E. (2016) *The Importance of Being Little: What Preschoolers Really Need from Grownups*. New York: Viking Press.

Clapton, G. (2013) *Where's Dad? Father-Proofing Your Work*. Edinburgh: Fathers Network Scotland.

Clapton, G. (2014) *Dad Matters: Why Fathers Should Figure in Your Work*. Edinburgh: Fathers Network Scotland.

Clough, P. and Nutbrown, P. (2010) *A Student's Guide to Methodology, 2nd ed*. London: Sage.

Clutton-Brock, J. (ed.) (2015) *The Walking Larder: Patterns of Domestication, Pastoralism and Predation*. Abingdon: Routledge.

Collier, L. (2014) 'Why we cry: new research is opening eyes to the psychology of tears.' *American Psychological Association: Monitor on Psychology 45*, 2, 47. www.apa.org/monitor/2014/02/cry.aspx

Connor, J. and Wheeler, H. (2006) *Parents, Early Years and Learning: Training Guide*. London: National Children's Bureau.

Cox, M. J., Owen, M. T., Henderson, V. K. and Margand, N. (1992) 'The prediction of infant-father and infant-mother attachment.' *Journal of Developmental Psychology 28*, 474–483.

Csikszentmihalyi, M., Abuhamdeh, S. and Nakamura, J. (2007) 'Flow.' In A.J. Elliot and C.S. Dweck (eds) *Handbook of Competence and Motivation*. New York: The Guildford Press.

Dahlberg, G., Moss, P. and Pence, A. (2007) *Beyond Quality in Early Childhood Education and Care: Language of Evaluation, 2nd ed*. London: Falmer.

Darwin, C.R. (1872) *The Expression of the Emotions in Man and Animals*. London: John Murray.

Della Sala, S. and Anderson, M. (2012) *Neuroscience in Education: The Good, The Bad and The Ugly*. Oxford: Oxford University Press.

Denworth, L. (2015) 'The social power of touch.' *Scientific American Mind 26*, 30–39.

Deoni, S.C.L., Dean, D.C., Remer, J., Dirks, H. and O'Muircheartaigh, J. (2015) 'Cortical maturation and myelination in healthy toddlers and young children.' *Journal of Neuro-Image 15*, 115, 147–161.

Department for Education (DfE) (2014) *Statutory Framework for the Early Years Foundation Stage; Setting the Standards for Learning, Development and Care for Children from Birth to Five*. London: DfE.

Department for Education (DfE) (2015) *Working Together to Safeguard Children: A Guide to Inter-Agency Working to Safeguard and Promote the Welfare of Children*. London: DfE.

Department for Education (DfE) (2017) *Statutory Framework for the Early Years Foundation Stage; Setting the Standards for Learning, Development and Care for Children from Birth to Five*. London: DfE.

Department for Education (DfE) and WAVE Trust (2013) *Conception to Age 2: The Age of Opportunity*, 2nd ed. (Addendum to the Government's vision for the Foundation Years: 'Supporting Families in the Foundation Years'.) Surrey: Wave Trust Surrey.

Dewey, J. (1953) *How We Think*. Boston, MA: Heath and Co.

Ditzen, B., Schaer, M., Gabriel, B., Bodenmann, G., Ehlert, U. and Heinrichs, M. (2009) 'Intranasal oxytocin increases positive communication and reduces cortisol levels during couple conflict.' *Journal of Biological Psychiatry 65*, 9, 728–731.

Dodds, S. (2016) *Health and Early Years, Children and Young People: A GCPH Synthesis*. Glasgow: Glasgow Centre for Population Health (GCPH).

Donaldson, M. (1992) *Human Minds: An Exploration*. London: Allen Lane/Penguin Books.

Downer, J., Campos, R., McWayne, C. and Gartner, T. (2008) 'father involvement and children's early learning: a critical review of published empirical work from the past 15 years.' *Journal of Marriage and Family Review 43*, 1, 67–108.

Duffy, B. (2014) 'The Early Years Curriculum.' In G. Pugh and B. Duffy (eds) *Contemporary Issues in the Early Years*, 6th ed. London: Sage.

Dunsworth, H.M and Eccleston, L. (2015) 'The evolution of difficult childbirth and helpless hominin infants.' *Annual Review of Anthropology 44*, 55–69.

Early Education (2012) *Development Matters in the EYFS*. London: Early Education.

Edwards, S. (2013) 'Digital play in the early years: a contextual response to the problem of integrating technologies and play-based pedagogies in the early childhood curriculum.' *European Early Childhood Education Research Journal 21*, 2, 199–212.

Eggebean, D.J. and Knoester, C. (2001) 'Does fatherhood matter for men?' *Journal of Marriage and the Family 63*, 2, 381–393.

Eisenberg, N., Cumberland, A. and Spinrad, T.L. (1998) 'Parental socialization of emotion.' *Journal of Psychological Inquiry 9*, 4, 241–273.

Eisenberg, N., Smith, C.L. and Spinrad, T.L. (2016) 'Effortful Control: Relations with Emotion Regulation, Adjustment, and Socialization in Childhood.' In K.D. Vohs and R.F. Baumeister (eds) *Handbook of Self-Regulation: Research, Theory and Applications,* 3rd ed. New York: The Guildford Press.

Elfer, P. (2014) 'Facilitating Intimate and Thoughtful attention to Infants and Toddlers in Nursery.' In L. Harrison and J. Sumsion (eds) *Lived Spaces of Infant-Toddler Education and Care: Exploring Diverse Perspectives of Theory, Research, Practice and Policy.* (International Perspectives on Early Childhood Education and Development Series.) New York: Springer.

Elfer, P., Goldschmied, E. and Selleck, D.Y. (2012) *Key Persons in the Early Years: Building Relationships for Quality Provision in Early Years Settings and Primary Schools,* 2nd ed. Abingdon: Routledge.

Farb, N.A.S., Segal, Z.V., Mayberg, H., Bean, J., McKeon, D., Fatima, Z. and Anderson, A.K. (2007) 'Attending to the present: mindfulness meditation reveals distinct neural modes of self-reference.' *Journal of Social Cognitive and Affective Neuroscience 2,* 4, 313–322.

Farquhar, S.E., Cabik, L., Buckingham, A., Butler, D. and Ballantyne, R. (2006) *Men at Work: Sexism in Early Childhood Education.* Porirua, New Zealand: Child Forum Research Network.

Fatherhood Institute (2007) *The Difference a Dad Makes.* Abergavenny: Fatherhood Institute.

Felitti, V.J., Anda, R.F., Nordenberg, D., Williamson, D.F. *et al.* (1998) 'Relationship of childhood abuse and household dysfunction to many of the leading causes of death in adults: The Adverse Childhood Experiences (ACE) Study.' *American Journal of Preventive Medicine 14*, 4, 245–258.

Fifield, S. and Swain, H.L. (2002) 'Heteronormativity and Common Sense in Science (Teacher) Education.' In R.M. Kisson (ed.) *Getting Ready for Benjamin: Preparing Teachers for Sexual Diversity in the Classroom.* Lanham, MD: Rowman and Littlefield.

Fischer, K., Daniel, D.B., Immordino-Yang, M.E., Stern, E., Battro, A. and Koizumi, H. (2007) 'Why mind, brain, and education? Why now?' *Journal of Mind, Brain, and Education 1*, 1–2.

Fisher, A.V., Godwin, K.E. and Seltman, H. (2014) 'Visual environment, attention allocation, and learning in young children: when too much of a good thing may be bad.' *Journal of Psychological Science 25*, 7, 1362–1370.

Forman, G. and Fyfe, B. (1998) 'Negotiated Learning through Design, Documentation and Discourse.' In C. Edwards, L. Gandini and G. Forman (eds) *The Hundred Languages of Children: The Reggio Emilia Experience in Transformation,* 3rd ed. California: Praeger.

Fredrickson, B.L. (2003) 'The value of positive emotions: the emerging science of positive psychology is coming to understand why it's good to feel good.' *American Scientist 91*, 4, 330–335.

Fredrickson, B.L. and Joiner, T. (2002) 'Positive emotions trigger upward spirals toward emotional well-being.' *Journal of Psychological Science 13*, 2, 172–175.

Fuster, J.M. (2002) 'Frontal lobe and cognitive development.' *Journal of Neurocytology 31*, 373–385.

Gagné, R.M. (1985) *The Conditions of Learning.* New York: Holt, Rinehart and Winston.

Garrard, J., Leland, N. and Smith, D. K. (1988) 'Epidemiology of human bites to children in a day-care centre.' *American Journal of Diseases in Children 142*, 6, 643–650.

Garvey, D. (2017) *Performance Management in Early Years Settings: A Practical Guide for Leaders and Managers.* London: Jessica Kingsley Publishers.

Garvey, D. and Lancaster, A. (2010) *Leadership for Quality in Early Years and Playwork: Supporting Your Team to Achieve Better Outcomes for Children and Families.* London: National Children's Bureau.

Gazzaniga, M.S and Mangun, G.R. (eds) (2014) *The Cognitive Neurosciences,* 5th ed. Cambridge, MA: MIT Press.

Gerhardt, S. (2015) *Why Love Matters,* 2nd ed. London: Routledge.

Giedd, J.N., Raznahan, A., Alexander-Bloch, A., Schmitt, E., Gogtay, N. and Rapoport, J.L. (2015) 'Child Psychiatry Branch of the National Institute of Mental Health Longitudinal Structural Magnetic Resonance Imaging Study of Human Brain Development.' *Journal of Neuropsychopharmacology 40*, 1, 43–49.

Gneezy, U., Meier, S. and Rey-Biel, P. (2011) 'When and why incentives (don't) work to modify behavior.' *Journal of Economic Perspectives 25*, 4, 191–210.

Goksan, S., Hartley, C., Emery, F., Cockrill, N. *et al.* (2015) 'fMRI reveals neural activity overlap between adult and infant pain.' *eLife Science Publications.*

Goleman, D. (1996) *Emotional Intelligence: Why it Can Matter More Than IQ.* London: Bloomsbury.

Gopnik, A., Meltzoff, A.N. and Kohl, P.K. (1999) *How Babies Think: The Science of Childhood*. London: Phoenix.

Goswami, U. (2006) 'Neuroscience and education: from research to practice?' *Journal of Nature Review Neuroscience 7*, 5, 406–411.

Gottman, J.M., Katz. L.F. and Hooven, C. (1996) 'Parental meta-emotion philosophy and the emotional life of families: theoretical models and preliminary data.' *Journal of Family Psychology 10*, 3, 243–268.

Gove, W.R. and Mongione, T.W. (1983) 'Social roles, sex roles and psychological distress: additive and interactive models of sex differences.' *Journal of Health and Social Behavior 24*, 4, 300–312.

Gross, J.J. and Levenson, R.W. (1997) 'Hiding feelings: the acute effects of inhibiting negative and positive emotion.' *Journal of Abnormal Psychology 106*, 1, 95–103.

Heath, D.H. (1994) 'The impact of delayed fatherhood on the father-child relationship.' *Journal of Genetic Psychology 155*, 4, 511–530.

HMSO (2010) *The Foundation Years: Preventing Poor Children Becoming Poor Adults: The Report of The Independent Review on Poverty and Life Chances* (The Field Report). London: HMSO.

HMSO (2011) *Early Intervention: The Next Steps* (The Allen Report). London: HMSO.

Hooven, C., Gottman, J.M. and Katz, L.F. (1995) 'Parental meta-emotion structure predicts family and child outcomes.' *Journal of Cognition and Emotion 9*, 2–3, 229–264.

Howard-Jones, P.A. (2014) *Neuroscience and Education: A Review of Educational Interventions and Approaches Informed by Neuroscience*. London: Education Endowment Foundation.

Howard-Jones, P.A. (2014) 'Neuroscience and education: myths and messages'. *Nature Review of Neuroscience 15*, 12, 817–824.

Howes, C. and Spieker, S. (2008) 'Attachment Relationships in the Context of Multiple Caregivers.' In J. Cassidy and P. Shaver (eds) *Handbook of Attachment Theory, Research and Clinical Application*, 2nd ed. London: Guildford Press.

Jack, R.E., Garrod, O.G.B and Schyns, P.G. (2014) 'Dynamic facial expressions of emotion transmit an evolving hierarchy of signals over time.' *Journal of Current Biology, 24*, 2, 187–192.

Jensen, A., Broström, S. and Hansen, O. (2010) 'Critical perspectives on Danish Early Education and Care – between the technical and the political.' *Journal of Early Years 30*, 3, 243–254.

Kabat-Zinn J. (1994) *Wherever You Go There You Are: Mindfulness Meditation in Everyday Life*. New York: Hyperion.

Kaplan, L., Evans, L. and Monk, C. (2008) 'Effects of mothers' prenatal psychiatric status and post-natal caregiving on infant biobehavioural regulation: can prenatal programming be modified?' *Early Human Development 83*, 4, 249–256.

Katz, L.G. and Chard, S.C. (2000) *Engaging Children's Minds: The Project Approach*, 2nd ed. Stamford: Ablex Publishing Cooperation.

Keng, S.L., Smoski, M.J., Clive, J. and Robins, C.J. (2011) 'Effects of mindfulness on psychological health: a review of empirical studies.' *Journal of Clinical Psychology Review 31*, 6, 1041–1056.

Kerridge, T. (2017) *Dopamine Diet: My Low-Carb, Stay-Happy Way to Lose Weight*. London: Bloomsbury.

King, J.R. (1998) *Uncommon Caring: Learning from Men Who Teach Young Children*. New York: Teachers College Press.

King, K.M., Lengua, L.J. and Monahan, K.C. (2013) 'Individual differences in the development of self-regulation during pre-adolescence: connections to context and adjustment.' *Journal of Abnormal Child Psychology 41*, 1, 57–69.

Knudson, R.S. (1979) 'Humanagogy anyone?' *Journal of Adult Education 29*, 4, 261–264.

Kochanska, G., Murray, K.T. and Harlan, E.T. (2000) Effortful Control in Early Childhood: Continuity and Change, Antecedents, and Implications for Social Development. *Journal of Developmental Psychology, 36*, 2, 220–232.

Kohn, A. (1993) 'Choices for children: why and how to let students decide.' *Journal of Phi Delta Kappan International 75*, 9–18.

Kopp, C.B. (1989) 'Regulation of distress and negative emotions: a developmental review.' *Journal of Developmental Psychology 75*, 2, 343–354.

Korb, A. (2015) *The Upward Spiral: Using Neuroscience to Reverse the Course of Depression, One Small Change at a Time*. Oakland, CA: New Harbinger Publications, Inc.

Kotelchuck, M. (1976) 'The Infant's Relationship to The Father: Experimental Evidence.' In M.E. Lamb (ed.) *The Role of The Father in Child Development*. New York: Wiley.

Laevers, F., Daems, M., De Bruyckere, G., Declercq, B. *et al.* (2005) *Well-Being and Involvement in Care: A Process-Oriented Self-Evaluation Instrument for Care Settings (SICS)Manual.* Flanders: Research Centre for Experiential Education, Leuven University.

Lamb, M.E. and Malkin, C.M. (1986) 'The development of social expectations in distress-relief sequences: a longitudinal study.' *International Journal of Behavioral Development 9,* 235–249.

Landau, W.M. (1988) 'Clinical Neuromythology i: The Marcus Gunn Phenomenon.' *Journal of Neurology 38,* 7, 1141–1142.

Lazar, S.W., Kerr, C.E., Wasserman, R.H., Gray, J.R. *et al.* (2005) 'Meditation experience is associated with increased cortical thickness.' *Neuroreport 16,* 17, 1893–1897.

LeDoux, J.E. (1996) *The Emotional Brain.* New York: Simon and Schuster.

LeDoux, J.E. (2002) *Synaptic Self: How Our Brains Become Who We Are.* New York: Viking.

LeDoux, J.E. (2005) 'Contributions of the amygdala to emotion processing: from animal models to human behavior.' *Neuron Journal 48,* 2, 175–187.

Lenroot, R.K. and Giedd, J.N. (2006) 'Brain development in children and adolescents: insights from anatomical magnetic resonance imaging.' *Neuroscience and Biobehavioral Reviews 30,* 718–729.

Leyhausen. P. (1979) *Cat Behavior: The Predatory and Social Behavior of Domestic and Wild Cats.* New York: STPM Garland Press.

Lieberman, M., Doyle, A. and Markiewicz, D. (1999) 'Developmental patterns in security of attachment to mother and father in late childhood and early adolescence: associations with peer relations.' *Journal of Child Development 70,* 1, 202–213.

Lindon, J. (2011) *Too Safe for Their Own Good? Helping Children Learn About Risk and Life Skills.* London: National Children's Bureau.

Lindsey, E.W., Moffett, D., Clawson, M. and Mize, J. (1994, April) *Father-Child Play and Children's Competence.* Paper presented at the biennial meeting of the Southwestern Society for Research in Human Development, Austin, TX.

Macdonald, K. and Parke, R.D. (1984) 'Bridging the gap: parent-child play interaction and peer interactive competence.' *Journal of Child Development 55,* 4, 1265–1277.

Magon, N. and Kalra, S. (2011) 'The orgasmic history of oxytocin: love, lust, and labor.' *Indian Journal of Endocrinology and Metabolism 15,* Suppl.3, 156–161.

Malaguzzi, L. (2007) *The One Hundred Languages of Children.* London: Nursery World.

Manning-Morton, J. (2006) 'The personal is professional: professionalism and the birth to threes practitioner.' *Journal of Contemporary Issues in Early Childhood 7,* 1, 42–52.

Martorana, A. and Koch, G. (2014) 'Is dopamine involved in Alzheimer's Disease?' *Frontiers in Aging Neuroscience 6,* 252, 1–6.

Mate, G. (2013) *In the Realm of Hungry Ghosts: Close Encounters with Addiction.* Canada: Random House.

McComb, K., Taylor, A.M., Wilson, C. and Charlton, B.D. (2009) 'The cry embedded within the purr.' *Journal of Current Biology 19,* 13, 507–508.

Mehrabian, A. (1981) *Silent Messages: Implicit Communication of Emotions and Attitudes.* Belmont, CA: Wadsworth.

Mischel, W., Shoda, Y. and Peake, P.K. (1988) 'The nature of adolescent competencies predicted by preschool delay of gratification.' *Journal of Personality and Social Psychology 54,* 4, 687–696.

Mooney, C. (2000) *Theories of Childhood: An Introduction to Dewey, Montessori, Erikson, Piaget and Vygotsky.* St Paul, MN: Redleaf Press.

Najafi, M., Kinnison, J. and Pessoa, L. (2017) 'Intersubject brain network organization during dynamic anxious anticipation.' *bioRxiv*, p.120451.

Nutbrown, C. (2012) *Foundations for Quality: The Independent Review of Early Education and Childcare Qualifications, Final Report* (The Nutbrown Review). London: Department of Education.

Nutt, D. J., Lingford-Hughes, A., Erritzoe, D. and Stokes, P. (2015) 'The dopamine theory of addiction: 40 years of highs and lows.' *Journal of Nature Reviews Neuroscience 16,* 5, 305–312.

Oberlander, T., Weinberg, J., Papsdorf, M., Grunau, R., Misri, S. and Devlin, A. (2008) 'Prenatal exposure to maternal depression, neonatal methylation of human glucocorticoid receptor gene and infant cortisol stress responses.' *Journal of Epigenetics, 3,* 2, 97–106.

OECD (Organisation for Economic Co-operation and Development) (2002) *Understanding the Brain: Towards a New Learning Science.* Paris: OECD Publishing.

Ofsted (2005) *Early Doors: Experiences for Children in Day Care During the First Hour of the Day.* London: Ofsted.

Ofsted (2006) *The Logical Chain: Continuing Professional Development in Effective Schools.* London: HMI.

Ofsted (2008) *Early Years: Leading to Excellence.* London: Ofsted.

Ofsted (2015a) *Teaching and Play in the Early Years – A Balancing Act?* London: Ofsted.

Ofsted (2015b) *Early Years Inspection Handbook.* London: Ofsted.

Ofsted (2016) *Inspecting Safeguarding in Early Years, Education and Skills Settings.* London: Ofsted

Opondo, C., Redshaw, M., Savage-McGlynn, E. and Quigley, M.A. (2016) 'Father involvement in early child-rearing and behavioural outcomes in their pre-adolescent children: evidence from the ALSPAC UK birth cohort.' *British Medical Journal (Open) 6,* 11 .

Organisation for Economic Cooperation and Development (OECD) (2006) *Starting Strong II – Early Childhood Education and Care.* Paris: OECD Publications.

Ozer, E.M., Barnett, R.C., Brennan R.T. and Sperling, J. (1998) 'Does child care involvement increase or decrease distress among dual-earner couples?' *Journal of Women's Health 4,* 4, 285–311.

Page, J., Clare, A. and Nutbrown, C. (2013) *Working with Babies and Children from Birth to Three,* 2nd ed. London: Sage.

Page, J. (2015a) 'The Legacy of John Bowlby's Attachment Theory.' In T. David, K. Goouch and S. Powell (eds) *The Routledge International Handbook of Philosophies and Theories of Early Childhood, Education and Care.* Abingdon: Routledge.

Page, J. (2016) 'Educators' Perspectives on Attachment and Professional Love in Early Years Settings in England.' In E.J. White and C. Dalli (eds) *Under Three-Year-Olds in Policy and Practice. Policy and Pedagogy with Under Three-Year-Olds: Cross-disciplinary Insights and Innovations for Educational Research with Very Young Children* Series. London/New York: Springer.

Palmer, S. (2016) *Upstart: The Case for Raising the School Starting Age and Providing What the Under Sevens Really Need.* Edinburgh: Floris Books.

Paredes, M.F., James, D., Gil-Perotin, S., Kim, H. *et al.* (2016) 'Extensive migration of young neurons into the infant human frontal lobe.' *Science 354,* 6308, p.aaf7073.

Park, H.J and Friston, K. *(2013)* 'Structural and functional brain networks: from connections to cognition.' *Science 342,* 6158, 579–587.

Parke, R., and Swain, D. (1975, April) *Infant Characteristics and Behavior as Elicitors of Maternal and Paternal Responsiveness in the Newborn Period.* Paper presented at the meeting of the Society for Research in Child Development, Denver, CO.

Pascal, C. and Bertram, T. (2016) *High Achieving White Working Class (HAWWC) Boys Project: Final Report.* Birmingham: Centre for Research in Early Childhood.

Penn, H. (2014) *Understanding Early Childhood: Issues and Controversies,* 3rd ed. Maidenhead: Open University Press.

Perez-de-Castro, I., Ibanez. A., Torres. P., Sais-Ruiz. J. and Fernandez-Piqueras, J. (1997) 'Genetic association between pathological gambling and a functional DNA polymorphism at the D4 receptor gene.' *Journal of Pharmacogenetics 7,* 3, 45–48.

Peters, G. (2002) 'Purring and similar vocalizations in mammals.' *Journal of Mammal Review 32,* 245–271.

Pleck, J.H. (1997) 'Paternal Involvement: Levels, Sources, and Consequences.' In M.E. Lamb (ed.) *The Role of The Father in Child Development,* 3rd ed. New York: John Wiley and Sons, Inc.

Poehlmann, J., Schwichtenberg, A. M., Shah, P. E., Shlafer, R. J., Hahn, E., and Maleck, S. (2010) 'The Development of Effortful Control in Children Born Preterm.' *Journal of Clinical Child and Adolescent Psychology 53,* 39, 4, 522–536.

Pruett, K.D. (1997) 'How men and children affect each other's development.' *Zero to Three Journal 18,* 1, 3–11.

Purdy, N. (2008) 'Neuroscience and education: how best to filter out the neurononsense from our classrooms?' *Journal of Irish Educational Studies 27,* 3, 197–208.

Purves, D., Augustine, G.J., Fitzpatrick, D., Hall, W.C. *et al.* (2007) *Neuroscience,* 4th ed. Sunderland, MA: Sinauer Associates, Inc.

Rajmohan, V. and Mohandas, E. (2007) 'The limbic system.' *Indian Journal of Psychiatry 49,* 2, 132–139.

Rakic, P. (2009) 'Evolution of the neocortex: perspective from developmental biology.' *Journal of Nature Reviews Neuroscience 10,* 10, 724–735.

Read, V. (2009) *Developing Attachment in Early Years Settings: Nurturing Secure Relationships from Birth to Five Years.* Abingdon: Routledge.

Reggente, M.A.L., Alves, F., Nicolau, C., Freitas, L. *et al.* (2016) 'Nurturant behavior toward dead conspecifics in free-ranging mammals: new records for odontocetes and a general review.' *Journal of Mammalogy 97*, 5, 1428–1434.

Rosenberg, K. and Trevathan, W.R. (2002) 'Birth, obstetrics, and human evolution.' *BJOG: An International Journal of Obstetrics and Gynaecology 109*, 11, 1199–1206.

Rutherford, E.E. and Mussen P.H. (1968) 'Generosity in nursery school boys.' *Journal of Child Development 39*, 3, 755–765.

Rutter, M. (1972) *Maternal Deprivation Reassessed.* Harmondsworth: Penguin.

Rutter, M., Beckett, C., Castle, J., Colvert, E. *et al.* (2007) 'Effects of profound early institutional deprivation: an overview of findings from a UK longitudinal study of Romanian adoptees.' *European Journal of Developmental Psychology 4*, 3, 332–350.

Ryan, R.M. and Grolnick, W.S. (1986) 'Origins and pawns in the classroom: self-report and projective assessments of individual differences in children's perceptions.' *Journal of Personality and Social Psychology 50*, 550–558.

Sagvolden, T., Johansen, E.B., Aase, H. and Russell, V.A. (2005) 'A dynamic developmental theory of Attention-Deficit/Hyperactivity Disorder (ADHD) predominantly hyperactive/impulsive and combined subtypes.' *Journal of Behavioral Brain Science 28*, 3, 397–419.

Schaffer, H.R. and Emerson, P.E. (1964) 'The development of social attachments in infancy.' *Monographs of the Society for Research in Child Development*, 1–77.

Schmidt, J. (1999) *Overcoming Challenges.* Unpublished Doctoral Dissertation. Chicago: University of Chicago.

Schore, A.N. (2016) *Affect Regulation and the Origin of the Self: The Neurobiology of Emotional Development.* New York: Routledge.

Schore, J. and Schore, A. (2008) 'Modern Attachment Theory: the central role of affect regulation in development and treatment.' *Clinical Social Work Journal 36*, 1, 9–20.

Schultz, A. (1949) 'Sex differences in the pelves of primates.' *American Journal of Physical Anthropology 7*, 3, 401–424.

Schultz, W. (2007) 'Multiple dopamine functions at different time courses.' *Annual Review of Neuroscience 30*, 1, 259–288.

Shaver, P., Schwartz, J., Kirson, D. and O'Connor, C. (2001) 'Emotional Knowledge: Further Exploration of a Prototype Approach.' In G. Parrott (ed.) *Emotions in Social Psychology: Essential Readings.* New York: Psychology Press.

Sheese, B.E., Rothbart, M.K., Posner, M.I., White, L.K. and Fraundorf, S.H. (2008) 'Executive attention and self-regulation in infancy.' *Journal of Infant Behavior and Development 31*, 501–510.

Shen, H. (2015) 'Neuroscience: the hard science of oxytocin.' *Journal of Nature 522*, 410–412.

Shonkoff, J.P. and Phillips, D.A. (eds) (2000) *From Neurons to Neighborhoods: The Science of Early Childhood Development.* Washington, DC: National Academy Press.

Simons, L.E., Moulton, E.A., Linnman, C., Carpino, E., Becerra, L. and Borsook, D. (2014) 'The human amygdala and pain: evidence from neuroimaging.' *Human Brain Mapping 35*, 527–538.

Siraj-Blatchford, I., Sylva, K., Muttock, S., Gilden, R. and Bell, D. (2002) *Researching Effective Pedagogy in the Early Years.* London: Department for Education and Skills.

Snaidero, N. and Simons, M. (2014) 'Myelination at a glance.' *Journal of Cell Science 127*, 2999–3004.

Snarey, J. (1993) *How Fathers Care for The Next Generation: A Four-Decade Study.* Cambridge, MA: Harvard University Press.

Solter, A.J. (2001) *The Aware Baby.* Goleta, CA: Aware Parenting Institute.

Spinrad, T.L., Stifter, C.A., Donelan-McCall, N. and Turner, L. (2004) 'Mothers' regulation strategies in response to toddlers' affect: links to later emotion self-regulation.' *Journal of Social Development 13*, 1, 40–55.

Stiasny, K., Robbecke, J., Schuler, P. and Oertel, W.H. (2000) 'Treatment of idiopathic restless legs syndrome (RLS) with the D2-agonist cabergoline – an open clinical trial.' *Sleep: Official Publication of the Sleep Research Society 23*, 3, 49–54.

Striedter, G.S. (2006) 'Précis of principles of brain evolution.' *Journal of Behavioral and Brain Sciences 29*, 1, 1–36.

Sylva, K., Sammons, P., Melhuish, E., Siraj-Blatchford, I., Taggart, B., Hunt, S. and Jelicic, H. (2004) *Effective Pre-School and Primary Education 3-11 Project (EPPE 3-11): Influences on Children's Cognitive and Social Development in Year 6.* Nottingham: DCSF.

Taylor, M. (1999) *Imaginary Companions and the Children Who Create Them*. New York: Oxford University Press.

Trevarthen, C. and Panksepp, J. (2016) 'In Tune with Feeling: Musical Play with Emotions of Creativity, Inspiring Neuroaffective Development and Self-Confidence for Learning in Company.' In S. Hart (ed.) *Inclusion, Play and Empathy: Neuroaffective Development in Children's Groups*. London: Jessica Kingsley Publishers.

Valiente, C., Lemery-Chalfant, K. and Reiser, M. (2007) 'Pathways to problem behaviours: chaotic homes, parent and child effortful control and parenting.' *Journal of Social Development 16*, 2, 249–267.

Venterand, C. and Harris, G. (2009) 'The development of childhood dietary preferences and their implications for later adult health.' *Nutrition Bulletin Journal 34*, 4, 391–394.

Waldinger, R.J and Schulz, M.S. (2016) 'The long reach of nurturing family environments: links with midlife emotion-regulatory styles and late-life security in intimate relationships.' *Journal of Psychological Science*.

Warin, C. (2013) *How to Improve and Maintain your Mental Wellbeing*. London: MIND. Accessed on 31 July at https://mind.org.uk/information-support/tips-for-everyday-living/wellbeing/#. WX8jLTVK02o

Weems, L. (1999) 'Pestalozzi, Perversity and the Pedagogy of Love.' In W.J. Letts and J.T. Sears (eds) *Queering Elementary Education: Advancing the Dialogue about Sexualities and Schooling*. Lanham, MD: Rowman and Littlefield.

Wells, J.C.K., Desilva, J.M. and Stock, J.T. (2012) 'The obstetric dilemma: an ancient game of Russian Roulette, or a variable dilemma sensitive to ecology?' *Yearbook of Physical Anthropology 149*, 55, 40–71.

Westbrook, J., Durrani, N., Brown, R., Orr, *et al.* (2013) *Pedagogy, Curriculum, Teaching Practices and Teacher Education in Developing Countries. Final Report. Education Rigorous Literature Review*. London: Department for International Development.

Wheeler, H. and Connor, J. (2006) *Parents, Early Years and Learning: Reader*. London: National Children's Bureau.

White, J. (2013) *Playing and Learning Outdoors: Making Provision for High Quality Experiences in the Outdoor Environment with Children 3–7*. Abingdon: Routledge.

Wiking, M. (2016) *The Little Book of Hygge: The Danish Way to Live Well*. London: Penguin Life.

Wing, L. (1981) 'Asperger's Syndrome: a clinical account.' *Journal of Psychological Medicine 11*, 1, 115–129.

Wood, D., Bruner, J. and Ross, G. (1976) 'The role of tutoring in problem solving.' *Journal of Child Psychology and Child Psychiatry 17*, 89–100.

Youngblade, L.M. and Belsky, J. (1992) 'Parent-child antecedents of 5-year-olds close friendships: a longitudinal analysis.' *Journal of Developmental Psychology 28*, 4, 700–713.

Zeedyk, S. (2013) *Sabre Tooth Tigers and Teddy Bears: The Connected Baby Guide to Understanding Attachment*. Dundee: Suzanne Zeedyk Ltd.

Zero to Three and the Bezos Family Foundation (2016) *Tuning In: Parents of Young Children Tell Us What They Think, Know and Need*. Washington: Zero to Three.

Websites and Web-Based Documents

The following are some websites, or organisations and individuals, as well as web-based documents that I have found useful, and some are mentioned in the book. (All last accessed March 2017.)

Aces Too High: A news and information website covering a wealth of research and information, across a range of fields and disciplines, looking at Adverse Childhood Experiences (ACEs). https://acestoohigh.com/aces-101

Albrecht, K. *What's Play Got to Do With It? Understanding and Encouraging Toddler Play*. (undated) www.communityplaythings.co.uk/learning-library/articles/whats-play-got-to-do-with-it#

Allan Schore. www.allanschore.com see also www.youtube.com

Andy Man Club: Any man who is going through a storm, been through a storm or just wants to come along and meet a good group of people with the aim of improving one another. http://andysmanclub.co.uk

The Baby Room: Researching principles, policies and practices of early childhood education and care for babies and very young children in group-care settings in the United Kingdom and internationally. http://canterbury.ac.uk/education/our-work/research-knowledge-exchange/research-centre-for-children-families-communities/baby-room/baby-room.aspx

Backlund Wasling, H. (2014) *Fight Off Loneliness with Touch*. TEDx. www.youtube.com/watch?v=omIWt3xq648

Barker, E. (2015) *A Neuroscience Researcher Reveals 4 Rituals That Will Make You Happier.* www.businessinsider.com/a-neuroscience-researcher-reveals-4-rituals-that-will-make-you-a-happier-person-2015-9?IR=T

Barnardo's Policy, Research and Publications Unit. www.barnardos.org.uk/what_we_do/policy_research_unit/research_and_publications.htm?pub_subject=andpub_type=andpub_phrase=Resilienceandsubmit=Search

Bailey, D., Duncan, G. and Odgers, C. (2017) *Preschool Can Provide a Boost, But the Gains Can Fade Surprisingly Fast: What Children Typically Learn Are Skills They Would Pick Up Anyway.* www.washingtonpost.com/posteverything/wp/2017/02/17/preschool-can-provide-a-boost-but-the-gains-can-fade-surprisingly-fast/?utm_term=.4aaeeda76cea

Bains, R. (2017) *Shattering Stereotypes: Breaking Barriers: How Rugby League Is Embracing Mental Health.* https://sports.vice.com/en_uk/article/shattering-stereotypes-breaking-barriers-how-rugby-league-is-embracing-mental-health

BBC (2016) *Clumsy Teenage Boys 'Can Blame Brain'.* www.bbc.co.uk/news/health-36327280

Beddoe, L. (2017) *Brains, Biology, and Tests for Future 'Burdenhood' – Misguided Blind Faith in Science?* www.reimaginingsocialwork.nz/2017/01/brains-biology-and-tests-for-future-burdenhood-misguided-blind-faith-in-science

Bergland, C. (2016) *Harvard Research Shows How the Cerebellum Regulates Thoughts: The Cerebellum is Responsible For Monitoring Both Motor and Non-Motor Functions.* www.psychologytoday.com/blog/the-athletes-way/201605/harvard-research-shows-how-the-cerebellum-regulates-thoughts

The Brain from Top to Bottom (n.d.) A wealth of information, anything and everything to do with brain development. http://thebrain.mcgill.ca/index.php

The Brain from Top to Bottom (2012) *History Module: The Triune Brain/Limbic System Model – What to Keep, What to Discard.* http://thebrain.mcgill.ca/flash/capsules/histoire_bleu09.html. (See also www.blog-thebrain.org/beginner/2012/10/29/dusting-off-the-triune-brain-and-the-limbic-system)

Briggs, H. (2016) *Watching Films Releases 'Natural Painkiller'.* www.bbc.co.uk/news/science-environment-37418551

Brill, A. (2016) *Why Choosing Positive Guidance over Punishment Helps Reduce Attention Seeking and Other Unhelpful Behaviors.* www.positiveparentingconnection.net/why-choosing-positive-guidance-over-punishment-helps-reduce-attention-seeking-and-other-unhelpful-behaviors/?utm_content=bufferbff3aandutm_medium=socialandutm_source=twitter.comandutm_campaign=buffer

Brodie, K. (2009a) *Sustained Shared Thinking: How Important is it?* www.kathybrodie.com/viewpoint/sustained-shared-thinking-important

Brodie, K. (2009b) *Lost Boy: What Would You Do?* www.kathybrodie.com/viewpoint/lost-boy-what-would-you-do

Brodie, K. (2015) *The World of the Newborn.* www.kathybrodie.com/articles/newborn

Brodie, K. (2017) *Many Faces of Anxiety.* www.kathybrodie.com/guest-post/many-faces-anxiety

Brody, J.E. (1982) *Biological Role of Emotional Tears Emerges Through Recent Studies.* www.nytimes.com/1982/08/31/science/biological-role-of-emotional-tears-emerges-through-recent-studies.html

Campaign to End Loneliness: The Campaign to End Loneliness inspires thousands of organisations and people to do more to tackle the health threat of loneliness in older age. The Campaign to End Loneliness is a network of national, regional and local organisations and people working together through community action, good practice, research and policy to ensure that loneliness is acted upon as a public health priority at national and local levels. www.campaigntoendloneliness.org/loneliness-research

Children Act 1989, 2004, and all other UK legislation. www.legislation.gov.uk

Clothier, S. and Poppe, J. (2004) National Conference of State Legislatures. *New Research: Early Education as Economic Investment.* www.ncsl.org/research/human-services/new-research-early-education-as-economic-investme.aspx

Cook, P.F., Prichard, A., Spivak, M. and Berns, G.S (2016) *Awake Canine fMRI Predicts Dogs' Preference for Praise Versus Food.* http://biorxiv.org/content/biorxiv/early/2016/07/07/062703.full.pdf. Also at: http://mrcvs.co.uk/en/news/14843/Dogs-prefer-praise-over-treats,-study-finds

Coughlan, S. (2017) *Schools Should Teach Pupils How to Spot 'Fake News'.* www.bbc.co.uk/news/education-39272841

DANA Foundation (n.d.) Private philanthropic organisation that supports brain research through grants, publications, and educational programmes. http://dana.org/About

Dads Rock (2017): Exist to help all dads be the best they can, to spend time with their children, have a fun, positive and rocking experience! Dads and their children get invaluable 1:1 time, have the chance to make new friends and chat about what it means to be dad! www.dadsrock.org.uk

Davis, J. (2015) *The Opposite of Addiction is Connection.* http://upliftconnect.com/opposite-addiction-connection

Department for Children, Schools and Families (DCSF) (2008) *SEAD (Social and Emotional Aspects of Development): Guidance for Practitioners Working in the Foundation Stage.* Nottingham: DCSF Publications. www.foundationyears.org.uk/wp-content/uploads/2011/10/SEAD_Guidance_For_Practioners.pdf

Dickens, M. and Williams, L. (2017) *Listening as a Way of Life: Listening to Young Disabled Children.* London: NCB. www.ncb.org.uk/sites/default/files/field/attachment/Listening%20to%20Young%20Disabled%20Children.pdf

Education Endowment Foundation (2015) *Self-regulation Toolkit.* https://educationendowmentfoundation.org.uk/resources/early-years-toolkit/self-regulation-strategies

Fisher, J. (2012) *Personal Transition Curve.* www.businessballs.com/personalchangeprocess.htm

Furnivall, J. (20170 *Choosing to Love.* www.celcis.org/knowledge-bank/search-bank/blog/2017/03/loving-unlovable-child

Gallagher, J. (2017) *Prize for Cracking Brain's 'Feel Good' System.* www.bbc.co.uk/news/health-39183178

Geddes, L. (2015) *Why Your Brain Needs Touch to Make You Human.* www.newscientist.com/article/mg22530100-500-why-your-brain-needs-touch-to-make-you-human

Geddes, L. (2017) *Premature Babies Brains Respond Differently to Gentle Touching.* www-newscientist-com.cdn.ampproject.org/c/s/www.newscientist.com/article/2124885-premature-babies-brains-respond-differently-to-gentle-touching/amp

Goleman, D. (2016) *Emotional Intelligence: How Competent Are You?* www.linkedin.com/pulse/emotional-intelligence-how-competent-you-daniel-goleman

Guardian, The (2017) *12 Statistics to Get You Thinking about Mental Health in Young People.* www.theguardian.com/mental-health-research-matters/2017/jan/20/12-statistics-to-get-you-thinking-about-mental-health-in-young-people

Handwerk, B. (2010) *Chimp 'Girls' Play With 'Dolls' Too – First Wild Evidence Nature and Nurture May Both Influence Gender-Based Toy Choices.* http://news.nationalgeographic.com/news/2010/09/101220-chimpanzees-play-nature-nurture-science-animals-evolution

(The) Happiness Institute: The Happiness Research Institute is an independent think tank. Mission is to inform decision makers of the causes and effects of human happiness, make subjective wellbeing part of the public policy debate, and improve the quality of life for citizens across the world. www.happinessresearchinstitute.com

Harris, B. (2013) *Taming Temper Tantrums.* http://bonnieharris.com/taming-temper-tantrums

Head Start: www.acf.hhs.gov/ohs/about/head-start or National Head Start Association: www.nhsa.org/why-head-start/head-start-model

Heads Together: Work with partner charities who have achieved so much in tackling stigma, raising awareness, and providing vital help for people with mental health challenges. The team of charity partners working on Heads Together covers a wide range of mental health issues. www.headstogether.org.uk/about-heads-together

Health and Safety Executive (undated) *Myth Buster Panel.* London: HSE. www.hse.gov.uk/myth/index.htm

Heckman, J. (2017) *Fadeout: Statement on Duncan et al. Paper.* https://heckmanequation.org/resource/statement-duncan-et-al-paper

Higgins, C. (2016) *The Hygge Conspiracy.* www.theguardian.com/lifeandstyle/2016/nov/22/hygge-conspiracy-denmark-cosiness-trend

Hormone Health Network (2017) *What Does Oxytocin Do?* www.hormone.org/hormones-and-health/what-do-hormones-do/oxytocin

Independent, The (2015) *Judith Hackitt: 'The Myths of 'Elf and Safety.'* www.independent.co.uk/news/people/judith-hackitt-the-myths-of-elf-n-safety-10016089.html

Joseph, S. (2016) *3 Things Authentic Parents Get Right.* www.psychologytoday.com/blog/what-doesnt-kill-us/201609/3-things-authentic-parents-get-right

Keyte-Hartland, D. (2017) *Pedagogical Documentation and its Links to Children's Personal Social, and Emotional Well Being.* https://debikeytehartland.me

Kirk, M. (2017) *Can We Bring Back Riskier Playgrounds?* www.citylab.com/navigator/2017/01/can-we-bring-back-riskier-playgrounds/513929

Literacy Trust (undated) *Involving Dads – Literary Review.* www.literacytrust.org.uk/assets/0000/0790/Parentsandcarers_Dads_Key_Findings.pdf

McGlone, Francis (Professor) www.ljmu.ac.uk/about-us/staff-profiles/faculty-of-science/natural-sciences-and-psychology/francis-mcglone

Mantality: A media platform…which doesn't shy away from publicising mental health or touching upon the hard parts of life that everyone can go through…is to inspire the everyday male to live a more comprehensive version of themselves; with their mind to be the first point of address. http://mantalitymagazine.com

Men in Childcare: Rolling out the recruitment and training of more men into childcare throughout Scotland. www.meninchildcare.co.uk/index.htm

Merriam-Webster Dictionary. www.merriam-webster.com

Miller, A. (2016) *Dumb-Ass Stuff We Need to Stop Saying to Dads.* www.huffingtonpost.com/rosie-devereux/dumbass-stuff-we-need-to-stop-saying-to-dads_b_9186948.html

Mind (2015) *Search and Rescue: How to Manage Your Mental Wellbeing.* www.mind.org.uk/media/2199593/managing-mental-wellbeing-searchrescue_4.pdf

National Children's Bureau Listening and Participation Resources. www.ncb.org.uk/listening-and-participation-resources

NCH: The Children's Charity (2007) *Literature Review: Resilience in Children and Young People.* www.actionforchildren.org.uk/media/3420/resilience_in_children_in_young_people.pdf

New Economics Foundation (NEF) and Foresight (Government Office for Science) (2008) *Five Ways to Wellbeing.* www.fivewaystowellbeing.org and www.neweconomics.org/publications/entry/five-ways-to-well-being-the-evidence

Nguyen, T. (2014) *Hacking into Your Happy Chemicals. Think Better, Live Better.* http://theutopianlife.com/2014/10/14/hacking-into-your-happy-chemicals-dopamine-serotonin-endorphins-oxytocin

NHS Choices (2017) www.nhs.uk/Conditions/Sick-building-syndrome/Pages/Introduction.aspx. www.nhs.uk/Conditions/tongue-tie/Pages/Introduction.aspx (updated page from 23/02/2017)

Nursery World. Various men in childcare articles. www.nurseryworld.co.uk/men-in-childcare

Ockwell-Smith, S. (2017) *The Secret Reason Why Your Toddler Misbehaves.* www.huffingtonpost.co.uk/sarah-ockwellsmith/reasons-toddlers-misbehave_b_15079568.html

Orson, K. (2016a) *'The "Other" Reason Babies Need to Cry (and Why It's Parenting's Best Kept Secret).'* https://kateorson.com/2016/06/24/the-other-reason-babies-need-to-cry.

Orson, K. (2016b) *The Hidden Reason Why Toddler Tantrums are Hard to Handle (and What We Can Do About It).* https://kateorson.com/2016/06/21/the-hidden-reason-why-toddler-tantrums-are-hard-to-handle-and-what-we-can-do-about-it/?utm_content=buffer8f48candutm_medium=socialandutm_source=twitter.comandutm_campaign=buffer

O'Sullivan, J. and Chambers, S. (2012) *Men Working in Childcare: Does it Matter to Children? What Do They Say?* London: London Early Years Foundation (LEYF). https://issuu.com/leyf/docs/leyf-research-report-men-working-in-childcare-2012

Oxford Dictionary. www.oxforddictionaries.com

Packham, A. (2017) *Mum Judged For 'Babying' Son After He Got Hit In Face, Pens Important Message About Boys' Mental Health: The Notion that Boys Can Never Hurt is So Damaging to Them Long Term*. www.huffingtonpost.co.uk/entry/mum-open-letter-boys-cry_uk_589886b8e4b0a1dcbd0316fb?

Page, J. (2015b) *Professional Love in Early Years Settings (PLEYS) Summary of Findings*. https://pleysproject.files.wordpress.com/2017/06/pleys-report_singlepages.pdf; see also http://professionallove.group.shef.ac.uk/pleys/summary-of-findings

Parkinson's UK: Providing research, information and support to those living with, or affected by Parkinson's. www.parkinsons.org.uk/content/what-causes-parkinsons

Phoenix, S. (2017) The Phoenix Cups. *Kathy Brodie's Early Years Spring Web Summit*. See also www.phoenix-support.com.au

Play England: Vision is for England to be a country where everybody can fully enjoy their right to play throughout their childhood and teenage years, as set out in the UN Convention on the Rights of the Child Article 31 and the Charter for Children's Play. www.playengland.org.uk/about-us/why-play-is-important

Public Policy Institute for Wales (2016) *PPIW Report Publication: Promoting Emotional Health, Well-being and Resilience in Primary Schools*. http://ppiw.org.uk/ppiw-report-publication-promoting-emotional-health-well-being-and-resilience-in-primary-schools

Restom, D. *Why Most Women Carry Babies on Their Left Side*. www.kidspot.com.au/baby/real-life/in-the-news/why-most-women-carry-babies-on-their-left-side

Rolnick, A.J. and Grunewald, R. (2003) *Early Childhood Development: Economic Development with a High Public Return*. Minneapolis: FedGazette. www.minneapolisfed.org/publications/fedgazette/early-childhood-development-economic-development-with-a-high-public-return

Rugby League Cares: Charity dedicated to supporting the Rugby League family and its local communities. Mission is to enhance and enrich people's lives through the power and positive influence of Rugby League. www.rugbyleaguecares.org

Saltman, B. (2016) *Can Attachment Theory Explain all our Relationships?* http://nymag.com/thecut/2016/06/attachment-theory-motherhood-c-v-r.html

Schiller, B. (2016) *Meet the Billionaire Philanthropist Placing Big Bets on Early Childhood Development*. www.fastcoexist.com/3062654/future-of-philanthropy/meet-the-billionaire-philanthropist-placing-big-bets-on-early-childho

Simply Psychology: Aim of the site is to write engaging and informative articles in an academic style, but still clear and simple enough to be understood by psychology students of all educational levels. www.simplypsychology.org

Spark, A. (2016) *Step Away from the Laminator*. www.teachwire.net/news/step-away-from-the-laminator-and-remember-what-outdoor-areas-are-for?utm_content=buffer46173andutm_medium=socialandutm_source=twitter.comandutm_campaign=buffer

State of Mind: Established in 2011 with the aim of improving the mental health, wellbeing and working life of rugby league players and communities. www.stateofmindsport.org

Stephen Covey. www.stephencovey.com/7habits/7habits-habit5.php

Steavenson, W. (2017) *Ceausescu's Children*. www.theguardian.com/news/2014/dec/10/-sp-ceausescus-children

Sukel, K. (2015) *When the Myth is the Message: Neuromyths and Education*. http://dana.org/Briefing_Papers/When_the_Myth_is_the_Message__Neuromyths_and_Education

Szalavitz, M. (2010) *How Orphanages Kill Babies: And Why No Child Under 5 Should be in One*. www.huffingtonpost.com/maia-szalavitz/how-orphanages-kill-babie_b_549608.html

Tomlin, A. (2017) *Early Life Deprivation, Neurodevelopment, Mental Health And Resilience: ERA Study*. www.nationalelfservice.net/learning-disabilities/autistic-spectrum-disorder/early-life-deprivation-neurodevelopment-mental-health-and-resilience

Tovey, H. (2014) *All About...Risk*. London: Nursery World. www.nurseryworld.co.uk/digital_assets/291/LDAllaboutRisk.pdf

Turner, C. (2016) *What Kids Need from Grown-ups But Aren't Getting*. www.npr.org/sections/ed/2016/02/09/465557430/what-kids-need-from-grown-ups-but-arent-getting

Walters, A. (2016) *Did You Have A 'Blankie' As A Kid? Here's What That Says About Adult You*. https://dose.com/did-you-have-a-blankie-as-a-kid-here-s-what-that-says-about-adult-you-e9e91c160fa7#.xj1d7nbwr

Watson, T. (2016) *Whales Mourn their Dead Just Like Us.* Washington: National Geographic. http://news. nationalgeographic.com/2016/07/whales-death-grief-animals-science

Weiler, N. (2016) *Human Neurons Continue to Migrate After Birth, Research Finds.* UCSF website. www.ucsf. edu/news/2016/10/404486/human-neurons-continue-migrate-after-birth-research-finds

What Is the Difference Between Cognitive Science and Neuroscience? www.quora.com/What-is-the-difference-between-cognitive-science-and-neuroscience

Wiking, M. (ed.) (2014) *The Happy Danes: Exploring the Reasons Behind the High Levels of Happiness in Denmark.* Copenhagen: The Happiness Research Institute. https://media.wix.com/ugd/928487_7f341890e9484a279416ffbc9dc95ff4.pdf

World Bank and UNICEF (2016) *World Bank Group and UNICEF Urge Greater Investment In Early Childhood Development.* www.worldbank.org/en/news/press-release/2016/04/14/world-bank-group-unicef-urge-greater-investment-in-early-childhood-development

World Health Organization (2016) *Mental Health: Strengthening Our Response (Factsheet).* www.who.int/mediacentre/factsheets/fs220/en

https://youngminds.org.uk/about-us/media-centre/mental-health-stats

YoungMinds: UK's leading charity committed to improving the emotional wellbeing and mental health of children and young people. Driven by their experiences YoungMinds campaign, research and influence policy and practice. www.youngminds.org.uk/about/whats_the_problem/mental_health_statistics

Zaske, S. (2017) *Teaching Children to Play with Fire.* New York: New York Times. www.nytimes.com/2017/02/23/well/family/teaching-children-to-play-with-fire.html?_r=0

Zeedyk, S. (2012) *Babies Come into the World Already Connected to Other People.* Dundee: Suzanne Zeedyk Ltd. www.suzannezeedyk.com/wp-content/uploads/2016/03/Suzanne-Zeedyk-Attachment-v1.pdf

Zeedyk, S. (2014a) *We All Carry With Us the Fear of Disconnection.* Dundee: Suzanne Zeedyk. www.suzannezeedyk.com/wp-content/uploads/2016/03/Suzanne-Zeedyk-Attachment-v1.pdf

Zeedyk, S. (2014b) *Human Brains are Built on Connection.* www.suzannezeedyk.com/wp-content/uploads/2016/03/Suzanne-Zeedyk-Human-brains-v3.pdf

Zeedyk, S. (2014c) *How Dementia Helps Us Understand Our Common Humanity.* Dundee: Suzanne Zeedyk. www.suzannezeedyk.com/how-dementia-helps-us-understand-our-common-humanity

Zeedyk, S. (2016) *There Is Nothing Shocking About This Image.* www.suzannezeedyk.com/nothing-shocking-childs-image

Zeedyk, S. (2017) *Childcare Practice.* www.suzannezeedyk.com/childcare-practice-suzanne-zeedyk

Zeedyk, S. (n.d.) Suzanne Zeedyk: Connected Baby. www.suzannezeedyk.com and www.connected baby.net

Well-Meaning Debate

The following books, articles and websites are additional to the main bibliography and may be useful in your reflections, particularly around some of the wider thinking regarding Chapter 3. (All last accessed March 2017.)

Christmas

Brodie, K. (2014) *Sustained Shared Thinking in The Early Years: Linking Theory to Practice.* Abingdon: Routledge.

Douglas, L.V. (1930) *The Importance of Play.* Fordham University: Education Student Dissertations. Paper 3. http://fordham.bepress.com/gse_student/3

Kelly (2016) *Should Children be Told the Truth about Father Christmas?* www.earlyyearscareers.com/eyc/latest-news/should-children-told-truth-about-father-christmas

Kimberley (2016) *Should Early Years Setting Participate in Nativities and Christmas Concerts?* www.earlyyearscareers.com/eyc/latest-news/should-early-years-settings-participate-nativities-christmas-concerts

Myers, M. (2016) *A Slice of Autism: Christmas Survival Guide.* http://asliceofautism.blogspot.co.uk/search?updated-max=2016-12-14T08:51:00-08:00andmax-results=7

Newman, T. (2004) *What Works in Building Resilience? A Summary Sheet.* London: Barnardo's. www.barnardos.org.uk/what_works_in_building_resilience__-_summary_1_.pdf

New York Sun (2012) 'Is there a Santa Claus?' Reprinted from the 21 September 1897, *The New York Sun.* www.nysun.com/editorials/yes-virginia/68502

Nordqvist, C. (2016) *What is Neuroscience?* Brighton: Medical News Today. Accessed February 2017 at www.medicalnewstoday.com/articles/248680.php

Packham, A. (2015) *The Truth About Santa: How And When To Tell Your Children About Father Christmas, According to Parents.* www.huffingtonpost.co.uk/2015/12/07/tell-children-about-santa_n_8509224.html

Press Association (2016) *Parents Urged to Stop Pretending Father Christmas is Real.* www.telegraph.co.uk/science/2016/11/24/parents-urged-stop-pretending-father-christmas-real

Silver, S. (2016) *The Sweetest Way to Tell Your Kids the Truth About Santa.* www.popsugar.co.uk/smart-living/Telling-Kids-Truth-About-Santa-42837952

Thomas Russell, W. (2015) *How to Navigate the Santa Myth.* www.pbs.org/newshour/updates/what-i-said-when-my-daughter-asked-me-about-santa

Welch, A. (2016) *Santa Claus: What Should Parents Tell Kids?* www.cbsnews.com/news/santa-claus-what-should-parents-tell-kids

Zeedyk, Z. (2012) *Disconnection in the Midst of Family Cheer.* www.suzannezeedyk.com/disconnection-in-the-midst-of-family-cheer

Graduations

Benham, K. (2016) *The Cap and Gown Thing.* https://sparklingpreschool.wordpress.com/2016/06/29/the-cap-and-gown-thing

Espinoza, J. (2015) *Debate over American-style Nursery Graduation Ceremony.* www.telegraph.co.uk/education/educationnews/11742013/Debate-over-American-style-nursery-graduation-ceremony.html

Kimberley (2016) *Should Preschool Graduation be Encouraged?* www.earlyyearscareers.com/eyc/learning-and-development/preschool-graduation-encouraged

Miscellaneous

Blume, A. (2017) *Exclusive: Refusing to Touch Pupils is a Form of Child Abuse, Psychologists Say.* www.tes.com/news/school-news/breaking-news/exclusive-refusing-touch-pupils-a-form-child-abuse-psychologists-say

Dewar, G. (2015) *Stress in Babies.* www.parentingscience.com/stress-in-babies.html

June, L. (2016) *Well Here's the Most Depressing Possible Study About Body Image.* http://nymag.com/thecut/2016/08/body-image-issues-start-as-young-as-3.html

Lansbury, J. (2009) *You'll be Sorry!* www.janetlansbury.com/2009/12/youll-be-sorry

Ockwell-Smith, S. (2016) *Don't Make Your Child Kiss or Hug Relatives.* www.huffingtonpost.co.uk/sarah-ockwellsmith/making-your-child-kiss-or-hug-relatives_b_9663604.html?

PACEY (Professional Association for Childcare and Early Years). (2016a) *Body Confidence.* www.pacey.org.uk/bodyconfidence

PACEY (Professional Association for Childcare and Early Years). (2016b) *Children as Young as Three Unhappy with their Bodies.* www.pacey.org.uk/news-and-views/news/archive/2016-news/august-2016/children-as-young-as-3-unhappy-with-their-bodies

Pickles, K. (2016) *The Children as Young as THREE with Body Issues.* www.dailymail.co.uk/health/article-3765487/The-children-young-THREE-body-issues-Nearly-nursery-staff-heard-youngsters-fat-ugly.html#ixzz4YTO4U9Tx

Silva, M.J (2017) *Handling the Jolting Yet Universal Truth: All Children Get Angry.* www.huffingtonpost.com/entry/handling-the-jolting-yet-universal-truth-all-children_us_589ceba3e4b0e172783a9a48

Thomas Russell. W. (2016) *Why You Should Never Use Timeouts on Your Kids.* www.pbs.org/newshour/updates/column-why-you-should-never-use-timeouts-on-your-kids

Willgress, L. (2016) *Children as Young as Three have Body Image Issues While Four Years Olds Know How to Lose Weight, Study Finds.* www.telegraph.co.uk/news/2016/08/30/children-as-young-as-three-have-body-image-issues-while-four-yea

Rewards and Stickers

Dewar, G. (2008) *The Effects of Praise: What Scientific Studies Reveal About the Right Way to Praise Kids*. www.parentingscience.com/effects-of-praise.html

Evans, J. (2017) *Why are Rewards and Consequences Sill Used in Early Years Settings?* www.thejaneevans.com/why-are-rewards-and-consequences-still-used-in-early-years-settings

Harris, S. (2010) *How Heaping Praise on your Child Could Damage their Chance of Success*. www.learningandthinking.co.uk/How%20heaping%20praise%20on%20your%20child%20could%20damage%20their%20chance%20of%20success.pdf

Hurley, K. (2016) *The Dark Side of Classroom Behavior Management Charts*. www.washingtonpost.com/news/parenting/wp/2016/09/29/the-darkside-of-classroom-behavior-management-charts/?utm_term=.27197c4dc946

Lai, E.R. (2011) *Motivation: A Literature Review (Pearson Research Report)*. http://images.pearsonassessments.com/images/tmrs/Motivation_Review_final.pdf

Lowe, K. (2012) *When Rewards Systems Don't Work...What Next?* https://kathrynlowe.wordpress.com/2012/12/10/when-rewards-systems-dont-work-what-next

Mann, S. (2013) *Why '100% Attendance Awards' at School Don't Work*. www.huffingtonpost.co.uk/sandi-mann/why-100-attendance-awards_b_3414693.html

Ockwell-Smith, S. (2016) *The Problem with Rewards and Sticker Charts*. www.huffingtonpost.co.uk/sarah-ockwellsmith/the-problem-with-rewards-and-sticker-charts_b_9827014.html

Reischer. E. (2016) *Against the Sticker Chart: Priming Kids to Expect Rewards for Good Behavior can Harm their Social Skills in the Long Term*. www.theatlantic.com/health/archive/2016/02/perils-of-sticker-charts/470160

Weese, K. (2016) *How to Raise Kinder, Less Entitled Kids (According to Science)*. www.washingtonpost.com/lifestyle/on-parenting/how-to-raise-kinder-less-entitled-kids-according-to-science/2016/10/03/1a74fa3a-7525-11e6-b786-19d0cb1ed06c_story.html?postshare=7401475683730743andtid=ss_twandutm_term=.080c7ced61cf

Schoolification

Anderson, J. (2015) *Stanford Researchers Show We're Sending Many Children to School Way Too Early*. https://qz.com/546832/stanford-researchers-show-were-sending-many-children-to-school-way-too-early

BBC (2017) *Exercise Levels Decline 'Long Before Adolescence'*. www.bbc.co.uk/news/health-39255005

Christakis, E. (2016) *The New Preschool Is Crushing Kids: Today's Young Children Are Working More, But They're Learning Less*. www.theatlantic.com/magazine/archive/2016/01/the-new-preschool-is-crushing-kids/419139

Dubiel, J. (2016) *Wellbeing and Good Mental Health Should be Seen as Equally Important as Academic Success*. www.tes.com/news/school-news/breaking-views/wellbeing-and-good-mental-health-should-be-seen-equally-important?platform=hootsuite

Gladstone, A. (2016) *Why 'School Readiness' is Backwards Thinking*. London: Nursery World. www.nurseryworld.co.uk/nursery-world/opinion/1158827/why-school-readiness-is-backwards-thinking

Gopnik, A. (2011) *Why Preschool Shouldn't Be Like School*. www.slate.com/articles/double_x/doublex/2011/03/why_preschool_shouldnt_be_like_school.html?wpsrc=sh_all_dt_tw_topandutm_content=bufferbc582andutm_medium=socialandutm_source=twitter.comandutm_campaign=buffer

Gowman, V. (2015) *The Core Reason We Ready Children Too Early and Too Much*. www.vincegowmon.com/the-core-reason-we-ready-children-too-early-and-too-much

Whitebread, D. (2014) *Hard Evidence: At What Age Are Children Ready for School?* https://theconversation.com/hard-evidence-at-what-age-are-children-ready-for-school-29005

Self-Soothe and Self-Settle

Campbell, D. (2016) *What Happens to Your Brain when a Baby Cries*. www.utoronto.ca/news/what-happens-your-brain-when-baby-cries

Molloy, A. (2015) *Sleep Training at 8 Weeks: Do You Have the Guts?* https://parenting.blogs.nytimes.com/2015/03/26/sleep-training-at-8-weeks-do-you-have-the-guts

NHS (National Health Service, UK) (2013) *Dubious Claims That Crying Babies Self-Soothe.* www.nhs.uk/news/2013/01january/pages/dubious-claims-that-crying-babies-self-soothe.aspx

Ockwell-Smith, S. (2014) *Self Settling – What Really Happens When You Teach a Baby to Self Soothe to Sleep.* https://sarahockwell-smith.com/2014/06/30/self-settling-what-really-happens-when-you-teach-a-baby-to-self-soothe-to-sleep

Ockwell-Smith, S. (2016) *Don't Try to Teach Your Baby to Self-settle to Sleep.* www.huffingtonpost.co.uk/sarah-ockwellsmith/baby-sleep-self-settle_b_9779138.html?utm_hp_ref=ukand

Ockwell-Smith, S. (2016) *The Cry it Out Debate – Is it Safe, or Not?* https://sarahockwell-smith.com/2016/05/24/the-cry-it-out-debate-is-it-safe-or-not

Wright Glenn, A. (2015) *Screaming to Sleep, Part One: The Moral Imperative to End 'Cry It Out'* (Part One of a Two-Part Series On CIO). www.phillyvoice.com/screaming-sleep

Wright Glenn, A. (2015) *Screaming to Sleep, Part Two: The Moral Imperative to End 'Cry It Out'* (Part Two of a Two-Part Series On CIO). www.phillyvoice.com/screaming-sleep-moral-imperative-end-cry-it-out

Wright Glenn, A. (2015) *It Doesn't Take Guts to Sleep Train an 8-Week-Old.* www.phillyvoice.com/-it-doesnt-take-guts-to-sleep-train-an-8-week

Subject Index

Author Index